Kabbalah & Ve

He said, She said

PAUL COPPER

&

DEVI HARJEET KAUR aka Brigitte Calloway

Brumdu

New Zealand

ISBN: 978-0-473-58488-7
978-0-473-58489-4
978-0-473-58490-0

DEDICATION

To Paul's sons, Matthew and Jacob

and

Devi's children, Miriam and Amos.

CONTENTS

Acknowledgments   i

Preface   Page 1

1   Us   Page 3

2   The Divine Energy   Page 19

3   Ether   Page 54

4   The Universe   Page 84

5   Monism versus Dualism   Page 136

6   Creation and dissolution   Page 166

7   The Dark Night of the Soul   Page 181

8   Vibration   Page 221

9   Death   Page 237

10   Magic   Page 267

11   A world of order   Page 280

References   Page 321

ACKNOWLEDGMENTS

We are forever grateful to the ancient Rishis, who decoded the eternal truth. Without their wisdom, knowledge and dedication, this book would not have been possible.

We would like to acknowledge our families, who supported and encouraged us during the process of writing this book. Paul would like to thank his son Jacob for his forbearance in cups of tea and meals promised but never made as he sat and typed; also to Sybella, his stepdaughter for her endless support and encouragement. Devi's gratitude goes to her husband Ian, who put up with the simplest dinners for far too long; also to her children Miriam and Amos, who were always her biggest fans.

A huge thanks to all our friends who kept enquiring about the book.

.

PREFACE

This book is a dialogue, recorded in emails, text messages and phone conversations, between two contrasting people, living seven hours apart from each other, whom at a first sight may have nothing in common; different stages in life, nationalities, upbringings, interests and faiths.

Paul, a British man with a sharp and analytical mind, is a retired automotive engineer, living in Auckland, the biggest city in New Zealand. He built his life around the mystical Kabbalah that he studied and implemented in each aspect of his existence. On the Tree of Life and on pure science, research and data, he built his system of faith that gave his being peace that not many have achieved in their mortal existence.

Devi, a Clinical Hypnotherapist, born in the mythical Transylvania, now resides in the provincial town of New Plymouth. She modeled her life on the seed that is the Vedic philosophy, which, for the past few decades, was her prominent interest; her insatiably curious and fast learning mind being almost limitless in its quest for knowledge and understanding.

Their differences dissolved when they met in 2020 in a spiritual fraternity, based on ancient secrets and mysteries, which they are now both part of, he as an attentive mentor and she as his ardent pupil. Not long after they connected, when cancer hit Devi, Paul was the one who made a plan of surviving through surgery and medical treatments and beating the illness by throwing her into study. The endless conversations between the two developed into a body of work, which ultimately became a book when Devi was cured. Therefore, this book was written during a period of personal trauma, when Devi, an already published author of two hypnotherapy books, was dealing with cancer and completed when her illness was in remission.

"Kabbalah and Vedic wonderings" is a proof that different faiths, in this case Judaism and Hinduism have a common ground. The book analyses the main subjects of human existence, aspirations for eternal life from both perspectives, evidencing similarities between faiths and proving that Oneness is the only option for the survival of humanity.

CHAPTER 1

US

HE SAID

I had been a member of a fraternity that had a spiritual focus for a number of years and, in 2020, became mentor to new members. Membership came from across New Zealand and with the onset of Covid 19, face-to-face meetings would not be possible. Since mid 2019 I had coordinated a dialogue group using Zoom video conferencing so it was a simple matter to introduce the same technique to my mentoring meetings. It was agreed we would meet weekly on a Saturday.

The meetings commenced in March 2020. It was a joy to see people communicating with open minds and I got and still get much satisfaction in being with them. In July 2020, a new lady joined the group, at this time I knew her as Brigitte. As we got to understand each other, I found she had a spiritual name and from then on Brigitte became Devi Harjeet. When we first talked, Brigitte was so full of herself and she knew everything and seemed to feel we should be honored by her presence. Karma, astral projection, Vedic

3

philosophy and on she let us know her skills, even to being fluent in Sanskrit. How she though an Englishman with a Brummie ascent could use that she never said. If only she knew how this made me laugh, but strangely not at her but in some weird way, I enjoyed her company. To me, humbleness is to be admired not displaying knowledge.

To my surprise, Devi Harjeet started emailing me, asking questions. I thought it would be good to be able to sit over a cup of tea, English tea of course, and discuss, but living over three hundred eighty miles apart, this was not an option. I find trying to discuss using a keyboard intensely frustrating, but worked hard to answer her questions. What started as the odd email, became three or four a week and, in the end, a daily occurrence. I found I enjoyed communicating with this blonde lady who so intrigued me and who worked so hard to project a *"don't mess with me"* image, but I could see the odd chink; was that a little girl inside. Obviously I dared not even speak of what I saw; Devi spoke of some sort of projecting so even at three hundred eighty miles I felt I might get a slap.

Around the turn of 2020, our friendship had grown and we enjoyed talking about and looking for links between the Kabbalah and Vedic writings and the emails had become a daily occurrence. Late January 2021, I had a retreat from the world; seven days no conversation, laptop or phone. My retreat ended on a Saturday and I was so at peace. I felt as if clear spring water was running through my mind, but the real word said read your emails. I read one that just tore into me. Devi had written, telling me she had cancer. She would have just received a formed reply saying I was not available. Two words still live with me *"lonely and frightened"*. I had not been there when my now dear friend asked for help. I now saw the little girl I had glimpsed all those months earlier.

With Devi's inherent strength and me throwing philosophical challenges at her, the cancer was defeated. During this time, the stream of emails had become a torrent, which became a flood as Facebook messenger joined in. I noticed that we had starting playing email tennis. One of us would write a spiritual hypothesis, fire it over the net, and then the other would counter it and fire their hypothesis back refuting the previous suggestion and usually Devi would claim victory.

I was not aware but Devi was keeping all these words and one day, the lady whose arrogance I so laughed at eight months earlier, said *"Paul, could we put this dialogue together and perhaps tell our story"*. I may have spotted the little girl but still knew when not best to argue.

SHE SAID

2020 was the year of the Corona virus outbreak around the world, the year of lockdowns and social hysteria and the year I joined a spiritual kind of fraternity that changed my life. I remember that cold mid Winter New Zealand evening. How could I forget it? The one that had to travel for seven hours just to be able to step into the building was an accomplished hypnotherapist, with a practice that boomed, owning everything a human would dream for…. I mean everything! None of my achievements seemed important when I left.

At the end of the evening, I was given a mentor, somebody who would help me grow spiritually and deep down I doubted if anybody would be able to handle me; so I looked at this guy and thought to myself, is he aware of what he is taking on... but if I joined in, I had to abide by the rules. Therefore I was wondering what on earth this guy, or any person, was able to teach me because for the last thirty years my only focus was self-development and spirituality. Just to get closer to the light, for the last three decades, I studied verse by verse of the Vedas, the Upanishads, Bhagavad-Gita, Srimad Bhagavatam, Sri Isopanishad and all the other Hindu writings. I even learnt enough Sanskrit to help out myself and became able to adhere to Vedanta school of philosophy. Everything I learnt, I experienced in my Kundalini/ Laya yoga practice, so I asked myself, has this man any idea of the difficulties ahead. Did he know that, just a year before, I taught eighty seven workshops in meditation, past lives, karma, astral projection, energetic systems, sounds and vibrations... and a year before even more? Hundreds and hundreds of workshops, thousands of people listening to me speaking... Did he understand that I achieved a level in meditation that wasn't necessarily designed for humans?

I always needed challenges; I was never able to put my brain to rest and I acted upon my instinct. This is how I always functioned, so I looked at the guy again as he was talking to me and thought to myself that he may have been too gentle and too soft to handle me. To be perfectly honest, I liked him from that very moment. This is how I met Paul, my mentor who lived hours and hours away from me; the guy with beautiful white long hair, a sharp and logical mind and a kindness I have never seen in others.

He wasn't that soft after all. He made me work hard and for that I owe him much. For that and for so much more... I started attending his weekly Zoom virtual study groups and I felt very comfortable. Not being a team player; I therefore love my own company, but his groups were different. I was never forced to believe in something I didn't and I was never pushed to accept things just because somebody smarter than me wrote them. So, suddenly here I was, the one who thought she knew it all, wanting to know more. So I started emailing him any time I had doubts... and I had so many! I often pestered him and yet he always replied with that kindness, gentleness and softness, which is his nature. So I emailed even more and our dialog and friendship grew to the point where it became a necessary daily routine. In my emails, I was talking about the Vedic philosophy and he replied with his Kabbalah knowledge and everything blended in together. Pure symbiosis! Therefore, I began adding together our dialogue about gods, devas, beliefs, rituals, time, space, the Universe, energies, love, harmony and saved it all in a file... just in case. At that stage, at the end of 2020, I realized that the fraternity I was part of picked me the only mentor who was able to mould me and, to be perfectly honest, I am not sure now I would have stayed if it wasn't for Paul.

And when my life seemed so perfect, I was diagnosed with cancer and I haven't yet shared this news with others... but I told him. I am not sure why I felt like I had to, but now I know that it was the right choice. Again my instinct that lead to more... My mentor wasn't sorry for me; he was there for me. He understood that, in order for me to heal, I had to focus on study instead of feeling pity for myself. I had to forget the cancer, the surgery, and the treatments... He gave me work and I delivered as I always did in this life. And as the cancer went away, our dialogue recorded on my laptop in a *"He said, She said"* file got bigger and bigger.... and our friendship too. So if you wonder what two totally different people have in common, I have the right answer: nothing... or absolutely everything.

HE SAID

As a child, I was confirmed into the Church of England. My confirmation was in the Church of St. Mary, which stood in the Hamlet of Temple Balsall. As may be guessed, the hamlet was built on Knights Templar[1] land, which they farmed. I was expected to take part in the usual bible study classes and the church youth club. Being an antisocial child, I attended these rarely.

For a while, every Sunday, I wore a white surplus and served at high alter in my local church. I had many questions for my vicar but these Q & A sessions always ended with my queries not satisfied and the vicar disappearing at high speed on the ecclesiastical bicycle. There was little logic in what I was told and the more I dug, the vaguer the answers became. Perhaps some super brain has developed a formula for this *"Non temporal exploration equals indefinite response"*. So in my teens and twenties, religion played no part of my life and, as I compared the wealth of the major religions with the abject poverty of so many people, the gap between religion and I grew. But I never lost a feeling that a Divine Power lay somewhere.

Temple Balsall was to feature in my life some years later. The hamlet is situated on a notorious bend and more than once, on a dark and icy morning, my motorbike and I parted company as, on my way to work, I rounded the bend. The language that came out of a hedge bottom would have confirmed that vicar's thoughts about me ten years earlier.

As I headed toward my thirties, I went through a period that I have described as *"my difficulties"*. Despite this being a black time for me when indeed my life may have ended, I ultimately came out of it thinking more about a God of some description and, every Monday, I could be found attending a Buddhist Hermitage in Lower Fullbrook in Warwickshire. These evening meditations were recommended by my councilors who also gave me a copy of Alice Walker's book *"The Colour Purple"*. In the book, a young African-American girl named Celie Harris writes letters to God to help her cope with a life of abuse and loneliness.

So I meditated under the guidance of Venerable Luang Por Khemadhammo and wrote prolifically, but to no one. I remember one day lying by Afron Dwyryd in my beloved North Wales, I wrote ten pages all consigned to my waste bin but, oh, so cathartic. My job would see me travel across Europe, in some cases with only a few hours notice and as pressures grew, my visits to the Forest Hermitage and my writings became less and less until they vanished into my memory.

For many years, I had read the Tao te Ching[2] and although translations varied widely, I always felt an empathy with Lao Tzu's[3] words, so peaceful, so beautiful. Emphasizing that the Divine Being was above our comprehension, the words *"The Tao that can be named, is not the eternal Tao, the name that can be named, is not the eternal name"* have lived with me for over forty-five years. So as I travelled, these words came with me.

The nature of my work saw me travel, in most cases on my own, so I had time to myself. I sat in Carlow Cathedral, the Dom in Cologne, the Shinshoji Temple in Narita City among others and tried to understand what was this Divine Energy and where was I being taken? In Mishima City, in Shizuoka Japan, I found in a park, a simple shrine and it was here that I learned my love for Lao Tzu's words that had taught me to live a simple life, be calm and full of peace. Occam's Razor[4] sprang to mind; if there are a number of hypotheses the simplest is the best.

I had always thought psychological knowledge a constraint; you read words written by someone and you end up believing them as your own. I preferred to contemplate on an issue, form my opinion and then see if anyone else came to the same conclusion. If they did not, so what? They were my thoughts, my beliefs, not an imposition from outside. Here yet again I drew upon Lao Tzu's philosophy *"have the confidence to be yourself without caring what others think"*.

So I concluded that all matter came from the same source and all matter must be connected. It is only the rate of a vibration that separates us from the animals, flora and fauna and the very earth we stand upon. Everything in the Universe is cyclical, so at some point, all matter must be re-united with itself. There had been a great shattering at some point; was this the shattering of my Divine Unity or perhaps the Cosmic Soul, to which we all must return? Once we have become the spiritual being that faces us when we look into the mirror, our task is to retrace our path upwards so we return to the source of our emanation and once again become reunited with the Cosmic Soul from whence we emerged.

Occasionally I had read Kabbalistic[5] writings, concluding that their complexity was not for me. Remember for me simplicity had become my personal mantra. But there was this Tree of Life[6], a simple plan, its structure being based upon the emanations flowing down from the unknowable source of creation. *"From the void comes creation, the mother of a myriad thing"*, the Kabbalah complimenting Lao Tzu.

It is believed that a physical diagram of the Tree was built into the first Temple of Solomon, but it was lost when that Temple was destroyed by the command of the Babylonian king Nebuchadnezzar. The Tree stands upon three columns or pillars. The pillar on the left side representing Structure, the one the right being Dynamic, with the central pillar Equilibrium, yet again my old friend Lao Tzu appears *"Embrace opposites to hold the centre"*.

The Tree of Life image is based upon the emanations flowing downwards following the initial impetus of Creation. I believe everything must follow this path. Just as the Universe was created following a massive serge of Divine energy, the so called *"Big Bang"*, everything emanates from a spark.

The progress down the Tree is referred to as the Lightning Flash, which zig zags downwards. This flash crosses the Tree seven times, pillar to pillar, with a final movement directly downward. The zig zagging passes through ten Sephirot[7]. These are channels of Divine creative force or consciousness from which our being or personality is structured.

The Sephirot are formed in groupings; the three at the head of the Tree are the flows of the mind and below them we find the remaining seven Sephirot, the flow of emotion. These are in two groups, internal emotions and external emotions. It is the higher three Chochma, Binah and Da'at, the Seichel, that I use to test my spiritual hypotheses.

I have spoken of my long held belief in what I term a great shattering. This had started when considering the inflationary epoch that followed the Big Bang. After I had concluded my contemplations on this issue, I decided, as is my way, to read and see if I could find synchronicity within spiritual writing. It was there, *"the collective soul of Adam HaRishon[8], the supreme essence of mankind broke into 600,000 pieces"*. I then uncovered other synchronicities but this from the Kabbalah was the most dramatic. So I was able to assemble my simplistic postulation upon which I would establish my life.

All matter came from a unity to which it must return and, as a small part of that matter, I could use the Tree of Life as my under structure.

SHE SAID

As a teenager, I got myself involved in a meditation group, ran by some Russian yogis and everything there fitted my personality. I was a tinny blonde girl, independent, stubborn, very ambitious and I couldn't accept being just one of many in the crowd; and yet suddenly there I felt at home. With me in that group, there were maybe another twenty people, men and women of all ages, very carefully picked. I was the youngest and the most opinionated of them all. The yogis, who were our gurus, accepted me just the way I was, always enquiring, always wanting to know more. They knew I was in the search for the light and they understood that I would do whatever to find it!

The group was the spark that ignited the rest, mostly because it was totally illegal in a country based on a communist so called *"equality"*. I enjoyed sneaking out of my home every Sunday night, without my foster parents' knowledge, walking in circles on the streets, just in case somebody would follow me, going underground in that cold building, where mysteries were revealed and listening to those old yogis talking about the unseen world of God. I was familiar with the concept of God, but in a totally different way. As a child, my foster parents dragged me to the church every Sunday morning, but God may have had another plan for the day because he was always absent from the church. At least this is how I felt...

The inevitable happened in September of that same year. It was just after my birthday when the yogis told us that they have to return to their own country. I believe that they ran out of money because none of us paid them a dime. Not that they asked for money anyway! Just before they said their good byes, they showed us that everything was possible with the power of the brain… and the grace of God. So when I have seen them levitating, I surrendered and accepted that there is more than the eyes can see. But then they left and I felt alone in my search for the light!

The next day I was in the hunt for a church, a retreat, an ashram, a system of philosophy, whatever could have helped me to grow spiritually. I was hungry for the light! I didn't know back then that the light was in me!

A year later, I was still dull and in darkness, but one day I remembered that, in a similar situation, one of my gurus said *"Lead us from unreal to real"*, so good old Google gave me the answers: the Vedas… and this is how I started my journey in Vedic philosophy. I sucked in every verse from the Vedas, the Upanishads, the Puranas and moved on to Ramayana and Mahabharata, Bhagavad Gita, Srimad Bhagavatam, the Sutras, the Shastras, the Dharmasastras, Sri Isopanishad, and, when I got myself again to that crossroad with no visible roads ahead, I decided that it was just about time to learn a bit of Sanskrit. And I did it with such enthusiasm and desperation because I knew that I had found the light. But, to be perfectly honest, it was only when I started Kundalini yoga that the light revealed itself. I have taught in the past the most acrobatic styles of yoga and I loved everything about them, but I found my real identity in Kundalini yoga, maybe because it derives from the secret Laya yoga… and secrets and I go well together.

The bare truth is however in my spiritual name I was officially invested with: Devi Harjeet Kaur, *"the angelic deva lioness princess, who is completely victorious over life's challenges. Devi is one who is angelic and divine. Har refers to the name of God, which carries the vibrations of kindness and creativity. Jeet means to be victorious or overcome all obstacles. All females receive the name Kaur"*. Once I accepted it, I realized that there is no need to keep searching for God. God was in me! In the moment I came to that realization, the knowledge of Hindu ancient writings and practice of Kundalini yoga blended together in the path I have chosen: Vedanta school of philosophy, which I have followed ever since.

In the Vedic ancient writings I found all the answers I searched for when I was younger and, thirty years later, I am still excited discovering more. They kept me company during the darkest moments of my life giving me hope and cheering me up. There is so much wisdom behind each word ever written by the Rishis! For me, the Vedic writings are everything I ever needed: poetry, science and philosophy... and the certainty that I will live forever in a shape or form!

God is in us, there is no doubt about that, as an energy we call Kundalini Shakti, a divine force that stays coiled up in the Muladhara, the Root chakra, and awaits patiently to be awakened.... and once that happens, the Shakti pierces all chakras, one by one, and stops in the Sahasrara, the thousand petal Crown chakra. This is the moment when we become one with the Supreme Energy that is everywhere. This is the moment when this Universe becomes our forever home!

HE SAID

Did I choose the Tree of Life to support my beliefs or did it choose me, I ask myself. I ask this because of the manner in which we met; rationale says it could not have been by chance. My acceptance of the structure and associated words of the Kabbalistic Tree of Life was just there. As you are more than aware Devi, I quote Occam Razor's proposal that if there are many hypotheses, the simplest will be the best. I could understand the Tree easily and its logic was perfect. Kabbalah has great depth and the erudite understands its nuances far better than I but from the fog the Tree emerged for me.

Over many decades I have searched for a meaning but my search was for logical simplicity and, as I write this, I realise my working life was similar my decisions being simply, yes or no, without qualifications. So I ask is that my spirit, simplicity?

When I think of my faith, the biblical story of Joseph's coat of many colours always comes to my mind. My faith is similar; my lining is the Tree of Life with upon it stitched feelings from Daoism, Buddhism, Judaism, Christianity, the Baha'i faith and more. I call them my feelings because I feel the logic of simplicity. I do not want to have to think of a Divine Being I need to feel she, he, it around me. If I need help I just want to say *"Hey, I could do with a hand"*. I know that there are the most eloquent prayers written, a hundred wonderful words, but my six mean the same. So I could conclude that if my spirit is simplicity that is what I have looked for in many traditions, always rejecting any complexity. My Divine Being is not complex just simply the most wonderful Energy.

One thing more Devi, I have to admit that your Vedic Philosophy is slowly adding a sleeve on my multi patchwork coat. At first sight, I thought it is complex, but I just let it lie and the simplicity has started to surface. As with my other faiths I suddenly find it there. We live in a wonderful world if you only believe in Unity and of course you have guessed it Devi, Simplicity.

SHE SAID

I chose the Vedic path over thirty years ago, but of all schools of philosophy, Vedanta[9] resonated most with my heart because of the way it teaches about the microcosm and the macrocosm.

I believe that knowledge in general is taught, especially these days, according to the Tantric concept of *"iti iti"* (this too, that too). In this case, the object of the study would be taught without making any correlation with similar objects. However, in Vedanta, learning is based on the concept of *"neti neti"* (not this, not that), which allows, through Atma Vichara (self discovery), encompassing the whole picture. As an example, if the topic is identifying one particular tree in a forest, through *"iti iti"*, the teacher would point out that tree only. Through *"neti neti"*, the teacher would negate each tree, allowing the student to discover the desired tree through a process of elimination. Therefore, through negation, Vedanta permits introspection into transcendence and reality, being aware of the big picture rather than focusing on one aspect only.

I also picked Vedanta, especially its branch called Advaita Vedanta[10], because of the solution it gives to the source of suffering, this being one of the main struggles humanity faces at the moment. The real pandemic these days is depression, anxiety and lack of self-confidence, but through Vedanta I found my own answers and my own inner peace. I have been on this path of self-discovery for years and, without saying that I encoded all the mysteries of this vast Universe, I reached that point where my doubts disappeared. I can only thank that to Vedanta school of philosophy.

CHAPTER 2

THE DIVINE ENERGY

HE SAID

You will never find my beliefs written in one book because my faith is just that the faith of the Copper. It is draw from Eastern philosophy, Indian cultures, out of the air and, as an English man with a strange accent and a humour that can start a fight, from the Christian tradition Bible, but you may comment the Bible? Yes, but as King James VI of Scotland knew when he became King James I of England, he was on a dodgy wicket; he decided to puritanise the Bible, this in 1604.

Many amendments took place before its publication in 1611, so I discard his falsehood as a guide and looked at the Geneva Bible[11] for guidance. Then I added, of course, my own myopic view of life plus the Hebrew scriptures.

SHE SAID

Fortunately, the Vedas and the Upanishads stayed as they are now. What do you know about the Vedas, Paul?

The Vedas (in Sanskrit *"Vedah"* means *"knowledge"*) are the main Hindu scriptures, all compiled in Sanskrit by Sage Krishna Dvaipayana, known as Veda Vyasa[12] or *"the splitter of the Vedas"*. There are four Vedas: Rigveda (Knowledge of the Hymns of Praise), Samaveda (Knowledge of the melodies), Yajurveda (Knowledge of the sacrificial formulas) and Atharvaveda (Knowledge of the magical formulas); dated before 2000BC and passed on by Rishies (Sages). Being transmitted orally, the Vedas are considered Sruti, which means, *"what is heard"*. Each of them contains Samhitas (metric text/ mantras), Brahmanas (rituals), Aranyakas (theologies written in the forest), Sutras (laws) and Upanishads that are philosophical writings. So volumes and volumes...

The beauty of the Vedas is that they talk about atoms, how they interact, the Universe, the expansion of the Universe, physics and chemistry. Therefore when I go back to a verse, I have the feeling that I read a science treatise. There are thousands of verses about the soul and there are chapters dedicated to Hindu gods too. People talk about the Vedas without ever reading a verse, so they have no clue that most of the Mandalas (chapters) start with a hymn to Agni, the fire, because the Sages believed that everything in the Universe and within us starts with fire.

The main topic in the Vedas is Atman (the Self) and Brahman (Supreme Consciousness), the dissolution of the soul and each verse is pure poetry.

The Upanishads have been added one by one later, around 1000BC, and are the real philosophical texts of the

Vedas. There are one hundred and eight Upanishads, composed by different Sages and their families, thirty-eight of them referring to yoga only and twenty of those thirty-eight to Laya yoga, which we now refer to as Kundalini Yoga.

But, Paul, that is not all. There is the Bhagavad Gita that has seven hundred verses, part of Mahabharata, written by Sage Vyasa around 200BC, which is a dialog between Krisha, an avatar of Vishnu, and prince Arjuna. The Gita is the main text for all branches of yoga. It is said that Lord Ganesha, being inspired by Sage Vyasa, may have transmitted it, but in fact Mahabharata is attributed to Vyasa only. But because I mentioned Mahabharata, I would just say that this is in fact an epic poem based on the narration of Ugrasrava Sauti[13], in the sacred forest of Naimisha after attending the twelve years sacrifice known as Kulapati[14] or Saunaka. Some of the Puranas were attributed to Sauti too. Mahabharata includes over a hundred thousand Sloka (ancient poetic form) and over two hundred thousand individual verses.

And then The Srimad Bhagavatam or Bhagavata Purana, one of the eighteen Mahapuranas[15] in Hinduism, *"The story of the fortunate one"*, three hundred and thirty five chapters in total; the fortunate one being the one known in different incarnation. I know that may sound weird, but let it just wash over you as it is. Bhagavata Purana is an eighteen-volume work, first of them attributed for sure to Veda Vyasa. Each Canto (book) is about a different topic, creation, structure of the Universe, reincarnation, souls, the duties of mankind, structure of

God and so on.

Another main text in Vedanta school of Vedic philosophy I often go back to is Brahma Sutra, five hundred and fifty-five Sutra (aphoristic verses) composed by Sage Badarayana[16]; all the Sutra are organized in four chapters, based on the ideas developed in the Upanishads. Because the Brahma Sutra is the main writing for the Vedanta philosophy, it is known as the Vedanta Sutra.

I have to also mention Sri Isopanishad, which contains the knowledge that brings one closer to Krishna[17]; eighteen mantras that would help one acknowledge the supreme personality of the Godhead.

There are so many other Hindu scriptures; some of them compiled or inspired by Sage Vyasa, whose son Shuka is believed to have worked on several Hindu scriptures too.

So, Paul, many volumes, many verses, all written in Sanskrit[18], all remained the same over centuries... all talking about us, human beings and the divine force in the Universe. I mentioned some important to me and perhaps you should tell me more about the Tree of Life.

HE SAID

The Tree of Life is found in many mystical traditions; it consists of ten spheres or nodes representing differing stages of development or manifestation of a complete entity. The spheres are connected by twenty-two paths or channels, twelve of these channels representing the signs of the zodiac, whilst the remaining ten, represent the heavenly bodies that travel through the signs. The spheres have a number assigned to them relative to their position upon the Tree.

These spheres are arranged on pillars, the pillar on the left having feministic attributes and having three spheres positioned upon it. The right hand pillar, which represents the male attribute, also has three spheres upon it. There is a central pillar and this holds the remaining four spheres. On some depictions there is a fifth sphere upon the central pillar; this is sometimes noted as the *"invisible"*. I work with the Isaac Luria Tree, which includes this sphere as Luria's diagram is The Tree of Return. The title of the central pillar is Clemency; the female pillar on the left is titled Severity and the male pillar on the right being Mercy.

In the Jewish Kabbalah the spheres are called Sephiroth or singularly Sephirah. The Kabbalists use the Tree as a *"road map"* following the flow of forces down from the Divine to the lowest word. This route is called the *"lightening flash"* as it zigzags back and forth across the Tree, from sphere to sphere, in its journey of descent. A return journey can then be made again in stages as we purify our Being until it achieves Enlightenment.

The representation I use is the one attributed to Isaac Luria. I will outline the ten Sephiroth that I use but not speak about the twenty-two paths as to clarify these would require several pages.

At the top of the Tree is Keter, this is the Crown, and above Keter there are three veils, En Sof Aur[19], En Sof and Aur. These veils take us toward the Absolute the Un-Imaginable energy that is the source of the All. Out of Keter came the energy force that drove the manifestation of the universe. As I believe Keter is also unknowable, I start my journey of manifestation from the Sephirah that lies to the right and slightly below the Crown, Chochma. You will notice I equate Chochma to the Singularity because at this moment all matter there will ever be streamed forth or burst forth like a spark fired toward Bina. This Wisdom from Chochma crossed the Tree at the start of what is to become a zigzag path known as the lightening flash. Binah is understanding, realising what the Wisdom is imparting.

The lightening flash then moves to the right and downwards to Da'at. Da'at is sometimes called the invisible Sephirah, which I mentioned, and is not included in the Cordovero depictions of the Tree. For myself, Da'at is the critical point in the Chochma, Binah, Da'at triad. Speaking very simply, this triad forms our spiritual or emotional being. Da'at is called *"knowledge"* because it is here that the knowledge gained enables the manifestation of our physical being.

From Da'at, the lightening flash moves to Hesed, which has the quality of mercy and generosity, inner emotions. Gevurah is next on the left where we find the outer emotions of judgement. Moving to the central pillar, we meet Tiphareth or *"beauty",* which develops the essential nature of our being; then focuses upon the essential nature of our being, the Sephirah Netzach or repeating is next. Here the physical and psychological processes are established; returning to the left Hod, reverberation follows. It is called *"reverberation"* because this is where our reaction to external stimuli is established.

We finally go to Yesod and Malkuth. In Yesod or *"foundation"* we form our ego or the persona, the mask we show to the world. Lastly we have Malkuth or *"kingdom"*; it is here that the earth elements form the body.

Well Devi, I have tried to make it easy to read, but as you know, I am no teacher so I just hope it enlightens you.

SHE SAID

I am anchoring myself to your last word, enlightenment, so I would link it to Moksha (liberation of souls) by saying that the Vedas have, for me, the magical formulas to enlightenment.

Perhaps the best illustration of Moksha is in Katha Upanishad[20], text written by Swami Ambikananda Saraswati[21], who taught Vedanta philosophy and yoga. In it, Nachiketa, the son of Vajasravasa[22], asked Yama, the God of Death, what is the secret of death and whether or not one can really achieve immortality.

To that, Yama replied *"The joy of spirit ever abides, but not what seems pleasant to senses. Both these, differing in their purpose, prompt us to action. All is well for those who chose the joy of the spirit, but they miss the goal of life who prefer to be pleasant. Perennial joy or passing pleasure? This is the choice one is to make always. Those who are wise recognise this, but not the ignorant. The first welcomes what leads to abiding joy, though painful at the time. The later run, goaded by senses after what seems immediate pleasure. Well have you renounced these passing pleasures, so dear to the senses, Nachiketa,*

25

and turn your back on the way of the world that makes mankind forget the goal of life. Far apart are wisdom and ignorance. The first leads one to Self-Realisation; the second makes one more and more estranged from one's Real Self".

In this case, Yama refers to both Avidya, as ignorance of the world and, Ajnana, ignorance of the Supreme Reality or incomprehension of the spiritual energy I call God within us. What is your perception of that energy, Paul?

HE SAID

I have always believed in a divine force and that all matter is connected; arrogantly I state these facts as irrefutable, just try to prove me wrong! You cannot despite what trickery you may try. But as I travelled and took a bit from this belief and a bit from that, I realised I needed a framework to place them on, perhaps like that frame I dry my washing on. Without them my beliefs like the washing became scattered and difficult to pull together.

Then I was presented with and told to read Henrietta Bernstein's *"Cabalah Primer"*[23]. I gazed at Henrietta's words and muttered darkly about my College officer who had presented it to me. But as I read it again and again, there stated to rise from the pages a structure I could possibly use. I then turned to *"Practical Kabbalah"*[24] by Rabbi Laibl Wolf and he showed me how to make the structure. My beliefs could hang from the Kabbalistic Tree of Life.

Kabbalah means *"to receive"* and I received the

Tree with joy, straight out of the box it fitted. It shows how power comes down from on high to emanate the being we are. We are the created entity that comes from the Creator. Yes, but then what do we do now here, just sit and gaze at our navel? We are here in a separated state, individualised, we say *"I"* or *"my"*, confirming our separation from our higher self. Just as we have moved down the Tree of Life, we can reverse the process and retrace our step upward until we are unified with our Creator.

SHE SAID

I use the Vedic scriptures as reference to my faith. I believe in a higher energy I call God, an absoluteness that is love and fairness. Call it Yehova, Allah, Ram Das, still one Creator! My beliefs are not part of any religion or dogma. My God is neither Christian, nor Hindu… my God is above dogmas made by humans to excuse their own intolerance and ignorance. Therefore, my faith is based on my feelings and experiences, a perfect symbiosis of Vedic philosophy and yoga. I believe that there is a God; also that we are of divine nature. How do you use the Tree of Life?

HE SAID

I use the Structure of the Tree to place my beliefs at each stage, to vigorously test them and move on once I am satisfied. There are ten Sephiroth or stages we pass through on the Tree. I have made a slight adjustment for I believe that the Sephirah at the head of the Tree, Keter or the Crown, represents the first level of the Creator.

There are three veils above. It is impossible to

comprehend our Creator until we become enlightened and are reunified with that Energy Source, so I use the Sephirah Da'at. Da'at is known as the unseen Sephirah and functions in particular conditions; it is known also as *"knowledge"*, so I use it as the junction between my corporeal and ethereal being. My ethereal being is found beyond Da'at.

Complementing Da'at, Binah, understanding, and Chochma, wisdom, manifest the mind. To get to this upper triad, we must pass through the Abyss; to myself this is similar to passing through the Dark Night of the Soul[25], we then enter the noumenal word where Chochma and Binah exist. I use the Tree in many ways, one being that before I meditate, I perform the ritual of the Kabbalistic Cross. Please remember as you read my words that I am describing my return journey towards unification with my Creator.

My first Question to you Devi is what is the structure that you place your beliefs on, yes, those wonderful Vedic texts, but how do you manage them on the skeleton of your faith? Vedic philosophy enables you to stand on a branch and reach upward, towards the one above, but what are these branches constructed from?

SHE SAID

As a yogi, I worship extravagantly. All the Vedic knowledge I acquired during the years are worth nothing in the absence of personal experience; I could not be who I am today without it.

Anytime I look at my orchids, I am reminded that there should be a miraculous creator behind all this beauty.

Yet, that energy is within us all, so I believe that we are all miniature gods on our own. We have the power to create masterpieces, heal ourselves and others and change the world. Therefore I look at people around me and I think to myself *"if you only knew how divine you are"*. I worship the God in others and am amazed by the God within myself. I call it my own *"groovy God"* because He/She throws me in dramatic situations and He/She pulls me out of them… just a path to Jnana (supreme knowledge).

I wasn't always like this though. I gave in to the God called money, technology, assets, success and fame. I had them all; they were worthless, Paul. With or without them, life is still the same. We can live without wealth, but we cannot without hope. In the darkest moments, our belief in something higher, good and fair, keeps us going. We need so little to be happy, a roof above our heads, a little bit of food in our bellies and love. So I believe that God is unconditional love and, since I have found the light of limitless and eternal absolute love, my life has a meaning.

But, as you have noticed, I haven't really answered your question. I will though after you explain what the Kabbalistic Cross is.

HE SAID

As I said Devi, I use the structure of the Tree in many ways, one being as the ritual before I meditate or pray. I perform the ritual of the Kabbalistic Cross saying the words Atah, Malkuth, ve Geburah, ve Gedulah, Le Olam and Amen[26].

I see the Cross grow within as I do this. In what

way do you use your spiritual structure?

SHE SAID

I would just remark on the fact that those words have no meaning to me, so I would ask you to describe your Cross ritual in detail. In the meantime, I will deepen my explanation about my personal ritual.

As a yogi, worshiping the union, because yoga means just that, I start the day with Shat Kriya[27], the six cleansing processes of my internal tracks, which are Trataka[28] for eye sight, Neti[29] for nasal tracks, Kapalabhati[30] for lower respiratory track, Dhauti[31] for digestive tracks and Nauli[32] for abdominal muscles. I won't say more about them, because they are techniques used in yoga only and need time mastering them.

However, I vary each day my Kundalini yoga Kriyas. This is the time I spend with the Divine Energy, my God. For me, yoga is not fitness; it is the real union of God with my soul. I have to admit though that I wasn't that precise with my yoga Kriyas[33] lately… because of my illness. But I always meditate at lunchtime and pray later in the day. My prayers are series of Vedic chants in Sanskrit that work perfectly for me. I also dedicate time reading the Vedic texts because, as you know, knowledge is really important to me.

So, as you see, Paul, my practice is not set in stone and it doesn't follow a plan made by others. It is true that the steps of a Kundalini yoga Kriya cannot be changed, but this is just part of my daily practice. Now, back to your Kabbalistic Cross.

HE SAID

I perform the Ritual of the Celtic Cross before and after I meditate Devi. I hope my explanation is clear.

I stand upright and face East, breath slowly and empty my mind. The ritual connects me with my higher self, creating harmony in the aura and balance between polarities. Reach above my head with my right hand, thumb and fingertips together, fill my mind with Divine light; lead my hand down my forehead, visualising a beam of light and intone Atah (Thou Art), touch the region of my solar plexus. I visualise the beam or pillar of light reaching down to my feet and intone Malchut (the kingdom), then touch my right shoulder and intone ve Geburah (and the Power). Touch my left shoulder, visualising a beam of light from my right shoulder forming a cross, and intone ve Gedulah (and the Greatness).

Finally, place both hands together in the centre of my chest and the centre of the Cross of Light and intone le Olam (in eternity). I would hold the visualisation of the Cross in my mind and intone So Mote it Be[34].

You may recognise that the cross corresponds to the Ancient Hebrew letter Tav[35]. I have tried to make this clear Devi, have I succeeded?

SHE SAID

There is a similarity between your devotion and mine. You use your words to tune in; I use mantras. Chanting is a big part of my spiritual practice.

There are thousands of mantras, all very profound, all designed with the science of *"naad"*, the cosmic vibration or the essence of all Svaras (sounds). Let me be more specific: 20,379 mantras in the Vedas, so heaps to choose from!

I use chanting to connect to the Supreme Energy, to cleanse my chakras and to tune into yoga kriyas (yoga practices) or to a meditative state. Therefore I learnt hundreds of mostly Vedic mantras that resonate with me. I chant the whole day, Paul, and somebody who doesn't know me well would find me weird. Maybe I am...

Every day, I chant a morning mantra and an evening one... and hundreds during the day! I chant walking my dog Hendrix and I chant organizing my orchids in the greenhouse!

Did you know that many of the Hindu mantras had no meaning? They are just high vibration sounds that are able to travel through the ether... sounds that have the same frequency as the cosmic vibration. The meaning of most of mantras was added later, only to give them relevance.

There is a whole science behind chanting. It is not the fact that one chants; it is the way in which they chant. You see, the tongue has to touch repetitively most of the eighty-four meridian points on the hard palate of the root of the mouth for a certain code to program our thoughts and minds. And then there is the rhythm of a mantra that can change our own consciousness. Even the word *"mantra"* says it. *"Man"* means mind and *"trang"* means wave or projection.

You do this and I do that... different ways of devotion. So we worship differently, but do we worship the same God?

HE SAID

Let us once and for all agree that the word God has too much baggage attached to it. For someone with an upbringing in the Christian tradition, I was told that God was an elderly white male with long white hair and a beard. Yes, as so many people say, looks like me. I told you before I have a purple goatee to avoid being expected to perform miracles. No confusion regarding who's who.

So I will speak of a Divine Unity, an energy or vibration. Each day we pray together, we may be nearly four hundred miles apart, but we synchronise our prayer and I feel us come together. So we become one in our thoughts and we appeal to one Divine Unity, as you know I insist that every atom is part of the same cosmic energy so a feeling of unity is natural.

You say we worship differently but do we? Go to the basics of your faith in the Vedic writings; they are much more structured than my beliefs, which come from all over but hang together on the Kabbalistic Tree of Life. Superficially they may appear different but look at the base line and you will find they are the same. They cannot be otherwise.

When I was an altar boy at St Peter's church, I queried this supposed difference between my vicar's beliefs and those of the local catholic priest. Is there, up in heavens hotel a different room for Catholics, Protestants, Buddhists and others? If so, I hoped I was with the group that got the best location and food. No proper answer was forthcoming and, as I say elsewhere, I soon realised the standard religious thought is based upon the power a specific order has and never the twain will meet.

So yes, my dear, we both worship the same Divine Unity found within us. The much more intriguing though is if we exist in that Divine Unity's mind? And is this energy source guiding us back to the Cosmic Soul? A couple of questions I expect you to answer. But no pressure…

SHE SAID

You know what? I will let Atharveda[36] talk to us both instead of me trying to prove a point: *"There is no second God, nor a third, nor is even a fourth spoken of; there is no fifth God or a sixth, nor is even a seventh mentioned; there is no eighth God, nor a ninth. Nothing is spoken about a tenth even"*. One God for all religions, traditions and schools of thinking… only one, the same for all; you call it Divine Unity, I call it God!

There is no need to search the path to the Cosmic Soul. Our Self is that! This is very obvious if we go back to Purusha (the soul) as defined in the Munduka Upanishad[37]: *"Splendid and without a bodily form is this Purusha, without and within, unborn, without life breath and without mind, higher than the supreme element. From him are born life breath and mind. He is the soul of all beings"*.

And, if you still have doubts, Paul, what about this superb verse in Isha Upanishad[38] 16:17 *"I am He, the Purusha within Thee"*.

The Cosmic Soul is us and we are it! You can believe me… or not; and you can have faith in the Upanishads or not… This leads me to my next question. Is there any difference between belief and faith?

HE SAID

Following your recent criticism regarding my suggestion that knowledge can be a hindrance, I decided to read what the dictionary says about faith and belief. So I looked the words up in Nelson's Bible Dictionary[39]. The result caused some head scratching; first how I intended to reply and then how the erudite Nelson sees the words. I will let you be the arbitrator. For me the word *"belief"* is a bit *"lose"*. I believed it would happen but…. so, when it does not, I am not surprised. Whereas if I have faith in something, my faith is explicit. Nothing or no one can shake my faith.

So now, how does the dictionary define the words? It says that faith and belief are similar words. It defines faith as a belief in or confident attitude towards God, presupposing a commitment to his will for one's life. So not quite a draw, but close except that I take exception with Nelson using the word *"God"*; it has the wrong connotation. Also I cannot accept the word as gender specific. For the unknowable being I have faith in no gender can apply. To quote Lao Tzu *"The name that can be named is not the eternal name"*. Factum est ita! (and it was so). Please notice the Latin is Copper, not Lao Tzu.

SHE SAID

I never said that knowledge resists to experience or to anything else, Paul. Our argument on the topic was one of polarities. But because *"alea iacta est"* (the die has been cast), I am decided to prove myself as a worthy pupil by explaining to my mentor my thoughts about belief and faith.

In my opinion, beliefs are concepts, true or just idealistic, made up by our minds. We believe in things based on our own preferences and deny others that don't sound analytical enough; or just don't fit in our lifestyle. Shraddha (faith) is in our heart, Paul, and it is never based on logic. Therefore, I sometimes believe that faith is a vessel to hope. A proper transcription from Sanskrit of Shraddha says exactly that, hope in something higher than us.

For the Vedic scriptures, the object of faith is Brahman, who is not God as we know it; being however the ontological substance everything comes from. *"Brahman is of the nature of truth, knowledge and infinity"* (Taittaryia Upanishad[40] 2.1).

How do you link your faith to Kabbalah, Paul?

HE SAID

The Kabbalistic Tree of Life is the perfect diagram of the forces working throughout creation; it hovers between All and No Thing. At its crown is the entry point for the forces that come from the negative existence of the Absolute, so it traces a path from the highest vibration through to the lowest vibration in dense matter. In reverse, the return of all matter from a shattering, to complete reunion, can be traced and the stages reached measured. I use the Isaac Luria[41] Tree of Return[42], I have explained why elsewhere. This form enables a link between the three highest Sephiroth Chochma, wisdom, Binah, understanding and Da'at knowledge.

In my belief, Da'at is the key; I passed through Da'at on my descent. The uppermost triad is associated with our mind; it is here that our spiritual essence is formed. Da'at is the knowledge of this and also the knowledge that we will move on to the middle knowledge, where our emotions are formed and thus still descending to the lower triad to form our instincts and ultimately descending into Malkuth, where our being receives the intervention of the Divine.

Our task is to retrace the path returning up the Tree. This is done by purification at each of the Sephiroth proving we are worthy for the next stage. I believe that I have been shown that I am passing through Da'at and will be allowed to start a process of final reunion with my twin soul and then this soul will become one with the Cosmic Soul which equates with Keter the Crown.

SHE SAID

Retrace the path through Suddhi (purification)? Beautiful words, Paul! So I will anchor my thoughts to your thoughts. *"The body is cleansed by water, the internal organ is purified by truthfulness, the individual soul by sacred learning and austerities, and the intellect by true knowledge"* (Manusmriti 1.109). Manusmriti I just quoted is a Sanskrit legal text, written around 1250BC, that contains twelve Adhyayas (chapters) about dharma, karma, reincarnation and Moksha (liberation).

You were so right in mentioning the truth of the Cosmic Soul and knowledge as a path to purification. What if I told you that we would become one with the Cosmic

Soul if we would get rid of impurities as Ajnanam (ignorance), Asha (desire), Aham (ego), Pasas (Attachment) and Danana Pravriti (evil acts)? In Hinduism, our mortal world is considered contaminated; the source of impurities being anywthing from Kala (time), karma, our own actions, Dhosas (impurities in our bodies) to even planetary influences. The only entity considered Sudha (pure) is the soul that is eternal and immortal.

HE SAID

Well, I sometimes envy you Devi. You have your Vedic Philosophy with everything explained and laid before you whereas I have my own beliefs put together like a coat made of many fabrics, patches from here there and everywhere. I use the Kabbalistic Tree of life to hang my coat on and use the progression up and down as my test for the logic of my thoughts. For many years I have used quantum physics to measure how my beliefs are being proven by science, so, from Tomas Young's[43] double slit experiment to the three veils of En Sof Aur, En Sof and En, there are many pieces of material from many places on this earth. Perhaps by now you may understand the chaos that is my mind.

I have never explained to anyone what or how I believe except to say that there has been some hand guiding my life. This hand has placed me in places of despair, which even though they were dark times, they ultimately pointed me to a joyous conclusion to my life. You appeared from the West coast of New Zealand's North Island and said let's write a book, so you nailed me down forcing me to put into words what had only been thoughts before. You forced a complete understanding of St Augustine's[44] words *"When I think I know, when asked to explain what I think I know not"*.

My dear Devi, this is an over simplification of my journey but even so, I would love to hear your feelings about my thoughts.

SHE SAID

I wished the Vedic philosophy was already *"explained and laid before me"*. Please imagine my smile when I am writing this... Nothing is explained, Paul. There are so many schools of Hindu philosophy, each with different branches that approach the scriptures differently. Also remember please that these scriptures are in Sanskrit, an archaic language that requires attention when translating. But I would give you this: thank God I have the Vedas on my side!

But because I mentioned the higher energy, I believe that it was God's hand that led you to the point where you are now! Does God really exist?

HE SAID

It is an interesting concept- is it not? If God exists, what does he appear as, for many people, a huge version of themselves? He must be huge because of what he has created.

As a young child, I was taught that God was a white elderly male with a beard, a bit like the older men in my society. I am sure you have noted *"women excluded"*! I have no doubt this will be commented on in your reply. I wonder that if we imagine that our God is a larger form of ourselves would your chooks; if you asked them about their God, say he was just like a huge chicken. So I suggest that, to define God, we have to look beyond our cultural definition of God. If we do that, should we conclude that God has no form that would caste a shadow?

Before I go further, I must comment that my words will be based upon an explicit belief in Divine Unknowable Energy. We both know ours was not a chance meeting so there is a power behind all our actions.

SHE SAID

I noticed indeed that you referred to God as a he. Almost everybody does that, so I will conform. I wonder however, who started this trend of a male God? I don't believe that it was a woman!

Instead of asking my chickens how they see their God, I endeavor to put together something on this topic that may please you. It is really interesting how you noticed people's perception of a higher energy that looks very similar to each... but a bit or much bigger! You are so right because for me, my God has characteristics of my own being.

For the Vedic texts I so love, there are gods and goddesses, but all just deities in charge with bits and bobs of the Universe. Brahman however is the infinite, the inexplicable, the unchangeable, the Cosmic Principle, the only truth. The Vedas and the Upanishads don't relate to Brahman as God; they associate Him with the source or the cause of everything created, the Ultimate Reality. There is a verse I really love in Taittariya Upanishad 2.1 that says, *"Brahman is of the nature of truth, knowledge and infinity"*.

But in a way or another, Brahman is not alone because there is a very similar trinity to the Christian one, called Trimurti[45], a union of Brahma, Vishnu and Shiva. Please don't confound Brahman with Brahma! I know I will be talking about it later on, but what I would mention now is that Hindus worship Brahman by devotion to either Vishnu (or one of his avatars, Krishna, Narasimha and Rama), Shiva or Shakti the goddess, known as Durga, Kali or Parvati.

HE SAID

The list of erudite atheists is almost endless, Bertrand Russell[46], Daniel Dennett[47], Christopher Hitchens[48] among many. Baron d'Holbach was an eighteenth century atheist. He was a prominent figure in the French Enlightenment. Yes, I know that Enlightenment was not a spiritual event, but I still find the play on words amusing. Despite such accomplished thinkers propounding atheism, my belief in a Divine Force is unshakeable. Why?

It may seem strange to talk about logic in connection with God. If it is believed by only half the population of the world that their God is a representation of themselves there would be 3.8 billion versions of the deity. The whole concept of a God just does not compute. At the age of seven, I decided this way of thinking was ridiculous but I never lost my belief in a divine being so, as I stepped away from the Church of England, seventy years ago, I started to assemble my belief in a divine being.

I suggest to you, my friend, that the complexities of the Universe cannot be a chance happening, Hermes Trismegistus'[49] macrocosm and microcosm considerations defy any suggestion that a divine energy is not present.

An unknowable force of energy equates to my Ultimate Maker; this energy permeates the whole universe. As we write our book, you occasionally hear me saying, *"His Beauty shines through the whole Universe"* a while later I conclude with *"May His beauty dwell in our hearts"*. This is where what many call God is found inside every atom that makes the universe. The power is within me and you and everyone.

SHE SAID

Yes, God's strength is with all helping us living on a planet that we made by choice far from being perfect. *"His Strength is omnipotent"*. So if His power is incommensurable, why do we doubt that we were invested with the same energy to change this planet back to where it supposed to be? The answer is simple: because, in this battle ruled by greed and egoism, we lost the connection with the Creator.

To understand the unity of Atman (self) and Brahman (Cosmic Principle), we would need to follow the four Mahvakyas (great sayings) of Advaita Vedanta Astika (school of philosophy): *"Brahman is Prajnana (pure consciousness)"* (Aitareya Upanishad[50] 3.3 in Rig Veda[51]); *"Atman is Brahman"* (Mandukya Upanishad[52] 1.2 in

Atharveda); *"That essence you are"* (Chandogya Upanishad[53] 6.8.7 in Sama Veda[54]) and "I am divine" (Brihadaranyaka Upanishad[55] 1.4.10 in Yajur Veda[56]). All I can add to that is my hope that we can live up to our divine nature!

HE SAID

When you walk in a wood, do not look at a tree and think that's a pohutukawa or a beech, for a name is not needed. Look at the wonders of the tree; look inside it at the activity going on and the failure to believe in a divine presence is impossible.

Just one final thought. If I give up my pedantic insistence that the word *"God"* has all the wrong connotations and use it to describe my ultimate maker, I will insist that this word is a verb a *"doing word"*.

Of course, Devi, I could just have said in answer to your query *"yes"* instead of my gentle diatribe against atheism. But where would the fun in that have been?

SHE SAID

Same atoms in the tree as in us, Paul, so if trees are beauty, so are we. Everything resumes to the concept of *"Zero and Infinity"*, so beautifully described in the Vedic texts.

The Bindhu (a dot in a circle) was for the Vedic Sages the symbol of reducing to nil, negating the egoic self; therefore accepting our divine nature, a symbol of pure consciousness or the ultimate reality. The same symbol has an identical meaning today. Thus, I am wondering what stops us annihilating our ego and surrender to our divine nature when we know that the prize is infinite: pure consciousness. Are we that fragmented already?

HE SAID

If we are fragmented, it depends on what level you consider the fragmentation occurring. I suggest that we are aware that our individual souls are not broken or fragmented; in fact you and I believe ours are linked but look around at the physical beings that inhabit our world. At that level fragmentation occurs, physical and physiological fragmentation is driven by our minds, activated by external forces. From childhood we are taught that we must compete, the words *"let the devil take the hindmost"* come from a seventeenth century children's game, but now seem almost deep in our psyche.

In Kabbalah, there is described Shevira, the shattering of the Sephirot vessels; this was the shattering of Adam Kadmon, the Primordial Man. I have great respect for Isaac Luria *"Ha ARI"*[57], but as ever I have to put the Copper philosophy and describe my thinking. The Comic Soul was shattered and, as I have said before, the separate parts then broke in two with the twins being parted. As we have discussed previously, the souls' task was then to purify and ascend upwards to be reunited with the Cosmic Soul.

SHE SAID

Just think at what you, as a Kabbalist, would call Tzimtzum, the contraction of God at the very beginning of time to create space for mankind and the world in general. That proves the essence of God-mankind, but what happened from then on is a totally different story.

Perhaps you are right in saying that instead of living the light as the emanation of the Divine Energy, we divided our existence in small pieces and, since then, our only mission is to complete the puzzle. We can however find our embodied soul, and ourselves, but do we dare to find God as part of our soul, too? As much as we ignore it, Atman, the Self, is Brahman, the Cosmic Soul.

How can we, humans, forget about our divine nature?

HE SAID

Devi, you say *"but do we dare to find God as part of our soul"*. I think we can, but I suggest it may be stronger than can. You know I do not use the word God because of the baggage that comes with it, but for ease, I will this time. My God is incorporeal; it has no material existence unlike the Abrahamic God who almost seems to be tangible. My God is not only all encompassing, but Its essence is within me and everything I can see, touch and feel. Our Universe is within God's essence.

I pray, but when I pray, I pray to the God inside me. In doing this prayer, there is also a wave, a vibration going outward. Gautama Buddha[58] said *"we are what we think"*; all we are arises with our thoughts and with our thoughts we make the world. So when I pray for your health I aim to be a change agent.

My dear, I have wondered away from *"is God part*

of our soul", but this is to explain how I believe that God is a part of it. I have just thought I could have been briefer in saying our soul is part of the Cosmic Soul, which in turn is within the Energy that created all this, so that our soul is part of God.

SHE SAID

Is the soul part of the Cosmic Soul or the other way around? You know my opinion! Based on my affiliation to Advaita Vedanta philosophy, Atman, the eternal Self, is Brahman, what you call the Cosmic Soul. That implies that all beings, people and animals, are part of the universal divine whole and the only way freedom can be achieved is by acknowledging our divine nature. The fragmentation, you referred to starts with separating ourselves from our souls.

I mentioned Advaita, because Dvaita[59], another branch of Vedanta sees Atman different to Brahman, whilst Akshar Purushotam[60] branch refers to Atman as being Jivatman. It may sound complicated, but it is not. Jivatman is the individual soul, whilst Atman refers to the universal self. Many people mistaken one for another, but they are totally different concepts. But again, I adhere to Advaita Vedanta, so I sympathise with their philosophy.

HE SAID

Now let us look at another aspect of fragmentation and return to that seventeenth century children's game. It was decided that we should call our species Homo Sapiens because that means *"wise or astute human"*, but I think you will agree, Devi, that those words are now such a misnomer. I have mentioned before Aesop's[61] words *"united we stand divided we fall"* but every day my belief grows that, unless we revise our separatist considerations and stop being divided, Homo Sapiens will fall.

It is 2021 when we write and the world has been and is being ravaged by a pandemic. Are we united in fighting this? If ever there was a time when people, countries, nations should combine it is now, but the old British naval saying *"pull the ladder up Jack I'm alright"* is writ large. I must apologise for so many aphorisms.

So Devi, thank you for listening to this ramble and I return to my first comment, which was a qualified yes. Yes, our souls have become fragmented, but as I say yet again that fracturing is being repaired; the soul is aware of what its task is. I have also a belief that despite the power bases, which urge man to be separated from man this fracturing, will be reversed.

I suggest that the realisation that man must reunite with man is starting to stir and a principle of the Oneness of Mankind is not only necessary but also inevitable and that a realisation of this is approaching and gaining speed.

On Saturday evening and again on the next morning I sat and discussed *"fractured humanity"* with a small group of friends who believe that mankind will return to wholeness. There are many such groups around the world. I suggest that the energy from the thinking of these groups will eventually combine and become a force that will change universal thinking from the insistence on the *"I"* to the realisation that our only salvation is *"Us"* as a unity.

SHE SAID

I agree that the only salvation is oneness, because at the end of the day there is a common source of Atman, the Self, and that is Brahman, the Ultimate Reality or the one and only Cosmic Principle. For me, as a Vedanta scholar, this is an obvious fact, as evident as the concept of oneness is. However our human nature tends to dissociate and separate from all and everything. It may be the rush of the present, greed or the desire to shine above others, forgetting that our common source is the same atom that formed identical interchangeable molecules.

You talked about the fragmentation of the soul and I am wondering if this is not again the separation of Atman, as the Universal Self, from the absolute and infinite Cosmic Soul. And if this is what you refer to, then the way back is the state of Samadhi (Self Collectedness), the only one in which oneness and unity with God can be experienced. As a yogi, Samadhi is a way of life really; therefore I will be reveling some facts about it you may agree with or not.

Samadhi is in fact the total contemplation of the Absolute with the desire of absorption into the cosmic identity. The word in Sanskrit has two roots *"sam"* meaning "together" and *"dha"* meaning *"to integrate in the aim of acquiring wholeness"*. I associate Samadhi with a state of super consciousness, achieved in deep meditation; therefore there are stages in order to master it. The first is Savitarka Samadhi or dissociating what is real from what is not. In this level, a yogi would know how to use the right words and decide what is useful to experience and what is not. In Sa-Amsita Samadhi, a yogi would purify their mind allowing it to spike deeper. What follows naturally is Savichara Samadhi, in some way, the Cosmic Mind replacing the ordinary thoughts produced by the mind itself; therefore the notions of time and space would have a different meaning. In the last stage, Sa- Anada Samandhi, the mind becomes Sattvic (angelic) allowing the total bliss to kick in that permits identifying ourselves with all and everything. This is the state of understanding our true nature in oneness. In this last level of Samadhi, my feeling was always that God's consciousness is the real source of our consciousness.

HE SAID

Devi, I have a question for you, is consciousness fundamental, ubiquitous and does this show that the Universe is God and that God is the Universe?

If you refute what follows you must explain when consciousness arrived on the evolutionary scene. My basis is that consciousness is a vibration that comes from the Divine Source; therefore it permeates the whole Universe whether the medium is tangible or intangible. Looking at it from the reverse direction, the intrinsic nature of everything is consciousness.

I will argue my suggestion from two platforms, the spiritual and that occupied by the theoretical physicist, let me commence with the latter. The ground of all being, or could I call it the Creative Principle, lies in the unified or Super String Field[62]. The strings are like small elastic bands with ten degrees of freedom and are continually vibrating. This is a field of potentiality and unity; all things are possible and are unified. As consciousness is fundamental, it emerges from the basis of mind and matter, which is an intelligence and pure being. Consciousness transudes upwards. As I wrote these words, I realised that trying to separate my thoughts on the physical and nonphysical is not possible. I suggest, my friend, that above I am describing our Creator and how the unknowable energy creates all. This being so, I will not use my suggested two platforms, but just discuss my premise regarding the advent of consciousness.

To continue, whether ethereal or tangible the base ground is just energy, intelligence; this may be alluded to but never described in a comprehensible manner. This base ground is pure Being and it is the Fountain Head or Godhead of consciousness. We are unable to understand the extent of consciousness, but all emerges from its vibrations. Perhaps this analogy will explain how the various forms are constructed. I walked by the ocean earlier; a strong wind was blowing from the east and from the same water a variety of waves formed, endless shapes and sizes. This is how pure consciousness is. It is suffused with all forms of the natural word all in unity. We are only aware of one consciousness and sadly our ego blocks us from seeing this unity as the ego insists on its individual uniqueness and prevents us being aware of our true nature.

Your thoughts on the formation of consciousness please Devi and if you disagree that it is fundamental, please advise how it was formed. As you know, I suggest we are consciousness and that our awareness allows us to recognise this and also recognise that our phenomenal world is a reflection of the universal mind.

SHE SAID

Do you realize how much pressure you put on me by starting with a question and finishing with another one? I will do my best though. So what came first, the hen or the egg… mind or matter; Cit (consciousness) or the Universe?

I am not very sure if you approach creation of the Universe and Cosmic Consciousness from an Abrahamic point of view, a Vedic perspective or just the Copper's standpoint. As you know the Abrahamic perspective admits that the Universe has a starting and an ending point, creation and uncreation; therefore consciousness develops from birth and ends with death.

From the Vedic perspective, the formation of the Cosmos has no beginning and no ending and it happens in cycles of creation and dissolution according to the energies involved into it or withdrawn from it.

The Vedic texts are complex and very tolerant by the way, accepting different arguments and approaches to the Cosmic Mind. The Puranas[63], for instance, describe that the mind came first. The story is quite fascinating and it starts with Vishnu awakening and Brahma rising from a lotus on Vishnu's navel. It was Brahma's mind that created living beings, perhaps because he felt lonely or he thought that he was the true creator.

Another myth talks about the pillars of fire that embodied consciousness and about both Brahma in a form of a swan and Vishnu as a boar trying to find it. These are just myths, Paul, but every legend starts from a seed of truth; in this case the Vritti (mental processes) as a creator of our reality.

My point is that for consciousness to ignite, it needs a spark and that is not necessarily produced in the mind, because there is no proof that consciousness is in the mind. That flicker, in my opinion, was the expanding thought of creation itself.

As you know, my views are in accord with the Vedanta school of philosophy that refers to Mayaopahita Chaitanya, consciousness linked to the Maya (illusion), Avidyaopahita Chaitaya, consciousness associated to Avidya (ignorance) and simply Chaitanya, the Pure Consciousness. Before you tell me that there is only one consciousness, I am rushing to explain.

Mayaopahita considers Maya (illusion) as being the source of creation of all existence whilst Avidya (ignorance) is the cause of mistaking Atman, the Universal Soul, with the body we see in the mirror. Therefore Chaianya, true Pure Consciousness, is the product of denying both Maya and Avidya.

To be perfectly honest, there is no way you would not agree with those three states because they are identified with perception and thoughts and consciousness in general is based on those. My personal opinion is that science was not able so far to put together the puzzle of consciousness, but the Vedic Sages had quite a brilliant go at it.

Is consciousness fundamental? What can be more fundamental than something that is infinite and is present with us day and night? So the link with God is simple, Paul, and stays in the essence of our eternal Atman, that relies on

Cit (consciousness) in order to allow the Sat (truth) of Ananda (total happiness).

CHAPTER 3

ETHER

HE SAID

Morning Devi. I had just sent you some pictures of the sun rising over the sea when you sent this text *"What are your thoughts about Ether?"*

Ether is silence, space, stillness; it is the element that holds us, binds all matter as one entity. It contains the essence of all the elements. Our thoughts and consciousness lie in this subtle field. Theoretical physicists accept that all is surrounded by a force that holds the orbs of the Universe in place; and call it dark energy because they are not able to explain it satisfactorily. One thing it is not is the concept we have of the word *"dark"*. In fact just the opposite...

SHE SAID

Science struggled, in my opinion, to define dark energy or ether, but what was difficult for science, it came so easy for the ancient Sages. I realised today that perhaps the best way to describe ether is in the starting of Isha Upanishad:

"Purnamadah Purnamidam
Purnat Purnamudachyate
Purnasya Purnamadaya
Purnameva Vashishyate"

There are all sorts of translations, but the correct one would define ether perfectly:

"That is Whole (infinite)?
The Whole arises from the Whole.
Having taken the Whole from the Whole,
Only the Whole remains."

Isn't that beautiful? As a logical guy you are, I assume that you mix your faith with bits of science; also that for you the Universe started with the Big Bang.

HE SAID

I often refer to the burst of energy that started everything, the so-called *"Big Bang"*. It is suggested that at that point, Chochma on the Kabbalists Tree of Life, something came from nothing, with the greatest respect, *"rubbish"*. Something came from something that we cannot possibly comprehend. It was energy containing the whole of creation that burst forth from the Creator. A thought I would like us to challenge ourselves on is do we live in the mind of that Creator? But that is for another time.

For a childlike analogy, try this Devi. My mother used to make a jelly with little square pieces of tinned fruit suspended in it. The fruit, planets and stars, the jelly that held everything in place, our ether... Take away the jelly and no wonderful dessert; take away the ether and no wonderful life. No Devi, no Copper.

SHE SAID

I loved the jelly analogy! I propose that Akasha (ether) is God that expands in us. In Sanskrit, Akasha comes from the root *"kas"* that means *"to be"* and in the Vedic texts is described as *"open space"* or *"open sky"*.

Most of the Vedic Darshana (philosophy) schools and especially Vaisheshika[64], one of the main one, believed that Akasha was a Padartha (category), they named Dravya (entity). The other five categories the Vedic texts described are: Guna (quality), Karma (activity), Samanya (generality), Visesa (particularity), Samavaya (inherence) and Abhava (non existence).

The Vedic schools of philosophy identified six Dravya that are eternal: Jiva (Soul), Pudgala (Matter), Akasha (Ether), Dharma (Motion), Adharma (Rest) and Kala (Time).

According to the Vaisheshika school of thought, which bases its doctrine on the Vedic atom theory, ether cannot be perceived because it doesn't have two primordial conditions: perceptible dimension and colour; therefore Akasha is eternal because it does not depend on any substances for its existence. For the Nyasa[65] school of thought, based on the philosophy of logic and reasoning, ether and time are nonmaterial, each being a whole in itself.

I would just highlight the fact that ether is not vacuum and not dark matter either, which behaves like an average particle having though no electric charge or interaction with other matter particles. So I totally agree with ether being what science calls now dark energy. I hope I don't step into your territory saying that dark doesn't mean black; it just means unknown. Like ether, dark energy is not a particle. (Big Bang versus Big Crush).

The Vedas talked about the expansion of the Universe. Science confirmed that the Universe doesn't expand at a constant rate. Just think of the Hubble's Law[66]; the expansion is accelerating. Therefore is it Einstein versus Karl Popper[67], science versus non-science, falsifiability versus non-falsifiability or theory versus evidence?

HE SAID

You mentioned expansion. Dark Energy is the name given to the suspected force that is causing the expansion of our Universe to accelerate. It is a property of space.

There is nothing sinister about it; it is just that it cannot be seen. As you know, the ancient Greeks believed that the Gods breathed ether. So for a good few years man has believed we are surrounded by something. Donald Hoffman's[68] hypothesis takes it further in saying that a form of matter/ energy lies in the substance and that our perception of reality is wrong; we are fooled by a perceptual illusion.

It is possible that evolution has done us no favors by natural selection selecting the attributes for survival of the species over other skills we may have had at one time. Some animals and birds still have these. Your few lines say it exactly: matter cannot be created or destroyed, only changed in form *"The Law of Conservation of Mass"*[69], in other words the whole was there in the beginning and the whole is still there.

SHE SAID

According to the Vedas, all material creation started with ether. *"What is the essence of this world? Akasha, said Pravahana; All these beings arise from Akasha alone and are finally dissolved into Akasha; because Akasha alone is greater than all these and Akasha is the support at all times."* (Chandodya Upanishad 1:9 1-2).

We both agreed that we are all one, part of this Universe that is part of us. If this is true, have you ever considered the ether within us? *"That is the ether within the heart (Atman/ soul). That ether in the heart (Brahman) is omnipresent and unchanging. He who knows this obtains omnipresent and unchanging happiness"* (Chandogya Upanishad 3.12:9). I would quote another verse as a proof of us being made of the same particles as the whole Universe: *"And the ether which is around us is the same as the ether that is within us"* (Chandogya Upanishad 3.12:8).

So, Paul, if it is true that ether is *"omnipresent, infinite, immortal and indestructible"* also that it *"is the element of which god and celestial beings are made"*, then the whole reincarnation process and divine nature of humanity is proven. Our souls are divine and eternal! ... and so much more: we are vibration and sound because *"The origin of ether is Shabda"*, which is the primeval space from which vibration emerges before it transforms in sound. That makes me think of mantras as vibration and sound...

HE SAID

It is Good Friday as I write this and so I thought I would walk along the beach and think before the park became crowded. I was thinking if our thoughts float in the ether in a similar manner to the quantum waves floating in a vacuum both thought and wave full of potential Where does our consciousness lie in relationship to this?

As I walked on the grass amongst the trees, the accuracy of my belief that all matter is connected was made clear. You were working, seeing clients, over three hundred seventy miles away. You must have had a break because suddenly you Devi Harjeet were with me. The intensity of the joy and peace saw me start to cry so we walked along together until you said *"I have to work now Paul"*. What else could have proven my belief with such power? A unity, wholeness...

Every morning the first thing we both do is chant a Shanti Mantra. There is a line that speaks of wholeness; you chant *"Sarvesan puridan bhavatu"* and I *"May there be wholeness for all"*. The wholeness we call upon is the ether you ask about. It is so simple, but we try to complicate it with hypothesis after hypothesis.

SHE SAID

We picked right when we agreed on chanting the same mantras in the mornings and evenings; two ancient Shanti (peace) mantras from the Upanishads, you chanting in English and I in Sanskrit, the language they were initially spoken and afterwards written.

The vibration of our chant penetrates the first Arupa Jnaha (level of meditation) that is ether and gives us a hope that every person on this planet feels peace and harmony within themselves. Ether rejoices itself when the right vibration penetrates it, because ether is Pheuma, the breath of the soul or the breath of God opposing to Psyche, which is the breath of life, the ego. I am basing my argument not only on Vedic texts; on Greek philosophy too. The Stoics[70] believed that our soul possesses the universal and eternal Logos, the power or force that controls the Cosmos... at least according to Heraclitus[71].

I would love to hear your thoughts.

HE SAID

The ether or indeed dark energy is filled with waves and vibrations of potential. Consider the old conundrum, *"if a tree falls over in a forest with no one around does it make a sound"*? This is rather like a particle becoming a wave until it is observed. The tree falls and sound waves are omitted, but it needs an ear, the observer, to turn these vibrations into sound.

When we chant our mantra early morning and late night our voices cause vibrations within the ether. If a thousand people chant or pray, many vibrations or waves are combining within that medium, this ocean of energy will start to see the words used introduce change. As the Lord Buddha said *"we are what we think, all that we are arise arises with our thoughts, with our thoughts we make the world"*.

Returning to the requirement for an observer needed to change a wave into a particle, our Creator is the observer, the change agent. So our waves are turned into action by our Creator and, if enough waves are calling for change, it will occur. We, as human beings have the potential to make the changes so desperately need if our race is to survive. Remember Devi, we are the only group of beings who are working to destroy our planet, not out of necessity but because of avarice, the extreme greed for wealth or material gain.

SHE SAID

We are what we think? Beautifully said, Paul. My verse to you says the same: *"You are what your deep desire is. As your desire is, so is your will. As your will is, so is your deed. As your deed, so is your destiny"* (Brihadaranyaka Upanishad[72] 4.4.5).

And yes, we constantly damage our planet with our desire, will and deed; therefore I am concerned about the destiny of our home planet. We are the only race that hunts for pleasure, destroys beautiful pieces of land only to build more shopping centers, like there are not enough around, and chops down forests for no reason... And we are the only race that eats dinner whilst watching people killed on television. Should I continue? What is your Tree of Life saying about that?

HE SAID

I use the Lurianic version of the Tree of Life rather

than the Cordovero Tree of Emanation[73] because Isaac Luria uses pathways across the upper Sephiroth that link Da'at to Chochma and Binah. Cordovero makes no such connection as he identifies Da'at as the invisible Sephirah. I believe that it is in Da'at where twin souls reunite and move forward toward the Godhead. This because Isaac Luria shows Da'at included in paths of emanation and return.

In her book *"The Secret Doctrine of the Kabbalah"*[74], Leonora Leet suggests that the Hebrew scholar John Milton[75] incorporated Luria's doctrine of the Tzimtzum (self-contraction) in his epic *"Paradise Lost"*[76]. This started me thinking.

I believe that if one looks around the present day world and notes how man is treating his fellow man, totally without compassion one must conclude a wrong turn must have been taken in man's psyche. Was it at the time of an event recorded as the fall of Adam and Eve that paradise was lost? Or was it much later when the church and science split apart under the input of Newtonian physics[77]?

So I ask you a question. What does Vedic Philosophy say? Has man taken a wrong turn? If not why is the world on a self-destruct path?

SHE SAID

We turn wrong perhaps when we lost the union Rig Veda talks about *"Matara, Pitara, Janitara"*. (*"Heaven is my father, brother my atmosphere is my navel and the great earth is my mother"*)...

The Rishis understood the Universe with all that it consists of as a big happy family. Everything started changing when we forgot that we shouldn't *"pollute the sky and destroying anything of Atariksha (atmosphere)"* (Yajur Veda 5.5.43), and *"poison the water and harm or cut trees"* (Yajur Veda 5.6.33) or to *"never kill animals"* (Yajur Veda 13.37).

You may be right to blame it on Adam and Eve… Perhaps our fall started once humankind killed the first animal whilst food grew naturally on the ground. *"The earth provides surface for vegetation which control the heat buildup. The herbs and plants having union with the sun rays provide congenial atmosphere for the life to survive"* (Atharveda 5.28.5). Cravings for blood, greed and avarice brought us where we are!

To be perfectly honest, I am worried for the future of this planet. I am sure you are too, Paul. Can God save us from what is gone too far? What are your thoughts on the concept of an omnipotent mighty God?

HE SAID

You asked me Devi to give you my thoughts about the concept of the word God. As I splashed through the surf on my walk this morning, I thought about your challenge, found a bench and wrote a few notes. This is the outcome.

Since an early age I have had a difficulty with the word God. As you know I was brought up in the tradition of the Church of England, here I was taught that God was an elderly white man with a beard and long white hair. In discussing this with friends? They often remark *"like you then"*. My response is *"that's why I die my goatee purple, so there is no confusion between him and I"*. But this image implanted at an early impressionable age has been difficult to dislodge. So I will talk about my Divine Energy because that is what my God is.

SHE SAID

Same Divine Energy is my God, Paul. I believe that Para Brahman, the Supreme Energy, is within us all! This opens a new topic, oneness. *"In very truth, the One has become the whole world"* (Rig Veda 8.58.2). As a joke, I refer to God as my groovy God, you know that…. but maybe I should put the goofiness aside and focus on how to expand the qualities of God within myself.

"Ong Namo Guru Dev Namo" ("I bow to the Divine Teacher within") is the mantra every Kundalini yogi from all around the world uses to tunes in to the God within us!

HE SAID

When you asked me to give you my thoughts about God. My first reaction was it is impossible to talk about something we cannot possible have any conception of? But you ask, so these are my considerations and feelings. On the Kabbalistic Tree of Life, above Keter, the crown, lies the unmanifest of negative existence; negative existence that lies between the Godhead and Creation. There are three veils there. The nearest, just above Creation is Ein Sof Aur, limitless light. As we move above creation, a second veil Ein Sof is found this is limitless, it is the first stage toward creation. We know little about Ein Sof as the intellect of our being cannot comprehend at this level. It is at this point that Ayin[78,] the ultimate void, starts to focus out of no thing into the limitlessness where there is something that is.

You will recall how I have used *"as above so below"* to describe the nature of the Universe? Well, that sequence occurs here also. The three veils Ein Sof Aur, Ein Sof and Ayin perform a crystallising of the being that permeates the whole of All. It is without form, space or time but as it manifests downward on the Tree as the lightening flash moving from side to side galaxies, planets, organic life, mankind form from no thing. As we travel down deeply, atoms, subatomic particles are found until eventually we again find an energy, but no matter as it was above Ayin.

So, my Divine Energy lies within this process but perhaps I should speak of a Divine Oneness because all matter is connected. On this basis, my Divine Oneness lies within me. If I want to find peace, I look inside and it is here wrapped in joy. I need no complicated dogma, endless books to study, say long wordy prayers; all I need to do is still my mind and say to the Divine Oneness *"I could do with a bit of help"* and it will come.

So, from a Paul Copper look alike with whom I felt no affinity I have moved to a certain knowledge that my creative force lies within, as it is within the orchids you brought for me. As ever I await your thoughts.

SHE SAID

If I only gave God as much time as I spend on my orchids…

Is there something, anything whatsoever beyond us

and, if there is, is that God? Some people believe that our destiny is to continuously search for God, when in fact there is nothing to search for and nothing to find because God is in us. We were born with a divine energy within that is coiled up in the Muladhara, the Root chakra area, more than likely around the Sacrum bone - in Greek Sacrum means sacred-, which can be awakened and released in the Universe. The sum energies released is God. Imagine how huge that force is! How many people have ever lived? Billions and billions of energies united in God.

Every religion ever invented by people, every dogma and every school of thought talks about this divine energy in us. They all agree that this Shakti (energy) is a feminine energy and that, acknowledging it and being aware of it, is the real spiritual awakening.

In the old and new Testaments, it is mentioned in several verses - six verses in Proverbs only -: *"She is a tree of life to them that lay hold upon her: and happy is every one that retaineth her"* (Proverbs 3:13.18); *"She is more precious than rubies: and all the things thou canst desire are not to be compared unto her"* (Proverbs 3:13.15). In the New Testament, this energy is referred to as the Holy Spirit.

Judaism calls it Shekhinah (Semitic root in: *"dwelling"* or *"settling"*); Rabis refer to it as *"the feminine attribute of the presence of god"*. In the Talmud (Tractate Shabbat)[79]: *"The Shekhinah rests on man neither through gloom, nor through sloth, nor through frivolity, nor through levity, nor through talk, nor through idle chatter, but only through a matter of joy in connection with a mitzvah"*.

Kabbalah followers, back to Assyrians actually, call it the Tree of Life within, because at the end of the day what is that diagram you study if not the true path within, the tree planted in us? *"A breath which comes from this world shakes the branches of the Tree of Life, Which spreads the fragrance of the future world in this world and brings the holy souls alive. These souls come up waking each other ... and the Tree of Life rejoices."* (Zohar[80]). But this is your territory; so I would not interfere!

The Egyptians referred to the Uraeus, the serpent or the staff of Osiris, as being the Divine Shakti. Lots to talk about here... one day perhaps! The medical system adopted it as Caduceus[81]. Islam calls it Shakina, the presence of God in us. You may know that in the Quran[82] *"Sakinah is a sweet breeze/wind, whose face is like the face of a human"*. Hindus call it Kundalini Shakti, the divine feminine energy within us, coiled up at the base of the spine. Hindus worked with it and learnt to release it in a practice called yoga, which means *"union"*.

Kundalini yoga, which is nothing other than Laya[83] yoga, the yoga practiced by our ancient Sages, bases its practice on awakening the divine energy, pushing it up from where it sits to Ajna, the Third Eye or the Brow Chakra; guiding it to Sahasrara, the Crown chakra, and then releasing it into the Universe. Instead of using our own energy, we access the sum of all energies called God. Kundalini yoga is sacred, Paul, and its mysteries and secrets are presented in twenty of the Upanishads. You would wonder what is secret about it if it is revealed in the

Vedic texts, but my answer is this: one has to be taught to be able to understand them.

Have you ever watched videos on You Tube of people going through an orgasmic Kundalini awakening? Or heard people speaking in tongues during episodes of enlightenment, mostly in Pentecostal churches? It is fascinating! We, the Kundalini yogis learn to awaken Kundalini Shakti in a natural way and are able to store the energy in different chakras. We learnt to play with it and access it when we need it. We believe that God is within us!

HE SAID

"Is there something, anything beyond us and, if there is, is that God"? What a wonderful title for a dialogue.

If the Universe is mental and in saying this we suggest that the Universe is the mind of what I shall call God, logic suggests that an essence of God is within every subatomic particle. 13.8 billion years ago there was an event followed by the expansion, so again logically every subatomic particle came from the same source ergo every creature and the very essence of the planet is linked. If this is disjointed it's because some blonde bombshell keeps texting me.

So I propose that the vibration of a Divine Being is in the rock up to the creature; the vibration is just at a differing speed... So QED must find the divine within us. The question is how do we find this energy and use its power to return us whence we came.

The Western regions have lost their way because they are controlled by the need for power and prestige, so they are little help in this search even though they allude to an awakening. But the other faiths mentioned in your paper call for the creature to look inside and I agree that is where the essence must lie.

Regarding your comment *"instead of using our own energy, we access the sum of all energies called God"*, this access will allow the creatures to combine and return to God. This has to be done if civilization is to continue. This is happening around the world, but it must accelerate.

SHE SAID

At this stage, for me at least, it is less important what came first, the egg or the chooks in my garden, nor why the rock is a rock and my dog Hendrix is a quadruped whilst I am human. Regardless of how it all started, we all share the same atoms and, as I have said for so many times, we just came packaged differently. Oneness with and within everything is not a hypothesis; it is a certainty. And because it is, all I can do, as a human, is to adhere and comply with the eight limbs of yoga, one of them being the Yamas[84] that refers to my own attitude towards nature, animals and the environment in general.

My point however is that, because I was reincarnated as human, I have the privilege of holding within myself a divine energy. I could die like an ignorant with it within me or I could choose to use it. I am not sure if my parrots for example have these options, but I know that I do... and you do too. And I understand that we are as divine as the concept of God is, because God is us and we are God. I know exactly how your brain works and I sense that you already picked on that and thought to yourself that if we are God, trees and animals are God too... and they may all be. Therefore instead of searching for flying horses to worship, we could just start purifying ourselves and, as you beautifully said, - as always! - look inside ourselves. And that perception within is called respect for us and for everything else. And it's called love!

"Ek Ong Kar, Sat Nam" (*"One Creator created this creation; truth is His identity"*).

HE SAID

There is that beautiful Mantra *"Ek Ong Kar"*, *"One Creator"*, so why do we insist on *"I"* or *"me"*? I will explore this from my perspective Devi, and then await your view.

We live in a totally material world where the more *"stuff"* we accumulated and the more financial wealth we display, the higher we sit upon society's ladder. To achieve this, we insist that I am better than you; I do not care if I damage you because I am very important. Let the Devil take the hindmost, those without do not matter. Look around the world and see where this attitude has got us. We are currently fighting a world epidemic; this could bring us all together but no, the rich nations squabble amongst themselves as to who has the most vaccine, not say how can we help our less prosperous neighbor.

Wherever you look at the basis of spiritual faith and religious traditions, they stand upon a Divine Unity. Even from the corporeal perspective, this unity was there at the inception. The cosmologists tell us that 13.8 billion years ago, from no thing out popped a fireball, which they call the Big Bang and, at the point of the *"popping"*, all matter must have been unified. So, having been part of a Divine Unity at some point in our history, were did Homo Sapiens go wrong? It's ironic is it not Devi that *"we"* decided to call ourselves Homo Sapiens as this means *"wise human"*. Oh what a misnomer!

SHE SAID

The veil of ignorance of *"wise human"* is the source of all misery. Is the salvation Vidya (knowledge) or that wisdom you mentioned, Jnana (supreme spiritual knowledge)?

"Into a blind darkness they enter who follow after the Ignorance; they as if into a greater darkness who devote themselves to the Knowledge alone" (Isha Upanishad 1.9).

Is that knowledge, Paul, a vessel to the union with the Creator? I actually believe that everything starts with knowing ourselves and discovering the macrocosm in our own microcosm, but, as you have said, things get messy in a world based on materialism only. Perhaps reconsidering oneness and unity, which should have been our main focus initially, is the knowledge of the absolute.

HE SAID

In many traditions, a breaking up or shattering is referred to Lao Tzu, the Kabbalah; in Hindu religion, four bowls reflecting one sun and can I suggest that even the Christian Old Testament, Genesis chapter 5 talks of Adam and Eve *"begating"* a whole population of beings. So do these writings refer to a breaking up of the Comic Soul? I wonder Devi, was this shattering accidental or by design? Has the Divine Unity given all beings a task? That of purifying ourselves and returning to the oneness with that unity... The Kabbalistic Tree of Life can be used as a road map for this, plotting our return course from Malkuth, the sovereign state that exists in all of us, to Keter the crown whence we enter Unity or become Whole again.

I find it ironic that Isaac Newton the physicist could be called the father of *"The Age of Reason"*[85], when in fact for thirty years or more, he explored Alchemy and so should, more accurately, be remembered as the *"last of the magicians"*. What Newton was doing was attempting to break down the base material, remove the dross and find the pure spirit within. This corresponds with our attempts to purify our base being, remove the falsehood of duality and return to the Divine Unity. The difference being his work lasted around thirty years, ours may last several life times, or longer, before we approach enlightenment.

So my dear friend, it's over to you to wipe away my ramblings with your razor sharp Vedic philosophy. If you can!

SHE SAID

So you, my mentor, are doubting me! Then I would start by mentioning Samkhya, one of the schools of Vedic philosophy that was and still is based on duality. Its followers believe that the Universe consists of two things,

Purusha and Prakriti. The tricky part is that the Samkhyas are both theists and atheists. Purusha is the Self or consciousness that connects everything and everybody, the soul, whilst Prakriti is the primal condition of everything, matter, mostly accepted as the feminine aspect of life. I have to quote Munduka Upanishad on the root of Purusha *"Splendid and without a bodily form is this Purusha, without and within, unborn, without life breath and without mind, higher than the supreme element. From him are born life breath and mind. He is the soul of all beings"*.

You mentioned dualism. Well, the Samkhya is based on duality... Purusha and Prakriti. Samkhya's dualism however is not necessarily denying oneness, which proves that there is always more than one solution to an argument.

HE SAID

Going back to Samkhya's followers being theists and atheists. So the theists believe in a God, but how do they see God's relationship to Purusha and Prakrti? How does the atheist's philosophy fit in with the Vedas writings?

SHE SAID

Samkhya is the oldest school of philosophy in Hinduism and all the Vedic views in this school are attributed to Sage Kapila[86]. He believed that the soul is confusing itself with the body; and this is the reason why I always said that the body is an instrument of consciousness; therefore physical pain is usually felt at the soul level too.

I said that the followers of Kapila's concepts about creation are both theists and atheists because initially Samkhya had no place for a creationist God. Their idea about creation was very simple: the Universe is enough to express itself. Therefore, an eternal and unchanging God cannot exist in a Universe in permanent change. Later though, Samkhya added Ishvara (God) to get themselves closer to the theistic views of Yoga school of philosophy, so, theists and atheists followers could express their opinions. Remember that freedom is rule number one in Hinduism!

Anyway, Samkhya's scholars obeyed to two laws: Satkaryavada, stating that cause and effect are the same; and Parinama, proving that the effect derives from the cause itself. Do you know that you would fit in so comfortable in Samkhya? As well as you fit in Panentheism. You are the master of that!

HE SAID

Panentheism comes from the Greek, *"pan"* that means *"all"*, *"en"* that means *"in"* and *"theos"* that means *"God"*; God and the world are inter-related with the world being in God and God being in the world.

In process philosophy, understanding God contains all possibilities and presents every possible response that an actual event might make to any events from the past that influence what that event becomes. Think of an event as a reflex to any other event. I am thinking that a thought is also a reflex driven by another thought but I need to contemplate that further.

As a panentheist, I cannot accept a dualistic nature of consciousness and matter. For me consciousness and matter are different manifestations of a basic ontological unity and all actualities have an element of mentality. The Universe is mental I suggest.

Thomas Young's *"Double Slit experiment"*[87] is used to confirm that particles can also be waves. The observer causes the change, but this proves that the mind can affect matter; this point is not driven home hard enough. Understanding the world as composed of relationships among particles that are physically separated provides a model based in science for understanding God's relation to the world. God's influence can be present at the level of individual events at quantum level so must be within all matter through entanglement.

Around 13.8 billion years ago there was an event from which our Universe has been formed. A surge of energy followed by an expansion these events taking nano seconds. This event is described in the Kabbalah Tree of Life on the plane of Beriya. Keter is the indescribable; it is on the plane of Atzilut, the subconscious. Think of the Dao *"et al" ("and others")*.

Then the first Sephirah Chochma. Chochma, wisdom, emits a spark of energy, the big bang. This is fired toward Benah, understanding, the expansion. Then Da'at, knowledge, the growth of the Universe, occurs over billions of years. Chochma, Binah and Da'at lay on Beriya the plane of the mind. In Da'at, the mind is linked with emotion and so the Universe grew. There is much more....

You will no doubt think this is questionable, but

ponder this Devi. 13.8 billion years ago there was a great unimaginable burst of energy. Was this the reformed cosmic soul shattering again? Various traditions I believe tell us so, but before this shattering, all was together so plain logic screams that at a point everything was one even God so every bit of stuff in the galaxy must contain the same essence, go on knock that logic.

God is in every atom, but the traditions tell us that there is a divine figure beyond this God. The Christian tradition volume of sacred lore says *"God was Told..."* Kabbalah tells us there are three veils above Keter, the divine self, En Sof Aur, En Sof, Ayin. Ayin is the ultimate void the no thing our mind cannot comprehend beyond this. And other traditions tell of an ultimate condition.

This will do for me; as ever it is been written in a vain attempt to clarify my mind's thinking so if you have got this far Devi, I thank you. These are my views no one else's so you may say Paul this is tosh but I will defend it.

SHE SAID

I told you that you are the master of Panentheism, but I have a point to prove too, so I would go back, if you don't mind, to Samkhya school of Vedic philosophy, and to Prakriti, which is the cause of the material world and Purusha that has no cause.

For Samkhya, dualism was straightforward. Imagine the shoemaker and the shoe. The shoemaker makes the shoe, but it remains outside of his creation or it doesn't identify itself with it; the shoemaker and the shoe are two different things. The shoemaker is God and the shoe is the Universe.... Purusha and Prakriti[88].

There are limitless individual Purushas, each infinite and unchangeable. There is no single Purusha that sits above any others; therefore nothing being in charge because Purusha is pure consciousness and Prakriti is unconsciousness. Togetherness... Samkhya believed that when Purusha is near matter, Prakriti begins to change. So with us, humans!

Samkhya philosophy created a map of the Universe, where each thing starts with or from another. Their motto was *"Liberation is freedom from Prakriti"*. They believed that the marriage between Prakriti and Purusha is a disaster; therefore a divorce is a must. But this is another story, so let's discuss it another time... or not!

HE SAID

You said that Samkhya School added God to get closer to the theistic views of Yoga school of philosophy, so, theists and atheists followers could express their opinions. Was it here that the deeper physiological aspects were considered?

SHE SAID

The deeper psychological aspects were always there. Just because you call God an energy or John or Mary it doesn't make it less God. The way Samkhya understood creation was that the Universe created itself and we are particles of the Universe so totally equal with everything in the Universe. We were all created at the same time; therefore there is no master over us. Then they decided to accommodate the yogis too and let them worship with them and they said yes, we call the Universe the only God, but we maintain what we said prior that this God and us all, plants and animals are all equal. The Universe or God is not the master of us and we are not the masters of it.

For Samkhya school of Vedic philosophy however the creator and the creation are two different things that have nothing in common other than the act of creation itself... the shoemaker and the shoe... Very different to other Vedic schools of thought, like Vedanta for example, which believes that God and us is one single aspect, all made of the same matter, all equal, blending the creator and the creation in, with God being God though!

HE SAID

How can anything be beyond God? I made a suggestion a few emails ago about a higher energy source. This being suggested in different traditions, I cannot accept that all is not united at the origin, shattered, but will be united again. Purusha is pure consciousness. I have already said that this is in line with my certainty that consciousness is fundamental. I agree that consciousness is all-pervasive but I also believe the Divine being is all-pervasive. So do you see this duality if it is a duality?

SHE SAID

This is the beauty of having so many ways of seeing things. You don't have to agree with all... or any. So let's just see what we are dealing with. In Hinduism, there are ten schools of philosophy, six Vedic and four non-Vedic;

all Asktika (Theistic) though. The Vedic schools based their statements on the Vedas, whilst the non-Vedic accepted other texts too. Don't confound these philosophies with religions, Paul. All these ten school interpreted the Vedas however suited them. Remember though that Samkhya was the oldest school in Hinduism, so for many years, it had no competition. I would keep this subject open if you don't mind for after we discuss cosmology and planetary systems.

I sometimes believe that the views of the ten Vedic schools of philosophy are as different as they can be on the more unconventional topics, one of them being karma. So, if you want something more exciting, I would continue my idea about karma by mentioning that in Jainism[89], karma is a physical substance that lingers in the Universe and our souls attract particles of this karma or to be more precise, karma particles stick to our souls according to our actions. These actions however are caused by thoughts of ignorance, not understanding ourselves, our mission, our path, our destiny, our... you name it! So what is the solution? Knowledge, but not necessarily passed from others; knowledge based on understanding Brahman, the cosmic principle that is within us.

HE SAID

So my soul would have attracted particles, but I was given the chance to understand and believe in a path. This path cleared the particles allowing my soul to meet with the Cosmos. Our meeting and journey was /is pre-ordained so was some form of divine being helping me meet you for instance. You see, I find the words very personal; for me they talk about my life as it was and as it is now and I believe from them that at some point my life became taken over, as I am now given more than guidance. I am still not getting things right, so I may upset you by each day until I become clearer on my path although I still do not fully know what is expected of me.

SHE SAID

Everything resumes to the soul's mission, doesn't it? Remember Sage Kapila who believed that the soul is confusing itself with the body; so, physical pain is usually felt at the soul's level too.

You may have heard that once the soul is released at death, it stays for a while in an area where it is healed of pain. It may be true, it may not be, but if it is, it means that the soul feels the pain exactly like the body does.

I am just thinking that maybe the vibrations of pain, excitement, happiness and sadness - because they all vibrate differently - are actually transmitted to the soul itself. The question I would like you to answer to is what is the relationship, if any, between soul and consciousness? Does the soul carry a sum of consciousnesses through each past life?

HE SAID

The soul and consciousness are differing entities. Consciousness is as the ether; it pervades everywhere and is fundamental.

Basic logic says that consciousness cannot be

individualised if we each have our own consciousness around us like a box. What happens when people are in close contact? Do the individual boxes bang together? I think not... it would be like a Monty Python sketch.

SHE SAID

I assume that you refer to an overlap of consciousness. Can my consciousness overlap yours? Good point, Paul. I believe that if it could cover yours, I could read your mind. But I cannot. Therefore, even if I would agree with a slight overlap of personalities, I couldn't prove my point because consciousness doesn't have dimensions; it is infinite. So where does mine stop for yours to start?

There is one consciousness however hidden in each being, all pervasive, the Eko Deva, shining, pure consciousness. All this means is that there is a bright, luminous aspect of each consciousness. Perhaps this is the overlap you mentioned.

HE SAID

For me, our soul is a much more complex part of the energy that drives our being. Of course the first question is when does the soul enter the body? This is my view and, by now, you should be aware that my view on life does not come from another's thinking but is Paul's. The soul joins what is to become a fetus at the point of conception the is a spiritual vibration at this point and a soul with a matching vibration is attracted and enters the mother's womb as the genetic process starts. I believe that the heart is one of the first organs to develop and it is here that the soul resides. No doubt in your response you will use the term Atman and I suggest that the soul or Atman starts to develop, as the fetus develops with the network that will eventually link and align the chakras.

The soul is the entity whose task is to return to whence it came and return to the creator. If you have read my thoughts on determinism, you will realise that I am certain that the Creator guides and give signposts as to the path the soul must take; the soul has energy of its own and may not take a direct a direct path, but over a number of life times it will gradually purify itself until it crosses the abyss near the top of the Kabbalistic Tree of Life and thence begins the final preparation for reunification with the Cosmic Soul.

SHE SAID

The soul? What a great topic. As usual, I will relate it to what it meant to our Rishis.

Atman (the universal Self) is the main concept in Hinduism, approached differently by different Askika (Theistic Vedic schools). They all agreed on one fact, which is that the soul is eternal, infinite and the purest state of everything that is. Atman is in fact the Self because it has no identifiable attributes.

The ancient Puranas, which are scriptures based on cosmology and creation, speak about the state of non-existence and a Triad forming at the end of it. This trinity contains Saguna Brahman, the Cosmic Soul, Jivatma, the individual souls that are described as the body of Vishnu, the Preserver and Prakriti, the nature or the matter.

Ribhu Gita, which is the sixth part of the Shiva Rahasya Purana, identifies the eternal and infinite attribute of the Self, comparing it to the Universal Soul: *"A god is entirely of the nature of the Self"* (Ribhu Gita 10:50).

I totally agree with Vedanta's philosophy in regards to the concept of the Self. Vedanta believes that Atman is the source of all existence; also that it is pure consciousness. Therefore for Vedanta, Atman and Brahman have the same characteristic of self- existence and self-brightness. As you can see, I mention again the state of luminous consciousness I referred to previously.

You say that the soul may reside in the heart; and you are right. The Upanishads are very specific about that in saying that the Self is in the heart. It can be true, Paul, because according to Svetasvara Upanishad[90] 5.9, the soul is very small and it could fit there: *"When the upper tip of a hair follicle is divided into one hundred parts and again each of such parts is further divided into one hundred parts, each such part is the measurement of the dimension of the spiritual soul"*.

In regards to the soul's journey though past lives, I would just say that this is called Samsara, the reincarnation cycle. In my opinion, as the soul is imprinted with all previous karmas in each life, it may be possible to be a blueprint of each consciousnesses in all past lives. I base my assertion on *"As the same fire assumes different shapes when it consumes objects differing in shape, so does the one Self take the shape of every creature in whom he is present"* (Katha Upanishad[90] II.2.9). And this is why perhaps some people are more evolved than others!

CHAPTER 4

THE UNIVERSE

HE SAID

During the opening of Dylan Thomas' *"Under Milk Wood"*, a play for voices, the First Voice says very softly *"Listen time passes. Listen...Time passes"*. But what is this thing called time?

Could we say that there are two types of time? There is the tick tock clock chiming time necessary as a frame of reference for when a number of people need to meet to perform a joint function. Or to measure a period of rest? We need a timetable to see when the train or bus leaves or do we?

I remember when I wanted to catch a bus from out in the sticks into Spanish Town in Jamaica, I asked what time does the bus leave and was told when it's full! No time, yet l did my daily task, then when I wanted to return home, the hand on my watch did not point to *"when its full"*, so I just got on the bus and sat looking in wonder at the sky then the bus was full and we left. No pressure no rushing... But yes, in modern life I am forced to concede that we need the ability to measure time.

At the opposite end of the time spectrum to my Jamaican bus journey comes the physicist's calculation of the periods of time associated with the Big Bang and the following Inflation. They talk of ten to thirty two of a second. Very impressive, but sorry it means little to me. They could have saved their money and just said it was quick. But as I say despite my jaundiced eye looking at time, we need such a measure.

May I suggest that there is a second type of time, physiological time and further ask is this a product of thought? We talk about *"when my time is up"* as mostly we fear death but what is time there. The word is used to convey movement from here living to there death.

SHE SAID

Is time a product of our thoughts? I would argue first that time is cyclic and my statement is based as always on how the Vedic Rishis defined time as an endless procession of creation, preservation and dissolution.

You talked so often about the Big Bang; so what was before it? Nothing, no space, no matter, no time.... just nothing... This is exactly what the Sages agreed on: *"Then was not non-existence nor existence: there was no realm of air, no sky beyond it. What covered in, and where? And what gave shelter? Was water there, unfathomed depth of water? Death was not then, nor was there immortal: no sign was there, the day's and night's divider"* (Rigveda 10.129.1- 7).

In this verse the word *"death"* used by the Sages is

not Mrtyu, which would be the correct word in Sanskrit; they believed that Kal (time) was death, which proves that you were so right in believing that time is a product of our own flow spent in this endless mind that creates thoughts. How weird and how amazing that you mentioned time and death too in the same sentence...

HE SAID

I woke thinking about Dylan Thomas and those words *"time passes"* came in my head. What started this, was me saying I may regret something I say?

In *"Under milk wood"*, there is apart when the voice describes PC Atila Reece waking up in the early hours after a night drinking gallons of *"warm flat Welsh beer"*; he reaches for the guzunda, but grabs his helmet by mistake and as I swishes in the dark a little voice in his head says *"you'll regret this in the morning"*.

SHE SAID

"In darkness, we may mistake a snake for a rope" is the main principle for Vedanta or Uttara Mimansa school of Vedic philosophy. Advaita, one of the main pure monism branches of Vedanta, bases its credo on life being Maya (illusion), Kal (time) not existing and the only reality being Brahman, the highest universal principle or the Absolute Reality. Illusion and time bring regrets. So what are your regrets, Paul?

HE SAID

I said I could have no regrets because of where I

am this day. As you well know Devi, my certainty is that
we are on a journey, a journey that may have lasted several
life times; the next stage is a return to the unity of the
Cosmic Soul.

So I should have a considerable list of regrets but
perhaps I should call these points of change. The *"Wisdom
Keepers"*[92] suggest, in their ageless wisdom, that human
spirituality has three core constituents: relationships, values
and life purpose. It is suggested that these three are so
tightly joined that it is nearly impossible to split them apart.
Relationships, a broken marriage is full of hurt for all
involved but would the hurt be more if a sham situation
emerged? So the relationship I held uppermost was that
with my higher self, in Shakespeare's *"Hamlet"*, Polonius
says *"To thine own self be true"* and despite the chaos
around me I held true often at considerable cost. The
onlooker would think *"that person must be full of regrets"*.
I regret that people were hurt but as I say the ultimate
mayhem around me would have been severe if I was not
true to myself. Each time I reached a point of change,
something told me what I had to do to move back to the
centre path in my journey. I always had a value I needed to
keep and maybe without realising it, I held fast to my life's
purpose. Perhaps my Divine Unity had given me that
purpose.

So the outcome was I ended up living on New
Zealand's North Shore. I arrived here very ill and, as I
passed through immigration, I had no idea where the other
seven members of my family were. There was one thing for
certain: I was here to be shown something. Until the last

couple of years I did not know what but now, well now I do. It may sound fanciful but I am here to complete the last few miles of my life's spiritual journey. So my dearest Devi, you now see in the written word what you already knew. I have not given you a list of regrets but hopefully you will understand. Oh, a final thought perhaps; you should now play Frank Sinatra's *"My Way"*! Of course our commitment is to *"He said She said"* so now it's your turn!

SHE SAID

Regrets? What is there to regret? And if I regret something, can I really change it? I am who I am because I was who I was. Would I have done things differently? I would say now that I would have, but I know that I didn't. I was sometimes strong, other times weak, selfish and selfless, happy and sad, different cycles of time I would argue... I made it so far though!

There is a beautiful story in both Bhagavata Purana or Srimad Bhagavatam and Vishnu Purana[93], one of the Mahapuranas, about the prince Dhuva and his younger brother Uttama, born to another mother. The story may sound similar to the biblical narratives of Abel and Cain or Jacob and Esau. The way it goes is like this. Uttama's mother, Suruchi, wanted to make sure that her son would inherit the throne; therefore she didn't let Dhuva get closer to his father, the king. She said that only God was able to unite him with his father.

Dhuva prayed, fasted and done everything in his power, hoping that God will notice him. He actually overdone things, so, worried for the young boy's life, Sage

Narada appeared in his dreams and taught him the famous Dwadasakshari[94] mantra *"Om Bhagavate Vasudevaya"* (I bow to the Lord who is within all beings). The story says that Vishnu also appeared in front of Dhuva whilst he was meditating, but being with his eyes closed, he couldn't see him. So Vishnu revealed himself again, this time in Dhuva's meditation and promised him to Varadana (grant a wish).

Having no regrets that he lost the chance of being a king, Dhuva asked instead for Stuti Vidya (knowledge of hymns). Vishnu granted the boy's wish and, on top of that, made him king at just six years old and gave him the state of Dhruva Pada, which is the state of a celestial body, untouched by Pralayah (dissolution). So, instead of regrets about time that passed, be like Dhuva and focus on timing, Paul!

HE SAID

"When something is comprised of parts and components which do not exit, how can that thing contribute to reality" (St Thomas Aquinas[95]); so if we discuss time are we talking of an illusion? So let's look at something that may not be there, bit like Alice in Wonderland; how deep is the hole.

I am going to be high handed and dismiss the thought of time as linear. Linear means *"arranged in or extending along a straight or nearly straight line"*. I can find no evidence to support this suggestion so can find no reason to do other than reject. "Nihil amplius"!

If I ignore my belief that time is illusory, a

manmade mental construct, put in place to ensure Mr Jones catches the 8:15 train to Birmingham Snow Hill, let us consider cyclical time.

For something to end it must have had a beginning; for something to start it must have had an ending. The form may change but the essence or original source must be there. I concede that divine intervention may not follow this proposition. But time is represented through change, such as the circular motion of the moon around Earth or the much more subtle changes of season. In this circular time, every object and event must return to its own beginning and repeat the process, the cycle of maturation and death. This cycle may vary between the twenty-four hour between the birth and death of a May Fly or theoretical physicists' suggest life cycle of the Universe at two hundred Billion years.

The Universe has gone through endless time cycles of creation, destruction and then rebirth, the big bang exponential expansion, implosion or collapse and another Big Bang. The largest time cycle we can comprehend.

You ask if time is cyclical, so I suggest yes, but does time in fact exist? As I write this, I am in the now even writing the word now was in the past so that point no longer exists.

SHE SAID

I thought we already agreed on cyclic time. I would add something though. Srimrad Bhagavatam talks about Kal (time) as a manifestation of God: *"Time is the potency of the almighty Personality of Godhead Hari, who controls all physical movement, although He is non-visible in the physical world".*

You would be quite surprised to hear that *"one can estimate time by measuring the movement of the atomic combinations of the bodies".* I am sure that you, the logical guy, liked that. Let me reveal a bit more. In the same Smirrad Bhagavatam, *"atomic time is measured according to its covering a particular atomic space, that time which covers the unmanifest, aggregate of all atoms is called the great time".* So now that I satisfied your love for science, I would go back to the Vedas and my dear Rishis.

The Sages calculated time in Tithis (lunar days). A lunar day was for them the time required for the longitudinal angle sunrise to sunset to increase by twelve degrees. Therefore Tithis were between nineteen and around twenty-seven hours, so different to our set up twenty-four hours day! They also defined time in Paksha or fortnight, in Masa, a lunar month, in Ritu, two lunar months and in Ayana, a half-year. This is why the moon was and still is so important for the Vedic yogis and this is why we, Kundalini yogis, sing to La Luna.

The Sages agreed on a year consisting of three hundred and sixty days for humans, measured by the sun's Northern and Southern movements in the sky. Their mathematical calculations were remarkable, but if they are true or not, it is up to you to decide.

HE SAID

Time must come in three stages the past, now and the future. Imagine the concept of time being an endless spiral, like infinity no beginning and no end. The spiral represents evolution and growth. Attached to the spiral, is a small dot traveling at 186,000 miles a second. This dot is the now; the frame of the spiral behind the dot is the past in front of the dot is the future. This is a little complicated because all matter has a spiral. The speed of the dot, the now, is the same, but the rate of change depends upon the rate of vibration of that segment of matter. You vibrate faster than say a tree, so your rate of change is faster than the tree, but you are both in the same segment of being, so you feel a consistency with each other. A bit like me watching an aircraft flying overhead. A person is walking down the aisle between the seats, the other passengers see him moving at one mile an hour I from the ground see him moving at six hundred and one miles an hour so our perception of same event is different as is the perception of the same event is different between you and the tree.

Sorry, I need to think this out a little but perhaps not today. But I have a question for you how does the world of spirits relate to time?

SHE SAID

Well, the Vedic Sages talked about Kala, time dilution, which may affect differently humans, the Devas[96], Manus (the first man), Pitris (ancestors' spirits) and even the Brahma, main deity for Hindus, related to creation. The Vedas referred to cycles of time according to cycles of creation, each cycle starting with God making energies active and ending with pulling them back into total passivity. But this is not all. Some of Vedic schools of

Hinduism mentioned time as being Maya (illusion), to be more specific time creating the illusion of life and death.

You may wonder if the Devas live forever. The Rishis believed that they are as long as their lifespan lasts... you figure this out!

If I remember well, according to the Big Bang theory, the age of our Universe may be somewhere between eleven and twenty billion years, but there are new theories including all sorts of other galaxies proving that the Universe may be way older. But again, I don't want to step into your territory. The Vedic Rishis believed that the total age of our Universe is around three hundred eleven trillion years, and based on their calculations, we may be now at the middle of that period.

They divided the age of the universe in four Yugas or cycles of time: Satya Yuga, 1.7 million years; Treta Yoga, 1.2 million years; Dwapara Yuga, 0.8 million years; and Kali Yuga, 0.4 million years. The Sages used in their calculation Days of Brahma and Years of Brahma. One year of Brahma is three hundred eleven trillion years, which they called one Maha Kalpa or *"one breath of Vishnu"*. They believed that when Vishnu will breathe out, many other Universes will be created with a new Brahma and Devas in each; but when Vishnu breathe in, Brahma is meant to die and a new one is created. This process is never ending. Therefore, like humans, Devas have their own lifespan. To cut the long story short, the age of the current Brahma, according to the Sages, is a hundred of his own years formed by twelve hour Kalpas (days) and twelve hours Pralaya (nights), each lasting for 4.3 billion years.

I remember a good friend of mine asking about how Devas were created. Well, the creation of the Universe followed nine steps only, described in details in Bhagavata Purana. So, everything started with the three Gunas (properties or tendencies) that had an influence on the further creation; ether to gas to liquid to solid matter. Time started to be manifested with Mahat tattva, the incarnation of the Supreme Reality. In the seventh step, for instance, fauna appeared, followed by some of the animals; human life was created in the last step of creation.

However, after creation was complete, there was an extra phase when demigods were made. The Purana identifies eight types of higher entities: demigods; forefathers, Devas and Asuras (opposites of Devas); Ganddarvas (angels) and Apsaras (water nymphs); Buthas (djinns), Pretas (zombies) and Pisacas (evil spirits); Shiddas, Caranas and Vidyadharas, all inhabitants of higher planets; Yaksas and Raksasas, tribes in constant war with Aryans; and superhuman or celestial beings. All these beings have their own lifespan.

You asked about the Devas; but what about the Asuras, Paul? People refer to them as evil entities, but in fact they just had a different mission than the Devas. The Asuras are said to be the children of Sage Kashyap[97], who fought against the Suras (Devas). Very complicated, I know, but remember that the Sages lived before 5000BC.

HE SAID

If we are going to talk about physiological time we must include thought and words. For this form of time is the time taken to move one thought in a string to the next and we must include language as mostly we think using words.

Time is change and thought is a process of change, so is time a construct of thought? For convenience we use words spoken in our head to establish a thought and language. I suggest words are another construct of thought. I would wish to consider the use of words in thinking shortly, Devi, but now back to time.

If I use an exaggerated example to explain my thinking, I say *"I hate that person"*, but I realise that I must change this to love. This change could be done in one movement of thought hate to love in an instant. In doing this, we have marginally used thought, sidelined it and dispensed with physiological time. We have not gone through the lengthy period of consideration of our feelings, deciding how we can change etc. So we have not used time or thought. As we find when we first start to meditate using an empty mind, thought demands to be used. There are many meditation techniques that use memory, which is thought but even in them though has to be disruptive. One is happily intoning a mantra and suddenly we are thinking about the loaf of bread we forgot to buy yesterday.

To accomplish this disruption thought had to introduce a vehicle and time was the answer. Put time in place and a gap appears which thought can fill however it feels. At some time in our past, we did not have a spoken language, we acted on instinct; if I saw a lion, I did not allow thought to consider which tree should I climb or perhaps should I fetch a ladder, maybe wave my shirt like a bull fighter, no I use no thought and up the nearest tree I went.

So the question I pose Devi is this. As we became more sophisticated as a being, did thought take control? Thought starts wars and the same process is used to end wars. Every action we make or take is a product of thought, if we acted on instinct, dispensed with physiological time, no thought, would life improve?

Earlier I commented on the use of words with our thoughts, I wonder could we replace thought words with images or would this require the introduction of physiological time again?

SHE SAID

Thoughts are vibrations… echo. Because they are instincts evolved into mostly involuntary thoughts, they can take any forms or shapes, depending on how much we focus on them.

You talk about words and images and they are all there in each though our minds process; words through the language we speak and images through visualization and meditation. And this is why I love Sanskrit. It gives me the chance to interchange words and make up my own mind on how much something can be something else. In Sanskrit, Aatma (consciousness), Jiva (soul), Chita (feelings) and Indriya (perception) are all words that can interchange depending on the context. Nothing is set in stone in Sanskrit.

By the way, Sanskrit comes from two roots, *"sama"* and *"akriti"*. Sama means returning to the initial thought or action or even returning to the first musical note of a scale, whilst Akriti means configuration or formula. What is the path of returning to the first thought? What a beautiful process, what a perfect way of perception! Would this be the psychological time you referred to?

Only the Western cultures draw a line between body and mind! The Sages visualized the body as being a series of concentric Koshas (circles): Anna Kosha (circle of flesh), Prana Kosha (circle of prana or breathing), Chitta Kosha (circle of feelings), Indriya Kosha (circle of senses) and Budhi Kosha (circle of intelligence).

For Hinduism, there is a Sthula Sharira (physical layer), a Sukshma Sharira (psychological layer) and Karana Sharira (karmic layer) that surround each body. And, as the psychological and physical aspects of the body were seen as togetherness, so is the notion of time! The Sages attributed a psychological aspect to time. There is never just this in Hinduism. If Vedanta school of Vedic philosophy says *"neti neti"* (not this, not that), Tantra complements with *"iti iti"* (this too, that too).

Can thoughts travel through ether as sounds and words do? I am patiently, or not, waiting for your answer, Paul.

HE SAID

Of course I will answer your question but first a correction. You say *"I am patiently, or not, waiting"*; we both know that patience is an anathema to you my dear friend, so I must answer instantly.

Yes, thoughts can travel through ether as sounds

and words do. It is believed that thoughts occur in our head but I cannot accept that. To date no cognitive physiologist has been able to more than hypothesise where thought originated from. So when I say the mind is the origin of thought and further say the mind lies outside the body, I say, prove me wrong!

So our thoughts float in the either as waves, we pick them up to manipulate and use. But am I the only one to select my thought. For many years, a large number of random generators working in over seventy differing locations across the planet have watched for and identified when large numbers of the 7.6 billion occupants of our planet have a similar thought. Typically this is when an event occurs that is reported across the world's media. The energy from this mass thought wave is measurable.

Now let us look at the possibility of a thought wave passing between two people this will not cause a fluctuation in a random number generator but it will cause the individuals involved to marvel at what has happened.

Elsewhere we have spoken of twin souls, such people have thoughts pass between them naturally it requires no technique it just happens as two people become spiritually aligned. It is not instantaneous but not far off person A has a thought and maybe, many miles distant, a person B has a similar thought. Until they physically communicate they each think that the thought was their own but no the thought has become available to both as it drifts about the ether.

So do these words convince you about thoughts floating in the ether, or, my dear friend, did you have my thought as your own and so there was no need for me to write this as you already thought it.

SHE SAID

We decided already that thoughts are vibration and Shabda (sound) is what characterises ether. You are also right referring to waves of thoughts. No doubt you are because you are the mentor. In meditation, our brain waves, or what you described as waves of thoughts, communicate with the waves of our planet. *"Oh, in the limitless great ocean of myself by the winds of consciousness are produced instantly waves of wonderful worlds"* (Ashtavakra Samhita[98] 2:23).

Our Rishis described in detail the process of meditation and its effects on our own consciousness. There are numerous pages in Rigveda dedicated to meditation where the term Upasana is first used to define the meditative state; in Chandogya Upanishad where the concept of Dyana or contemplation was beautifully described; in Katha Upanishad where the notion of self meditation is first used; and in Maitri Upanishad[99], where Sadhana yoga or the six fold yoga is a main concern. However, for me Paingala Upanishad[100] is the one that brings thoughts, meditation and devotion together; and of course Bhagavad Gita: *"When the perfectly controlled mind, free from longings for the objects of world, is turned towards the Self, it abides in the Self"*. In other words, you are what you think.

You mentioned synchronicity in thinking... maybe even telepathy. This is not uncommon for yogic practices and was somehow described in the famous *"Autobiography of a yogi"*[101]; Sriyukteshwar Giri giving telepathic commands and knowledge to Paramahansa Yogananda. So I ask you, Paul, if you believe that we can control thoughts.

HE SAID

Devi, we could consider thought, but why we cannot control it and what a power it would be if we could think on a global constant. 7.6 billion minds all with the same thought. Obviously I will not be able to reach an *"am right"* conclusion but these will be my considerations. You cannot reject them, as much as you may wish to, because you, Devi, will also be in the same situation. You may introduce a null hypothesis, but I will reject your words if there is any hint of QED within them.

Thought is a process of selecting items of knowledge and assembling them in a required order. The very word *"thought"* is in the past tense, so we should use the word *"think"* but who thinks? We assume it is the *"I"* or *"me"* that directs the thought process. But remember to assume makes an *"ass of u and me"* so ruminate again. You decide to do *"A"* but then consider *"no B"* may be better or perhaps even *"C"*. Eventually you decide *"A"* is the best option, but have you decided *"A"* or did thought decide for you?

The thought process must start from the basis of knowledge and sadly some of this knowledge will come from emotion, which can be highly suspect. How often do we find ourselves in a negative thought train that is both painful and destructive, next time this happens and it will and you eventually realise the absurd nature of what thought is doing. Do not just jump onto another more pleasant train, but take a hard look at the lunacy you have been forced to consider the truth. Have a close look at the nonsense of the words you were following and try to find where they arose. You will realise just how distorted thought can make memories or indeed knowledge. Our savior is intelligence because this moderates thought it makes us consider the fact of the matter not idiotic suppositions.

SHE SAID

You talked about thoughts as a process of Jnana (absolute knowledge). Which Jnana do you refer to? The Gross Jnana, knowledge from exterior sources, people, books and personal studies, the Subtle Jnana, knowledge from within, or the Casual Jnana referred to as unconsciousness? So which one would it be? Or maybe the supreme Turiya Jnana[102] that transforms an average human to a Jnani (enlightened master), the one who knows that the only way up is within and the one who sees through Jnanachakshu (the eye of wisdom).

Until you decide which knowledge you consider as a base of your thoughts, I will play with the concept of Jnana as described in ancient times. The Sages believed that there are eight sources of knowledge. Firstly, Pratyaksha (perception) that comes from our five senses; then Anumana (interference), which is nothing else than reaching a conclusion based on truth. Upamana (analogy) is us, humans, comparing knowledge to various sources, followed by Arthapati (postulation), which is a state of making our minds up based on previous knowledge and it sounds like an equation: if this means that, then that means this. The Rishis believed that Anupalabti (negative perception) is another source of knowledge because by knowing a negative thing we can prove the thing itself. We however sometimes rely on Sabda (testimony) by accumulating knowledge from people we trust. There are layers of knowledge and we have to peel them all, one by one...

HE SAID

I was sitting, reading the book you gave me for Christmas and I was thinking how you are making me look deeper into Kabbalah. As you know, I do not like or trust psychological knowledge. I want my thoughts to be mine, not those of someone else so I tend to take what I want from a subject just to check against what I have concluded without outside influence. Then I will move on, so I know very few subjects in depth. I know what I wanted to find out no more.

Earlier you spoke of peeling away layers and it struck me how my physiological knowledge was a mirror of my life with relationships. Take what I want, don't look deeper and become bored because there is no depth. But with you for the first time I wanted to know your mind. This is now what you are making me do in Kabbalah and other stuff, peel back the layers. You can only peel back the layers when you know something wondrous lies below. Is this rubbish or can you understand?

SHE SAID

I can understand that very well and I can understand you perfectly well, no matter how strong your accent may be. If you understand me, I understand you.

Wondrous? It is exactly what I wanted to hear because inspiration and imaginations make sense to me. So I am asking myself how much we allow ourselves to create Maya (illusion) and how much we dare to Kalpana (imagine).

Well, in the Western world, Kalpana is based on Avidya (ignorance) whilst in the Vedic system of philosophy, Kalpana is a gift from God, a tool in creating and uncreating thoughts and dreams in our Aja (birthless identity). I would challenge you to dream huge, get inspired and imagine the future because all or just part of it may just become reality! Why, you may ask? Just because Kalpana comes from the Sanskrit root *"kalpanama"*, which has nothing to do with fiction; it means in fact *"planning on doing something you are able to create"*. Therefore when you are inspired, you create a path for the future.

For the Vedic Sages, the creation of this Universe started with Kalpana, so, why would you not create your own reality out of just imagining it? *"He, the first origin of this creation, whether he formed it all or did not form it, whose eye controls this world in highest heaven, he verily knows it, or perhaps he knows not"* (Rigveda 10.129.7).

A powerful verse in Shevashvatara Upanishad (5:5) says exactly that: *"Because it is taught that Pradhana is the creation of God, so there is no contradiction in calling her both created and uncreated, as in the case of honey"*.

Pradhana refers to the state of balance between the three Gunas (tendencies or attributes of matter); this equilibrium being nothing else than the matter from which the world has been created, because the Gunas are present in us as well as in everything in the Universe and the whole world started from them. Chaos to the aspired perfect order...

Honey knowledge or Madhu vidya is a concept in the Vedic philosophy, developed in Chadogya Upanishad, and refers to the knowledge transmitted from a teacher, mentor or guru to a disciple or student, the only knowledge that can take one to identify with Ananda (supreme bliss) of true self. So, thank you for everything you taught me, dear mentor!

HE SAID

As we have become aware, when you work closely with another the evidence of thought transfer becomes apparent, not in co-occurrence but in theme. So does this suggest that all thought lies in some external form or that thought waves are held amongst the information that resides in the ether? Do like minds become aligned and pass information to and from directly?

Socrates said that *"we are what we think we are"*, the Buddha went a stage further than Socrates when he said, *"We are what we think. All that we are arises with our thoughts, with our thoughts we make the world"*. Theoretic physicists tell us that there are forms before us that our brains are not able to interpret is this what the Buddha and Socrates meant, our thoughts will tell us what we see? So

Devi, lots of questions for you to ponder upon and I leave you with this thought.

Every morning and evening, we say our Mantras, in differing languages but the asking is the same. Just think if only a half of the 7.6 billion minds did it with us, all focused on the same intent, would the direction toward destruction that the world is embarking on be turned toward a more compassionate and positive direction? I await your challenges with expectancy.

SHE SAID

Very cheeky of you asking so many question, but I will manage somehow. One verse in Moksha Gita[103], also called the *"Song of Liberation"*, which is a treatise of wisdom of the Advaita Vedanta, pops into my mind *"The Mind has the power of creating or undoing the whole universe in the twinkling of an eye"*. So it is the power of our thoughts that creates mighty actions. Imagine the vibration a wave of billions of thoughts at unison!

But before I eventually go further, I would ask you, Paul, if you agree that either curiosity or intelligence is the source of our thoughts?

HE SAID

Now I ask you, Devi Harjeet, think about what you ask, are not curiosity and intelligence the result of thought? One theory explains that thoughts are generated when neurons fire in the brain, yes, but this is only a part answer. Let's split thoughts into two categories, common everyday thought such as *"shall I stop at this red traffic light or just go across?"* No, not a good idea; this activity causes a chemical reaction in the brain and is based in the brain full stop. Then we have physiological thought this occurring in our mind, which lies external to our body. It is here that your curiosity and intelligence are born; it is here that our consciousness and sub- conscious come out to play. The egoic mind sits here also. I do not suggest we have three minds, but we have differing states in our mind, a three-ring circus with our ego, the grand I am, the third ring and also the ringmaster.

Our understanding of the mind is like our understanding of the ocean; we know the upper 5% but the deep 95% we are puzzled by. Everything that has ever happen on this planet has been driven by thought, Pol Pot[104], the master of genocide, was driven by thought, as is Lhamo Thondup[105] the 14th Dalai Lama but what differing thoughts. We like to think it is the "I" or the "me" that decides but oh no it is thought.

Did we think before we had spoken language; if so in what format, pictures? How does a disruptive though train arise? The *"I"* does not want it, yet it is there and tries to come again after we have derailed it. Are there no new thoughts? Is there an Akashic Library of thought and they just come tumbling out?

So my dearest friend, I have answered your question *"Is the source of our thoughts curiosity or intelligence?"* with answer no, the two come from a differing source but have left you with two or three questions I have. So I close with *"Answers to Paul's questions please Devi".*

SHE SAID

So let's see what can alter thoughts. Have you heard about Vasanas (subtle desires)? The term of Vasana was first used in Srimad Bghagavatam, also called Bhagavata Purana. Advaita Vedanta school of Vedic philosophy believes that bondages are caused through Vasanas and the only way to freedom is by destroying Vasanas. But, you see, these Vasanas are conditioned by the Gunas (tendencies or properties of matter). Are you familiar with the Gunas?

Properly translated from Sanskrit, the word Guna means *"fibre"*. The ancient Sages believed that there are three Gunas in the human body as well as in everything around us, actually in the whole Universe. We cannot be one without the other; therefore we are the joint result of all three.

The Rishis referred to Sattva as balance, harmony or synchronicity; to Rajas, as passion and to Tamas, as imbalance, chaos or disorder. The essence of Sattva is transparency and Sat (truth), allowing awareness to be present. But then, we act on Rajas, passion, and on the energy of change, whilst constantly trying to get back to the sattvic mode and, tired and ignorant, after having no results, we allow the dullness and inertia of Tamas to take over and rule. And this cycle goes on and on forever and as hard as we would try, we can never break it! Therefore I would suggest that when in one of the Gunas, our thoughts are not very different from other people's thoughts in the same Guna. Intelligence may play a role; curiosity too, but per general the mechanism of thinking is very similar for all of us.

Are our thoughts a reflection of our desires or based on our own tendencies or moods, Paul?

HE SAID

But we respond to passion and are always looking for change, which causes us to fall back to tiredness and ignorance. This happens because to keep within Sattva's essence, truthfulness or transparency, may be hard work and we give up the hard path. When this happens, Tamas emerges, dullness, inertia, chaos. What's the solution then? I am not sure about this question, my dear, knowing you can be devious, I am wondering if you already have a subtle answer based on your philosophy. You can then pounce upon my observations and negate them immediately. So I start to write with the sword of ridicule hanging over me.

Are thoughts a reflection? If so how did the initial image arise? Was that not a thought also? If you examine an emotion, you realise it is caused by an initial thought. If someone thinks *"I am alone"*, that may become an emotion of loneliness of being rejected. You speak of tendencies, if a person is introverted, that is their tendency. In such a case I would suggest that the process would be; tendency, which may cause the thought of *"I am alone"* and then the mood may be despair. Tendency, thought, mood…

You equate tendencies with moods; if I may be so bold, that is incorrect; a tendency is an inclination toward a characteristic whereas a mood is less specific and changeable. Sorry if you think that I am being gloomy in using loneliness and despair as an illustration, but I feel it outlines the three conditions you ask about quite dramatically.

Now I have to reluctantly admit that I may have

negated my dismissal of you suggestion that thoughts are a reflection. If emotion is the trigger, perhaps that is what thought sees when it looks in the mirror. But as ever I await you arbitration on my comments with interest.

SHE SAID

You say that an introvert is under a tendency that makes them reserved. I agree, but remember that is their personality; and personality is nothing else than their spirit. However, even an introvert will be up and down, happy and sad, based on the predominant Guna in a particular point in time. Gunas have an effect on us exactly as they influence the whole Universe. So what is the way to balance them? I would say that the only hope is Upasana Suddha Satva, which means *"sit near pure goodness"*, observe, inspire and aspire.

For me, the Gunas are attributes of our own material substance. I would go even further in saying that they are the underlying blueprint for our physical world, so there is nothing wrong in being under the influence of one or another at different times of the day according to our moods, experiences and external events. But, I have to admit that all Gunas create attachments to our own ego. However *"When one rises above the three gunas that originate in the body, one is freed from birth, old age, disease and death, and attains enlightenment"* (Bhagavad Gita 14:20).

The Vedas go even deeper: *"Everywhere, in all material universe, the disposition of nature, gunas and prakriti perform all works. But deluded by egoism, man thinks, "I am the doer"*. Prakriti, here refers to nature and it is the primal matter that abides to the three Gunas too.

Thus, if we cannot alter the way the Gunas work, we can change our thoughts by Upasana Suddha Satva, sitting near the true light, focusing on the brightness of our divine being and on our own evolvement.

"You can't always have what you want" says a Rolling Stones song... especially when our desires are materialistic only. There is so much more to our beings than a mansion, sports car, fame and glory. So I would say that all we have to do is shifting our focus from what is not important to what keeps us steadfast on the path of enlightenment.

Can we change anything whatsoever, Paul, once the rule is already in place? Can we actually make order out of chaos?

HE SAID

You made me laugh when I read your question, why? Because as the Dutch graphic artist Maurits Escher wrote *"We adore chaos because we love to produce order"* I know a lady Escher's words fit exactly.

The answers you ask for causes chaos because I find writing chaotic. I start with a blank page, an emptiness in front of me, but a mind jumbled with thoughts, words rejections, so I sit and watch the mind sort itself out without me directing it and then words start to appear upon my blank page, order out of chaos.

I speak of the chaos in my mind and how order evolves, as I sat and thought about your question words from Nietzsche's *"Thus Spoke Zarathustra"*[106] came to mind: *"I say unto you: one must still have chaos in oneself to be able to give birth to a dancing star. I say unto you: you still have chaos in yourselves"*. Before you read on Devi, just sit and think about the beauty of Nietzsche's words.

The ability to make order out of chaos is there to see every time we look into the night sky. Following that incredible detonation of energy that started this Universe, there was an expansion, rigorous mathematical calculations have proven that this period and on into the early stages of our universe was totally chaotic. As the Universe continued its expansion, it cooled and slowly an order appeared.

I feel you may ask for more proof, but I feel none is needed. Nietzsche comments that, for something wonderful to occur, chaos must be a precursor. Mathematical analysis has proven that the wonders and symmetry of our Universe immerged from chaos and there is yet another proof of my answer yes from chaos comes order.

Its lunch time and, as I write this, I eat some marinated feta you kindly gave me. I look in the pot and it is a chaotic mix of feta, onion, sundried tomatoes and other delights, but once in my mouth wonderful order occurs. So from gastronomical chaos, I find a piquant order. I rest my response, Devi.

SHE SAID

Chaos is a very discussed subject in Hinduism. There is even a goddess of chaos, called Samhara Kali, the All- Destroyer, one that was more than likely in command of the Asuras, the opposites of the Devas.

The Vedic writings refer to chaos in several myths about creation too. According to them, Prajapati, the Lord of Creation, wanted to design a world, where the forces of order and chaos were in perfect balance. In his first attempt, there was too much Jami (order), which resulted in an imperfect world. His second attempt was a world with too much Prthak (chaos), which again lead to a fiasco. Therefore Prajapati decided that the perfect Praja (creation) should have both opposite poles, chaos and order, in equilibrium, which would design the perfect Ritam (universal order). It didn't turn up that way, as we both know! Is it because this world is imbalanced? I don't know if there is not enough good or too much bad in the world at the moment, but I do know that the equilibrium is lost for now. What is good and what is bad for you?

HE SAID

Is there such a thing? I wonder are good and bad the extremes of a similar event or action. My forefathers rode with the Inniskilling Dragoons at the Battle of Waterloo. For the British, the result was good; the French army was defeated but for the French the result was bad, twenty five thousand French soldiers killed or wounded and Napoleon defeated. So the same event on the 18th June 1815 was good or bad dependent upon your frame of reference.

So how do we identify what is good and what is bad? Can we suggest that a thing is good when it ought to be in place or prevail as an entity and bad when as an entity it ought not to exist? Could I suggest that good is desired whilst bad is not, that may seem somewhat obvious, but then I come back to Waterloo and, even if we say good equals what is desired, it still depends on the mind-set of the enquirer into what is good.

We could say that the dichotomy of good and bad are the tools a society judges an event by, but even societies judgment of good may also be wrong. We build a new highway so the vehicles can travel faster. Good for society, but bad for the flora, animals and Mother Gia. So Devi, yes, there is good and bad and it seems they always travel together, but I guess you will dispute my assumption and not be happy with a short answer.

SHE SAID

What is good for you Paul, may be less good or even bad for me. It is all about perception of reality, preferences and even moods. However, the Vedas state clearly what the two mean, by identifying good as Dharma, moral duties and bad as Adharma, everything that is immoral.

The boundary between good and bad is decided by the three Gunas (tendencies of matter). I totally agree with the fact that Sattva Guna is what we may call good, order, balance and God, whilst Tamas Guna is exactly the opposite, chaos, disorder and our own ego acting demonic. But remember that the Gunas exist in us as well as in the Universe. So, whilst our own acts of violence and aggression are bad, so is a cataclysm that is out of our control.

Perhaps the most accurate description of good is in Mahabharata, which is known as Manava Kartavya Satra or the code of duties of each human: *"Dharma sustains the society; Dharma maintains the social order; Dharma ensures wellbeing and progress of Humanity; Dharma is surely that which fulfils these objectives"* (Karna Parva 69:58). So if this is Dharma, then Adharma is everything that creates conflict.

However when I refer to good and bad, I have to consider that these days there is a slim line between the two. Maybe they both have to exist and the balance of them desires an ideal world. I would also argue that as acts can have a good or bad effect, so thoughts could.

We already agreed on the fact that thoughts are vibration that can travel through ether, so everything that is created by our own minds and becomes an action has results. Hinduism calls these results Karma and goes even further in saying that Punyam (meritorious karma) is part of the Mokshapath (path to liberation), whilst Papam (sinful karma) is a cause of suffering. So this takes us to another subject. If Tamas is the ego in action, is it the ego and its *"sinful"* acts that are continuously creating suffering?

HE SAID

First let us try to understand what the ego is. The word translated from Latin means simply *"I"*. Many years ago, I wrote about Sigmund Freud's early life and found that although the name or word ego is associated with him, it does not appear in any of his original Germanic texts he spoke only of *"das Ich"*. So terms that involve the ego are processes or reactions in which *"I"* or 'me' are the object being spoken of.

I would suggest that it is our minds that work within a background of our ego. The ego is not a separate being working from within our consciousness.

As you know, I think that consciousness is fundamental, so it is not possible for an individuality to operate from within it. Of course you may disagree. I will further suggest that we are all egocentric and we can never be free from our psychological vantage point, which is coloured by our experiences, biases and fears. It is easy to allow the ego to take over and we become locked into egocentric frame of reference and it is possible that the mind then follows a course that defies logic. The mind wants us to use it so will drive our thoughts before it. Developing thought after though after thought, even in extreme cases to the point of destruction.

You asked me about the *"ego's sinful acts"* so I will only speak of that but remember that egotism can make one consider oneself more favorably than is warranted. As I write this I am thinking that self-aggrandisement is also a sinful act! Just look around the *"bloated plutocrats"* who postulate that *"they"* are the major influences on society. Sinful or what?

So perhaps one last thought on the ego's part in suffering. I mentioned its ability to develop self-aggrandisement within persons who have a high opinion of themselves, but at the other end of the scale people who are self-critical and perhaps view themselves negatively are also egotistical. So would you agree, Devi, that the ego gives us a large range of options but not the option of ignoring it.

SHE SAID

Ego is not one of my favorite subjects unfortunately and this is because I, like all humans, have plenty of it! And please imagine the disappointment with myself whilst you read this.

You are right about Freud bringing ego into focus, but what he meant was more complex than what we associate these days with the word *"ego"*. I won't develop on this topic though.

In Hinduism, Aham or Ahamkara (ego) is related to the sense of self, more precisely to the polluted or contaminated Universal Self that creates duality between God and us. Shaivism, the Hindu tradition that worships Shiva, defines it as atomicity, feeling small and isolated. The Vedas tell us that only Brahman, the Universal Supreme energy, is Suddha (pure); so this is for me a relief because I am somehow assured that ego is normal for us, human beings.

The Yogasutras, which are Sanskrit aphorisms about practicing yoga, describe accurately the two selves we all have, one being a quiet observer and the other always on the go, creating worthless actions and chaos.

Ego is the cause of sufferance and separateness from our own divine nature, Paul. Rig Veda says it clearly: *"Ego is the biggest enemy of all people"*. Is there any relationship between ego and our own thoughts?

HE SAID

If I give you my thoughts, I then ask for yours. As you know Devi, we are on a journey returning to the Cosmic Soul; it is difficult to explain how I know. I have ascended my Tree of Life from Malkuth, the Kingdom, until I now am at Da'at, knowledge, and so perhaps I should consider what knowledge is but first let me look at the ego and thought. I will then question knowledge further.

Even in contemplation, I find I cannot separate my ego from my thoughts so that I can view them as separate entities. I will admit that my puzzle was such that I considered reading others on the subject. The choices are endless Freud, Ram Dass[107], Tolle and on, but I decided I will make my thoughts mine not someone else's; is this my ego at work?

SHE SAID

No, it is not, Paul! According to the ancient Rishis, Sabda (knowledge learnt from others) is just one of the sources we accumulate knowledge from. Those sources though, based on the Vedas, as reliable testimonies, oral or written, of people we trust. And to be perfectly honest, I am delighted you give credence to Ram Dass. One of my very favorites… You say that you cannot separate your thoughts from your ego and you are right. As long as we define ourselves as this person, the gap between God and us gets larger. *"I am this person, this body or this mind"* is a dangerous affirmation, Paul. The union exists only in *"I am"*.

HE SAID

I did see a quote from Talmudic origin which describes the outcome of egoic thinking perfectly *"We don't see things as they are, we see them as we are"*. Exactly, we are told by our mind and ego this is it and hence we believe this falsehood.

You are well aware that I have days when my negative ego takes over completely. Luckily for me Devi, you soon correct things, but on reflection I can study the absurdity of my thought process and how I believed it. Is my ego just the development area of my thought and does it contain energy packages of memories of the bad and good things parents and people have said in the past, so it uses these to point thought in a good or bad direction? When destructive thoughts flow endlessly there is always another component trying to intervene positively. Is this my awareness?

This awareness is like a drag anchor; it knows egoic thought is wrong in the direction it is taking me and keeps shouting *"Paul, you know this is rubbish"* and so a mental battle rages as to who is right or wrong, the ego or awareness. I find that a period of meditation is the answer still the mind so is freedom from ego freedom from thought. All I have done, my friend, is ask a number of questions with no conclusion but I have raised the issue of knowledge and this is what awareness uses to control things.

So you will answer, I guess as usual immediately and then I can tease your mind on the subject of knowledge and what lies beyond.

SHE SAID

Many questions that make me think further... Whilst reading your words, I suddenly remembered a quote from Buddha: *"With our thoughts we make the world"*... and with our egos we destroy it, I would add to that.

Instead of focusing on the ego, I would shift your attention to awareness. As an Advaita Vedanta scholar, I know that the Self, Atman is *"pure shining consciousness"*; therefore our Self's nature is awareness, because consciousness starts with awareness.

Based on the Vedic texts, consciousness has two distinct states: one universal and eternal with Brahman as a source; and the second one, a worldly awareness based on Prakriti (matter), Guna (tendencies) and Tattva (blockages). So here you have it, self-awareness versus ego-awareness. They both exist in us and they will always be present in the human race.

Do we raise our consciousness by working on perception and sensory awareness or cognition and reflective awareness? So which one is it, sensation or knowledge?

HE SAID

You say *"instead of focusing on the ego, focus on awareness"*. I was interested in your comment about awareness being our Self's nature, it is a lovely way to put awareness's role. It is like the backdrop on a stage watching the characters in the story act out their roles. The *"I"*, the positive thought, the negative ego all struggling for supremacy, slowly they merge into the backdrop and awareness becomes supreme and order is restored.

You ask about the relationship between perception, sensory awareness and cognition. Dare I suggest that you are only juggling with semantics, they are just variations upon a theme? So if I speak of awareness I include the other two. So we now have awareness and need to consider how consciousness plays its part.

If consciousness has two distinct states I will not be as bold as to say *"how can you conclude that"* but how can you differentiate between two parts of the same condition. Consciousness is fundamental it was there at the singularity or the spark of Chochma. To attempt to split it is like saying the water in your glass is different from the water coming out of the tap. If it comes from two sources do the two ever merge or do they oppose each other?

I am starting to come to the conclusion that awareness is within consciousness for in my search I am unable to differentiate the two. We use them to say the same thing, *"I am conscious that my hair is white"*, I mean silver, *"I am aware my hair is silver"* says the same thing, I suggest. So could it be that consciousness is fundamental but awareness is a refined consciousness that occurs as our soul enters our heart as it develops soon after conception?

SHE SAID

A multitude of shades makes a colour more interesting and the way one juggles them gives depth to the tonality. I agree that I played with the concepts of consciousness and awareness, but as a mentor, you taught me to think outside of the box.

You say that cognition, perception and feelings are variations of the same theme. Let me argue that they are if the theme is Vritti, human mental activity, but they are not if we look at them separately. What we see is not necessarily what we feel and what we know is different than what we feel too. I am awaiting your opinion on the role played by perception and knowledge on shifting the consciousness level.

HE SAID

Would you be prepared to consider that a sensation causes knowledge of that sensation? If I were to fall in love with someone, I would have a sensation that something was happening; I may know not what, so I would move the sensation into thought, which then becomes knowledge about my feelings. So would you accept that this is a process that takes place within our consciousness? I have not mentioned your saying by the Buddha; all I can comment is yes.

We are slowly starting to consider knowledge. I suggest that there is no new knowledge. Knowledge is a fact waiting to be discovered. The egoistical may say *"look what I have invented"*, but they should take a humility pill and say *"look at what I have uncovered or found"*.

SHE SAID

I am not sure if a feeling creates knowledge or just perception or awareness.

You said that there is no new knowledge; I would suggest that there is no absolute knowledge. I will prove it by quoting a verse from Nasadya Sukta or the Hymn of Creation, the tenth Mandala of Rigveda: *"When and how did Creation start? Did He do it or did He not? Only He up there knows maybe. Or perhaps not even He"*. (Rigveda 10:129). Many would find this verse quite controversial... but this is only because they have not read the rest of the hymn. However, I will maintain that knowledge is not absolute. Nothing is other than Brahman, the Supreme Reality.

I am wondering what is the link between ego and knowledge. Maybe you would develop on this, Paul.

HE SAID

Devi, we are considering the possible relationship between ego, consciousness, thought and knowledge. If we are now going to expand knowledge's relationship, could we first agree what knowledge is and how it arises? I speak of physiological knowledge here not the process that allows me to ride my motorbike to the local bakery. Of course you may say they are the same, let us wait and see.

How we obtain knowledge, I will give you my thoughts first. Then once you have responded we can discuss and see if we agree before moving on.

I draw my knowledge from two directions. Firstly, I like to contemplate on what I wish to know. Let's say I want to understand how the people of the earth have become spiritually separated (this I have done). First I had to confirm my conclusion regarding separation. I will not bore you with why I think this is, so just look around you. Then as I believe in a Cosmic Soul and concluded that the cosmological facts confirm that, at the time of the Separation all matter was unified, I state to myself there was an original unification. So from unity we have separated into isolated parts. I have my hypothesis so I need to confirm it.

I found many traditions words that suggested a fragmentation of the Cosmic Soul these varied from the gentle Hindu picture of ten copper vessels filed with water standing under the midday sun. Look at the vessels and you see ten suns, look above and there is just one. More dramatically, I found the Kabbalists shattering of the anthropomorphic form of Adam Kadmon into six thousand pieces. So without elaborating, I had found that my feelings regarding a shattered Cosmic Soul had support and I dug deeper to expand my knowledge.

As I say, my friend, I contemplate because I believe that all knowledge is found in the Akashic Library and then confirm my contemplations by reading. This then is how I have accumulated my knowledge which I shall use as we explore the relationship between ego, consciousness, thought and knowledge.

SHE SAID

You mentioned the Akashic Library, mostly known as Akashic Records, so I feel obliged to highlight the fact that even if Akasha is a Sanskrit word, there is no evidence that the records can be linked to the Vedic philosophy or Hinduism in general. We discussed Akasha as dark energy, ether or just *"open space"* as Sanskrit describes it. Therefore the meaning of a possible universal library would perhaps just mean the unknown matrix of all thoughts, ideas and experiences or of the universal consciousness. The term Akashic Records is mostly related to the Western world and to theosophy, Paul.

There is however another term that refers to Akahsa, described in the Vedic texts, and that is the Akashic Mind, you would refer to as the Cosmic Mind, whilst I would call it Mahat. And with this, I must mention again the Samkhya school of Vedic philosophy that defined Mahat as the first principle of the Universe, which derived from the union of Purusha and Prakriti. In Srimad Bhagavatam (2.1: 32-33), it is described as the Cosmic Person: *"Oh King, the rivers are the veins of the Cosmic Person and the trees are the hairs of his body. The air is his breath, the ocean is his waist, the hills and mountains are the stacks of his bones and the passing ages are his movements"*. In other words, everything in everything that forms everything...

I would suggest digging deeper into the concept of awareness because every answer is there.

HE SAID

Do you realise you are asking us to descend a rabbit hole Devi? Or is just I who descends whilst you watch with amusement? I feel that what you will read will be Paul raising mini-hypothesis and then seeing if they have logic. So possibly you may receive no direct answers but only suggestions for you to respond to.

Where is the line between consciousness and awareness how do these words differ? I once heard this suggestion, *"if you are being chased through a forest by a ferocious wild animal you are aware that a tree may be your means of escape but you are conscious that if the creature catches you, you will be torn limb from limb"*.

So is awareness a condition of specifisy, as you, Devi, are aware, I propose that consciousness is fundamental. If that is so and we live in a "field" of consciousness is our link to that field, our awareness? Awareness draws specifics to our being, from the all-encompassing field of consciousness.

So this is my fist mini-hypothesis for your consideration. As I sit here I realise that I must order a box of chocolates for my daughter-in-law's birthday. Now tell me did this realisation come from my memory or an awareness regarding the significance of the date. If it was because consciousness recalled that the month of May has four family birthdays it would be my awareness link that drew the fact to me.

Now another consideration arises is my awareness also the link to my memory. Second point for your consideration. Let us move to Copper's mini-hypothesis number three. Is the word aware just an adjective for the *"I"*? Does it just describe a condition of the *"I"* at a given moment?

At present, I am aware that it is very windy outside, I am aware I am feeling hungry, I am aware that later I will go for a walk, I am aware that the walk will be along the beach; it is endless this awareness lexicon. So Devi, I ask is awareness just another way of saying I have knowledge of, or is the *"I"* just pure awareness. The *"I"*, the mind, the thought are they all only awareness.

I have other considerations, but I long to read your retaliations, so I can couch my thoughts a little more constructively. I hope you are aware of this Devi Harjeet.

SHE SAID

This is what I believe. Awareness is the state of acknowledging and recognizing consciousness. I am aware of the *"I"* that makes me *"I am"*. But in the same time, is consciousness not a state of body awareness too? So which one prevails if any? I will let you answer for yourself whilst I move your focus to a topic that interests me: transfer of consciousness. I am sure I caught your attention because not many schools of thought, if any, other than some of the Vedic ones, agree on transfer of consciousness. Perhaps as an analogy just think at the process of hypnotic suggestions transferred to a patient. I can talk forever about this subject, but I will make it more challenging for myself by moving back to the Vedic knowledge.

Every school of beliefs argues that transfer of consciousness from one body to another one, or to another incarnation, is not a viable concept. I however may disagree even if I cannot totally prove my point... but I can give it a shot.

There is a practice in yoga called Samyana, which is in fact focusing on an object until the mind is able to separate it from the context by identifying it with one's own being; or perhaps taking over that object and transferring yourself into the subject observed or the other way around. Would it be possible to take over another body? Well, you judge for yourself: *"By making Samyama on the signs in another's both knowledge of that mind comes. By making Samyama on the form of the body the power of perceiving forms being obstructed, the power of manifestation in the eye being separated, the Yogi's body becomes unseen"* (Patanjali Sutra[108] 3.21)

But if you ask me if the transfer of a body is possible, I would gladly answer maybe, why not? I'll even quote a verse in my defense and I would say please, Paul, don't doubt me on this. So I will quote again Patanjali Sutra (3.39): *"When the cause of a bondage becomes loosened, the Yogi, by his knowledge of manifestation through the organs enters another body"*. I know it sounds complicated, but again, please be open-minded and admit that it may happen.

Then there is an ancient yogic practice, which is an advanced ritual, called Parakaya Pravesam (or Pravesh), which is the transference of a spirit into a body. It may sound out of this world for a logical guy like you, but it won't hurt you accepting facts as they are. At the end of the day, you believe in more than that... in electricity for instance without seeing the electric impulse or wave.

Therefore, for me, if shift of a body is possible, with that convey, there is a transfer of consciousness too... and this would prove that consciousness could be passed to a next incarnation... at least for me. Is that possible in your world, Paul?

HE SAID

But in the same time, Devi you are so aware that I

have experienced the transfer of mental and physical energy from one sentient being to another, so I am in total agreement with your words. Where I do not agree is in the manner or by what medium the transfer occurs.

You say it is consciousness that is transferred, you are aware that for myself consciousness is fundamental. You have never challenged me or pointed to an event in the timeline of the Universe when consciousness appeared. So if what I say is correct; consciousness cannot be broken into discreet packages and used to pass energy from one being to another.

I argue that we are aware that we are conscious, the addition of *"ness"* to the end of a word suggests the presence of a being. Therefore we are awareness and, as I have said, that awareness is used to channel information from consciousness. The more I think about it the more I feel that consciousness and awareness are mutually exclusive.

I will try to explain using two beings *"A"* and *"B"*. Being *"A"* wants to pass energy to being *"B"*. *"A"* is aware of the need to do this, so *"A"* uses this awareness of the need to pass the package of energy to *"B"* using the field of consciousness as the channel. Being *"B"* then becomes aware of the intention of *"A"* and *"B's"* body or mind reacts to the energy passed from *"A"*. *"B"* becomes aware of the transfer as their mind or bodily movements are managed from a source external to *"B"*.

You see Devi, I do agree with what you say, I only question the vehicle used to by the originator to enter the subject.

This is the only point I ask you to consider but fully expect you to patiently explain how wrong I am and attempt to straighten out the spaghetti of my mind. Remember I am not speaking of transferring a body but only specific functions such as movement or thought.

SHE SAID

Consciousness is important for everybody, Paul, not just for you. I don't ask you to agree with my point. All I asked you is to keep an open mind about my personal perspective; it may be valid, it may not be, but it is based on arguments I do understand. I know how hard it is to believe in things that sound a bit supernatural. Therefore, I would just say that certain advanced techniques in yoga are out of ordinary and very difficult to be explained; also not easy to be understood for those who are not part of the yoga movement. But I wonder if there is anything whatsoever impossible for the Cosmic Mind or for the Divine Consciousness. Because if there isn't, why would transfer of consciousness be impossible? How much of this can you admit?

HE SAID

In some ways, the basic activity is not unlike the process alchemists use to purify their base material. Previously I have written about the alchemical process but upon reflection, there is little I can cut and paste to satisfy you.

Transmutation of the soul can be effectuated by a spiritual revelation; a Zen Buddhist would call the event a *"satori"*, or a powerful charge of spiritual energy. So transmutation may be a slowly unfolding process or, as suggested, a sudden abreaction; in the latter case it may have a physical and emotional effect. In the former, a life of sensitivity to others, to their needs and comfort is a more gentle way of transmutation but the process may be congruent.

Transmutation occurs initially in the soul, but it permeates in ones thought waves and then in emotional patterns eventually being mirrored in the physical form. There will be external changes, an awakening of one's true nature will occur and the life path will change and emotions become more evident and unfortunately rawer. People who are close to the individual will perceive a difference perhaps not realising just what has changed.

For the fortunate few people, it may appear in their life and almost without knowing it intensify the transmutation and aid in what may be an intense spiritual period as what are found to be intense revelations are stumbled across.

Moses de Leon the primary author of the Zohar wrote *"the purpose of the soul in entering the body is to exhibit its powers and abilities to the world"* and in doing so undergo a tikkun, a perfection or repair. May I suggest that this is necessary to enable the soul to complete its return to the Cosmic Soul after it had become one with its twin.

I hope that my explanation satisfies you question Devi, I am confident that you will expand my conjecture.

SHE SAID

You seem to have a strong opinion about transmutation of souls. Therefore, I would not comment further, but I am so glad you mentioned Satori because this is the trigger for my answer. I will anchor myself to Advaita Vedanta school of philosophy, a familiar ground for me, and to Bodhi that is a Sanskrit word for awakening. A correct translation would however be *"perfect knowledge"*.

For Advaita, there are two main stages in awakening or Moksha (liberation): oneness and getting rid of the egoic mind. In other words, "I am one with all that it is". This is what the return to the Cosmic Soul requires, a pure soul that can go home to perfection.

Vedanta considers another four stages in achieving freedom by purifying from Vasanas (egoic tendencies); Sravana (understanding the teachings), Manana (contemplating on the teachings), Nidydhyasana (meditation) and Samandhi (total absorption). These stages take us to Ananda (total bliss).

Vedanta purification process is easy to achieve and it starts with non-dualism; Atman, the Self, being equal with Brahman, the Cosmic Soul, which means that we are all one. Contemplating and meditating on this would take us back home to God's soul.

But there is something else involved and that is the awakening of Kundalini, as I mentioned before. Both Kundalini yoga and Vedanta agree on this and, as I am both, I gladly admit it too.

Now going back to transference of a spirit into a

body that may result in a transfer of consciousness, I believe that everything is possible for the enlightened, one that purified themselves and is able to be absorbed into the higher reality. What is possible to Brahman may be possible to Atman too! All stand in perception and awareness...

HE SAID

You and I disagree on what the sense of awareness is. I know that for you, to concede is not an option, but I will expand my view a little. This more to confirm my thoughts than to persuade you...

Awareness is the vehicle that connects me to the all-pervading consciousness. Awareness is our ability to experience so it must be paramount to all existence.

You are alive, awake, hot, cold, conscious, how you know is because you are aware. If we were not aware, could we know of anything or any condition? Without awareness how would we know we had a body, surely you must agree, Devi, awareness is the foundation of the mind. Even when we sleep we are aware for it is ever present and without limit. There is a noise in your living room; it is awareness that wakes you from your sleep and so you become conscious that your cat is trying to eat one of your feathered friends.

Rene Descartes said or *"I think therefore I am"*; without awareness he could not have made that statement. Perhaps you will say he did not need to be aware to say, *"ergo sum"* but please explain. Only a few words but tell me where I fail.

SHE SAID

I would start with one of the main concepts in Vedanta, which is that consciousness is not necessarily a quality of the mind; it is what knows the mind. You see? In daily life, awareness is the focus also the response. I am aware of my body and I am aware of my body's limits. I can lose a part of my body in a surgery for example, but can I ever lose part of my consciousness? Let me explain myself please. We possess the body as we own our shoes, but we cannot ever possess consciousness because, as much as we are not the body, we are conscious beings; therefore we are our own consciousness.

Consciousness is limitless and present in every aspect of our lives, whilst awareness may not be infinite. There is only one statement I came across about awareness being infinite and that is *"I am aware that I am aware"*.

As a Vedanta scholar, I admit three aspects to Atma, the nature of our true Self: Sat (truth), Cit (pure consciousness) and Ananda (source of happiness, bliss). All three are limitless as the soul itself is. Therefore, we are inner conscious beings, unborn and uncreated as our true self, the soul, is, and because of the veil created by our own limits, we identify ourselves as the body, instead of as pure consciousness.

The difference therefore between consciousness and awareness is the distinction between Drik (seer) and Drishya (seen), amazingly described in a concept called Drik Drishya Viveka, based on the polarity seer versus seen. This is a Vedanta technique designed to differentiate the body from consciousness, attributed to Rishi

Shankara[109], a Vedanta philosopher.

We can agree and disagree forever on the terms of consciousness and awareness, thus I will draft a conclusion if you don't mind. As conscious people we are limitless, but the boundaries appear as embodied people in a temporary frame of body.

HE SAID

You suggest that consciousness is not necessarily a quality of the mind. I would respond that the mind is within the field of consciousness; the mind draws information pertinent to the individual by using awareness as the seeker.

I support the proposals regarding awareness and consciousness in the body of your reply, although I am aware that my road map differs from yours, but we both arrive at the same destination. Awareness is not infinite because it is our awareness, so it dies with us. To be accused of repetition consciousness is fundamental; have emerged with creation so the information held therein exists independently of human existence.

I find, Devi, your reference to three aspects of the soul (Atman) most interesting. If I comment would you expand please? Truth (Sat) yes, as the soul returns to purity, it must be filled with truth, source of happiness (Ananda), the joy of the soul when it returns to its Creator must be unbounded. But Cit, does the soul have awareness or consciousness. Not for the first time you have me perplexed so my comment on this is *"the jury is out for Copper"*.

SHE SAID

Consciousness is not evident; it is full evidence! What happens in our mind is known though consciousness only. This is why I have said that it is what knows the mind, not necessarily a quality of mind. Consciousness reveals our thoughts to ourselves. There is no scientific evidence that consciousness is in the mind, Paul.

To make a little light on my previous argument, I would say that the soul is neither the body, nor the mind or, in other words, it is not known to the body and not known to the mind either. However, that eternal and infinite entity, which is the soul, is not separate from our being or from our consciousness and to be our soul only, we would have to be aware that we are not the body, nor the mind. This is Sat, the real and absolute truth. Being the soul only would take us to that state of Ananda, which is Jivanmukta, or pure consciousness.

To answer your question, I will refer to the Advaita Vedanta's perspective, which you already know I agree with. Atman is self-realising awareness and self- luminous consciousness because Atman, the Self, is Brahman, the Cosmic Self.

CHAPTER 5

MONISM VERSUS DUALISM

HE SAID

This is the forerunner of the physicists' statements as to the formation and possible life of our Universe. There was a sudden violent burst of energy. Bringing Kabbalah into this, this was the spark from Chochma, from the energy made available by Keter. God made energies active. The Big Bang occurred followed by the Inflation; the spark enters Binah, and the process of development of the Universe begins. Ultimately the Universe expands exponentially only to collapse in on its self, swallowed by a black hole; the withdrawing of energies into total inactivity or the return up the lightening flash on the Tree of light to Ein Sof. But the process will be repeated again and again over trillions and trillions of periods.

SHE SAID

The Vedas described the dissolution similar to a Big Bang, where the Universe was created and recreated in multiple events. *"After a cycle of universal dissolution, the Supreme Being decides to recreate the cosmos so that we souls can experience worlds of shape and solidity. Very subtle atoms begin to combine, eventually generating a cosmic wind that blows heavier and heavier atoms together. Souls depending on their karma earned in previous world systems, spontaneously draw to themselves atoms that coalesce into an appropriate body."* (Prashasta Pada[110]). The Chit (Supreme Being) the Rishis referred to is in fact the pure Cosmic Consciousness.

I remember that, at some stage, we talked about Chit, perhaps when we defined time as cyclic, but I never came across something more beautiful than his: *"I am not the mind, nor the intellect, nor the identity of self, not even the consciousness; I am also not the sense of hearing, nor taste, nor smell, and nor even the sigh; I am not the ether, nor the earth, nor fire, and not even the air; I am the form of that Pure Cosmic Consciousness"* (Vedanta- Nirvana Shatakam[111])

I know you will love this, Paul. Our Sages had no doubt that the Universe has its own consciousness. They didn't referred to a God; they referred to consciousness. By the way, the Kundalini Shakti I mentioned so many times has the imprint of the Cosmic Consciousness, which is different from our own consciousness.

Allow me to quote Kundalini Yoga Upanishads, which is the eighty-sixth Upanishad of Muktika Upanishad: *"Then he sees the whole Universe in his body as not being different from Atman (soul). This path of the Urdhva-Kundalini (higher Kundalini), O chief of Kings, conquers the macrocosm ".*

The Rishis talked about the Universe expanding and changing, about ether, which they defined as black energy- they did that before science named it-, about time being cyclical and spiral - past, present and future all happening perhaps simultaneously - about the four Yuggas (world's ages), Krita, Treta, Dvapara, and Kali. They even defined how long those cycles of time lasted. They calculated ages in Days of Brahma, and they were spot on.

So you tell me, Paul, where should I find the truth if not in the Vedas? Because there is no water being turned into wine there; without denying that this is possible. Everything is logical in the Vedas... as analytical as you are by the way!

HE SAID

If you think about what I have said and written about the formation of the Universe and a shattering of the Cosmic Soul, you will understand that my comments will possibly have little in common with the Current Standard Model of Cosmology[112]. As I start, as in most things in my life, I have no idea where I will go.

In the beginning, there was a surge of pure energy (think of Chochma), then there was the inflation after which order started to develop from chaos until the current or now Universe is composed of about 5% ordinary matter, 27% dark matter and 68% dark energy. Note we have not a clue as to the nature of 95% of what is out there. Perhaps if Newton had not started the split between science and spiritual life, we may by now know a little more. Funny he is remembered for an apple dropping from a tree yet his main activity was that of an alchemist! Keynes[113] called him the *"last of the magicians"*.

In the last five hundred plus years, man has seen his belief in his importance in the Universe diminish. First in 1508, by Nicholas Copernicus although it was not until 1524, that he shared his findings; then Harlow Shapley and finally Edwin Hubble proved our insignificance. But during this diminishment humans horizons of knowledge expanded to a staggering degree.

But I suggest that something was missing. Physicists say they discovered the laws of physics but they only uncovered them. Do they comment that these laws were made by a Divine Being? No, not even as a footnote. So with no apologies, I return to my old gripe Isaac Newton and the *"Flower of Kent"* apple. If I had been rock that hit him, not the apple he may have just said *"ouch"* gone and had a cup of bromide leaf tea. You probably know he died a virgin, and instead of spawning materialism, gone back to his first love, alchemy, and science and religion would not have split.

This would have allowed the thoughts that the Universe is mental to establish itself and not have to wait for the *"Copenhagen Interpretation"*[114]. Yes, you being smarter than I, will mutter about Heisenberg's *"Uncertainty Principle"*[115] and the fact that now we know that the *"Copenhagen Interpretation"* was based upon a false notion, but it had started quantum physics moving back toward spirituality. The lost is found. Vedic writings *"all is cyclical"* spring to mind?

SHE SAID

No, I won't focus on Heisenberg, but how funny that you mentioned Copernicus. Can I please add something about the Vedas mentioning heliocentris? *"Sun moves in its orbit which itself is moving. Earth and other bodies move around sun due to the force of attraction, because sun is heavier than them"*. (Rigveda 1.164.13)

I would include something in regards to Newton too. The Vedanga Jyotisa, one of the earliest Hindu books on astronomy, mentioned the existence of the gravitational force. Same indicated in the Surya Siddhanta[116], eleven centuries before Newton was born: *"The spherical earth stands at the centre of space due to the Gurutvakarshan Shakti (gravitational force) of sun which prevents earth from falling away and helps it to stand firm"*.

To be perfectly honest, all three laws of motion have their roots in the ancient Vedic writings. This is how Kanada of Vaisheshika school of philosophy, described, in the Vaisheshika Sutras, the relationship between force and motion: *"Change of motion is due to impressed force"*; *"Change of motion is proportional to the impressed force and is in the direction of the force"*; *"Action and reaction are equal and opposite"*.

You beat this, Copper!

HE SAID

You beat this Copper! Stop being so smug Kaur; you know I cannot beat it, and by the way, I am forced to accept that your depth of knowledge is outstanding, but still worth a challenge.

All I can say for my words against yours is *"quod erat demonstrandum" ("what was to be shown")*, but do not forget that you have Vyasa on your side; I just have a feeble mind on mine.

Before Newtonian physics kick started the Industrial Revolution and Materialism, René Descartes split the church and scientific study by suggesting mind and matter are separate. I wonder what he would have made of the double slit experiment. He suggested that matter was the province of the physical, whilst mental was that of the church. So gradually the teachings of the Greek Philosophers, since two thousand years before Descartes, that the earth is a self-generating living process, divine and imbued with spirit, the roots of this lie even earlier in animism, were forgotten by all but a few.

Scientists now saw the Universe and its inhabitants as machines and they regarded natural forces, as obsolete and not needed, reality was in essence material.

So the Materialistic age became rampant with attempts to link mind and matter rebuffed. Even experimenters in the 1920, who discovered the *"wave particle duality"* seem to have missed the fact the effect the observer had proved that mind could influence matter. So if we use Descartes as a fulcrum point between a belief that the Universe is mind and the Universe is a machine, we could put another fulcrum in the 1970's, when scientist such as the sadly late Lothar Schafer started to question *"what is the ultimate reality"* and link quantum theory with the spiritual mind. So we will come full circle in the future when science finally accepts that the concept of animism is fact and that the Universe is mental.

SHE SAID

I cannot give up on this, sorry. Descartes? A while back, I emailed you this quote *"I think therefore I am"*. Do you remember what you replied? *"But is it your Cosmic Mind thinking?"* I had not responded then because I knew that you would disagree.

So I won't focus on the Cartesian dualism[117] - this is your area of expertise - I would however point out that true consciousness is beyond intellect and mind. The Yoga philosophy in thirty-eight of the Upanishads combines mind and Mana (conscious mind) into Chitta (thinking). Besides Chitta, there are two other aspects of the human mind, Buddhi (intelligence) and Ahamkara (ego), both developed differently by some schools of Vedic philosophy. There is no final solution of dualism in Descartes, but there is in the yoga philosophy that achieves the goal of unity.

For the Upanishads, the body is a Biswarupa (replica of the Universe itself), whilst the mind is just a property of the body, exposing therefore numerous emotions. Remember what Descartes said: *"I am resolved no longer to seek any science other than knowledge on myself"*. In fact Buddhi (intelligence) is the controller of both body and mind. Now let's be clear here. If there is no body, there is no decision about any action. So this is where the yoga philosophy creates that union of mind and body.

Chitta is in fact a sum of mind and body consciousness, which by the way envelops the soul, but pervades all five Koshas (layers), the mental body, the intelligence body, the breathe body, the food body and the soul body. So, going back to your initial question, yes Paul, it was my Cosmic Mind thinking!

HE SAID

"There is no final solution of dualism"? You cannot say that and just leave it you have to have a conclusion. Either the essence of a divine being is in all substance or it is not. For you which? Matter and spirit combined... no dualism!

According to Occam's Razor, if the spark from Chochma was energy from Keter, simple answer in my simple mind is no dualism. Yes, as the lightning flash moved downward, dualism occurred and where does this take us too? Fragmentation! Reverse up the tree and what happens the Cosmic Soul combines again.

I will not elucidate on my thoughts about the Vedic writings again, but look at them simply. The problem is your high-powered mind/brain likes to solve complex problems so it makes complexity. My mind/brain is empty except for a cobweb so I am unable to comprehend complexity. Probably why I still do not understand how the phone you so kindly gave me works.

SHE SAID

You should know by now that the hidden stuff is always in the detail.... and the detail is always hidden! I will therefore make an analogy only for you to understand the way I think... and the analogy is ... my dresses. When I

143

create something, the detail is always hidden; as you know by now the buttons are always at the back, therefore not visible. And then there is the sound! A dress is not a dress if it doesn't make a sound... again detail hidden in the under- fabric, a fabric that makes a sound when I walk.

Same with my thinking; but this time I was that open that I put the detail in front of your eyes! You looked beyond it though and read my cosmology answer to your words without noticing it. The detail was *"Cartesian dualism"*. I didn't say realism; I said Cartesian.

In Cartesian dualism, the mind phenomenon is non-physical. Now, you tell me, my friend, what in this world is non-physical? Can you ever dissociate body and mind? Have you ever had a mental experience that was non-physical too? Don't snap back... just think! Is the mind a non-physical substance? I doubt it! So dilemma sorted in *"there is no final solution in Descartes dualism"*.

By the way how is your Bohm- Krisnamurti[118] group going?

HE SAID

You asked for more information about the dialogue group meeting. Depending on the members' location, USA, Scotland, Germany or New Zealand, we meet on Sunday evenings or Monday mornings. We dialogue for ninety minutes or so talking about undivided wholeness as described by David Bohm in his book *"Wholeness and the Implicate Order"*.

We have also read Krisnamurti and Bohm's dialogues in the past. Some spoke of what they believed wholeness was. Then we talked about the concept of twin souls coming together and how I had experienced it happening and that I believed that our purpose was to restore the whole from the shattering mentioned in many traditions. We discussed our nature in relationship to the whole and then suggested that the whole could be a hologram and as parts of the shattering we are each the whole.

It went totally quiet for ten minutes, until we closed; I could feel the group seven of us as one.

SHE SAID

You suggested that *"the Whole could be a hologram and as parts of the shattering, we are each the whole"*... and I am still wondering how could you be that logical and intuitive to understand the essence of the Vedas without hardly studying them. Brilliant thought that got me challenged!

The whole essence of the Vedic philosophy is the soul. The Vedas suggest that the mind is the creator of the Universe through the process of Maya (illusion) versus Kalpana (imagination); therefore there is only one Cosmic Mind and that mind is of each of us. Vedanta goes even further in suggesting that there is only one consciousness, the Cosmic Consciousness, the creator, the pervader and the dissolver of everything in this Universe. Therefore, our own consciousness is a reflection of that cosmic dimension. So if there is only one Cosmic Mind and one Cosmic Consciousness, what about the soul? You see, the Vedic writings, especially the Rigveda, tell us that, in order to understand the Cosmic Consciousness, the only thing we have to comprehend is the soul itself because the soul is everything; each of us is everything and each of us is the whole: *"Know that (the soul), by which everything is known."*

"That eternal peaceful state, which is always auspicious, free from duality, and which the wise describe as the fourth state of consciousness, that is the Self, that is to be known thoroughly, scientifically" (Mandukya Upanishad 1.7). The Greeks said the same thing by the way: *"Gnothi Seauton"* (Know thyself)... my dear Socrates was always right!

I could go further and argue that the Vedic Sages built up beautifully the hologram: first letter is the particle, first syllable is the atom, first word is the molecule, first Pada (chant) is the being, first Richa (mantra) is the family, first Sukta (prayer) is the whole society, first Mandala (chapter) is the whole wide world.... and so on! The planets, the solar system, the galaxies, all these are the soul, the Universe as a whole because, according to the Upanishads, Jiva (individual being) is nothing else than the mirror of the Universal Soul. *"As is the individual, so is the Universe, as is the Universe, so is the individual"* (Yajurveda). Perhaps *"As above, so below"*...

Paul, the soul is the chip on a hard drive and the Universe is the hard drive itself. All the collective consciousness data is on that chip as well as on the hard drive.... because of that chip. The soul is the creation of the three Gunas; exactly like the Universe itself. I would quote now the Gita (7: 13-14): *"The whole of this creation is deluded by these objects evolved from three modes of prakriti- satva, rajas and tamas; that is why the world fails to recognize Me, standing apart from these and imperishable. For this most wonderful maya (veil) of Mine, consisting of three gunas (modes of nature), is extremely difficult to break through; those however who constantly adore Me, alone are able to cross it."*

To build up my point, I would look to another verse in the Gita: *"The soul is indestructible, the soul is incombustible, insoluble and unwitherable. The soul is eternal, all pervasive, unmodifiable, immovable and primordial"* (Bhagavad Gita 2: 24).

Now my question is this. Can an incomplete soul be the whole in the absence of the twin part? Wholeness or oneness? I think we both know the answer.

HE SAID

A while ago, Devi, you asked for my thoughts regarding wholeness. Now your new question asking for thoughts about unity and duality could be viewed as an extension of that discussion.

Some writers suggest that there are two fundamental possibilities for how human consciousness lies, on the dualistic or the unified planes. To suggest that there can be more than one fundamental condition only expands the destructive illusion of duality.

Fundamental is the essence of a condition; I suggest it cannot be either this or that. This dithering is when thought forces a delay, forcing thought to be used and so an immediate decision cannot be made. Shall I take the last cream donut not sure, yes or no? Well, just look at that someone else who did not dither is eating it.

So arrogantly, I say our fundamental plane must be a unified one. So, I guess I will need to explain by going back to my basic state, Chochma on the Kabbalistic Tree of life or the physicists Big Bang. In both the ethereal and physical words, the initial condition was a unity, a unified spark of energy from which all matter and non-matter emerged. So the fundamental condition is or was a unified one. Look into the night sky and you will see duality upon duality, but behind it all, the *"cosmic radiation background"* is there to remind us of the unity before inflation and expansion occurred.

May I be so bold as to suggest that the Kabbalistic Tree of Life described this change from Unity to duality long before Georges Lemaitre's discoveries of early 1900's?

Keter could be compared with Genesis 1:3 *"Let there be Light"*. This spark of light comes from second Sephirah Chochma, across to Binah and then to Da'at, the three Sephiroth of conscious divine intellect. The spark from Chochma then followed the lightening flash down the tree, moving left to right or from feminine to masculine until the manifestation of our being is complete.

In this manner the Cosmic Soul was split into many dualities. I would suggest, Devi, very briefly, that this shattering was caused by the divine to give our being the opportunity to journey upward, towards the Cosmic Soul and, in so doing, discover the nature of the Divine Being we are descended from. All matter being part of the hologram we call Our Maker. The ultimate Unity!

SHE SAID

"Let there be light"? This subject really suits me. For me, the answer is in the Pavamana mantras that open Brihadaranyaka Upanishad. They sound like this:

"Om, from Asat lead me to Sat,
From Tamas lead me to the Jiotir,
From Mytior lead me to Amarata"

Are we, earthly beings, aware of our journey from Asat (ignorance) to Sat (supreme truth); from Tamas (inertia) to Jiotir (knowledge through experience) and from Mrtyor (darkness) to Amarata (immortality)? The key is in the word *"Amarata"*, which translates to immortality; yes, but in fact it is the drink of Devas that lead them to infinity. So truth and knowledge are Devas' ambrosia, pure nectar!

Is Jnana (knowledge) or Anubhav (experience) relevant in life?

HE SAID

We have to feel the knowledge. Inside, we feel the wonder of what we learnt and are amazed by it. We use knowledge to develop and increase, so it's never static as long as we do not fear exploring and taking the knowledge to its limits and are excited about the amazing world we live in.

SHE SAID

So how important is what we feel and how crucial is what we know because knowledge is experience too. However, I believe that Einstein did not come up with a magical formula based on experience only. Knowledge comes in many ways; it is perception, but it is study too. You know that.

HE SAID

I feel reassured when someone else comes to the same conclusion. This is what I like about your Vedas.

SHE SAID

So I would ask you this. You are in front of a pyramid. What is more important, knowledge about that pyramid or your emotions about it? That shape brings back hierarchy, history, geometry, calculus, volume, area, art, colour; all based on your previous knowledge. What you feel is not really relevant, neither for you, now for others. So what is it then, Paul?

HE SAID

As I have said, you have to feel the knowledge, wonder, be amazed by the world we live in.

SHE SAID

The experience of the world we live in has nothing to do with that pyramid. Even science and faith in a God is based on knowledge because as more as you know, as more you agree that there should be a higher energy that made everything possible.

A person who experienced heaps is a wise man. A person who knows a lot is a smart man. A wise man is not necessarily clever, but a smart man can be wise too because knowledge is based on self-enquiry.

HE SAID

You say that the world has nothing to do with it. So you do not wonder at a huge tree that came from a tiny seed that had all the details in it for the tree to use; or how birds can fly thousands of miles to the exact same spot. So are not faith knowledge and science the same? Is that not how we are moving forward with them becoming one thought process?

SHE SAID

I know about thousand miles because I studied mathematics; I know about speed and velocity because I learnt physics and I know about seeds and trees because I studied biology. You will never change my mind, Paul. Knowledge is important to me!

HE SAID

You would have known because you would have looked and wondered what was happening around you; then you would have studied and enhanced your wonder. You did not study for the sake of it; you studied to develop what you wondered. I have no wish to change your opinion, nor would I ever be able to.

SHE SAID

Einstein, Newton, Galilei and so many others learnt from a very early age. Their brains developed more as they accumulated knowledge. Mozart and Beethoven studied and put hard work into music. Talent is nothing in the absence of knowledge. Here you have it. I threw in big names and I am sure you would pick on them... and you may even start with an atom!

HE SAID

A sudden thought I must get down. In the microcosm, an atom exists as a point when we ignore the point; it becomes a wave with no form or energy the wave just spreads out like a vast waving blanket, a wave of potentiality because the point can be anywhere within it and once we react with the wave the point returns

Is this how God is? When we seek the Divine with enough force, It makes Itself known to us otherwise it is there but not there with no energy of form so we do not feel its presence.

Sorry, this is not structured as it was a sudden thought I needed to get it down before it drifted away, I need to consider it more to make it more understandable.

SHE SAID

Same atoms within us as in everything in the Universe... unlimited oneness!

Vaisesika, one of the six schools of Vedic philosophy is based on metaphysics of substance and atomism. Its founder, Kanada[119], proposed the atomic creation of the Universe in Vaisesika Sutra[120], arguing that Paramanu (atom) is the smallest particle that cannot be divided; therefore is eternal and combines forming complex substances that are the foundation of everything matter is. I am sure that we both agree with this beautiful verse from Brahmanda Purana *"You are the part of infinite Universe, the same Universe is within you"*. The feeling I have writing down this verse? Pure happiness!

HE SAID

If you wish to find true happiness you must live in unison with the order of the Universe.

SHE SAID

This is my answer whilst I am driving to my radiotherapy treatment, hoping that cancer goes away. Happiness is always in front of your eyes. You just have to grab it!

HE SAID

You were not supposed to start so quickly go and talk to your beloved dog Hendrix and stop thinking faster that I can type. So I'd say, if happiness is in front of your eyes what is happiness and how do you recognize it?

SHE SAID

You recognize it in the same manner you recognize the light. If you know for sure that the light you see is the true light, the sacred fire, then that happiness you found is the one you have been supposed to find.

HE SAID

Why the light, as the words of Manfred Mann's song go *"Blinded"* by the light so we see no thing? There was a brilliant white light so I saw no thing... To be enlightened means to become aware and knowledgeable; to gain understanding, not to be blinded. If you are dazzled by a light, you see and understand no thing so why do we say it? I would argue it is meaningless or even a falsehood.

SHE SAID

Blinded? One of my very favorites! I have a little theory about how to find the light and that is based on the Pavamama mantras I already debated on. Now my question to you is how do you know that the light is the true light?

HE SAID

True light? You have gone back to light… is a true understanding being allowed to comprehend the source of all energy. I don't want to think that at the end of our journey someone will shine a torch into my eye so I can see nothing. We should say a *"glorious comprehension"*, an understanding of the true nature of the Divine Force, a realization that 99% of my and all matter is made of that force, that energy.

SHE SAID

Yes I will always go back to the light. One of my favorites mantras says, *"I am the light of my soul"*. The light is in us and it takes us, the human race, time to realise that! And going back to your first email, happiness is a choice. Even if it is always in front of your eyes, you can chose to be happy or not… free will!

HE SAID

But the light is understanding, realization, we are shown, not dazzled, by a hundred watt bulb. Total free will is an illusion we are given latitude, not total self-determination. I wanted to be alone and have no friends to bother me, just to be me, but I was told off Copper, that's not for you. I have a better path and the Divine was right... a much better path.

SHE SAID

Do you want me to quote the Pavamana mantras again? The light... yes, the light! Free will is an illusion, yes, if everything else, time and space for instance, is Maya (illusion).

HE SAID

So Devi concedes? That seeing the light is an allegory for enlightenment. Yes, what we see is Maya we see an illusion, not the truth. Plato's Cave[121]!

SHE SAID

It is not that I want to admit you are right. You were right from the beginning by the way! I knew that. I just wanted you to say more whilst been playful as naughty angels can be. So yes, you won the battle!

HE SAID

What? Devi Harjeet saying, "so yes, you won the battle"! Oh, be still my foolish heart. The words slid over me like a silk shirt but a little voice in my head said *"enjoy it whilst you may Paul, you will hear them not again"*.

SHE SAID

I have to go back to free will. I hope you don't mind. According to the Vedas, the Upanishads and the Gita, our lives are ruled by three forces or fundamental energies, one that we create and two independent to us. The first is Adhyatmika that is our individual free will; the second is Adhibhautika, which refers to the actions performed by people around us, sometimes as a response to our actions and other times just independently; and the third is Adhidaivika, the Universe's response to our action or God's grace. As you see, all those three words in Sanskrit start with the prefix *"Adhi"*, which means *"higher"*. Therefore, all those three energies in our lives are nothing else than: our higher free expression, their higher response and its higher grace.

If what I have said is true, it means that we have free will, but with it, there is a tricky part: Adhyatmika means free will, but in the same time it stands for 'free will to surrender to God". In other words, the only free will we have is to surrender to our destiny, accept it... or not!

Same thing is in Judaism actually, because *"bechiraf chofshit"("freedom of choice")* is based on the law of cause/effect or reward/punishment, almost similar to the concept of karma. So this free will for Judaism is nothing more than our free will to accept God's plan. But I'm sure you know more about that. Is your opinion about limited free will still standing?

HE SAID

The questioner asks, *"do we have free will"*? I answer no, and sit down, but this attractive but persistent blonde lady in the audience stands up and says *"don't just say that and sit down Copper; support your hypothesis"* and I then find an email which says *"cut out this preamble and get on with it Copper you are just fighting for more thinking time"*. True, but it was worth a whirl.

So, first a couple of initial ground rules; we are talking of physiological free will versus determinism and I am not considering a Divine control or the Akashic records. I believe these have an influence but would want to try and make an argument based on provable fact.

In his book the *"Audacity of Hope"*, Barack Obama wrote *"American values are rooted in a basic optimism about life and a faith in free will"*. The facts suggest not.

Darwin's first cousin, Sir Francis Galton commented *"If we have evolved, then mental faculties like intelligence must be hereditary. We use those faculties to make decisions. So our ability to choose our fate is not free but depends upon our biological inheritance"*. I would add, amongst other influences, such as social assumptions bound by culture. This is where our early years come in, when our thoughts were conditioned by our parents or carers. What they think is implanted in our minds.

Deeds are determined by something, every event has a cause, and all new events are caused by past events. I don't suggest that we are in a strait jacket, but we have guidelines within which we have degrees of freedom to choose.

I hope this makes sense, but events over the last twelve months have made me realise that my Maker must have had a plan for me, I was faced with trials, which I came through; he then has guided me into a joy I could not have believed and over which I have no control all I can do is just sit an wonder and, as I pray for my beloved's health, I now also thank my Maker for making her my friend and also showing me my spiritual home. I had no control over this and, Devi, I had no option but to accept it.

SHE SAID

Pure velvet! You are saying that the Maker brought you to joy, but you had free will to accept or decline it, didn't you? This is what I, in my blondeness, believe with respect to free will and destiny.

Paul, we can die in darkness, never using our free will based on the concept of Videhamukti, which says that Moksha (liberation) is granted only after death, concept developed by Meher Baba[122] or we can follow the light based on the concept of Jivamukta, achieving liberation whilst still alive. By the way, these two concepts are beautifully described in the Tejobindu Upanishad, the smallest Upanishad, consisting of just a few lines. This proves that beauty doesn't necessarily have to be grand.

My yoga asks me to look deeper within myself and stay away from five enemies: Mada (pride), Krodha (anger), Moha (delusion), Matsarya (envy) and Kama (non-moral behaviour). Without those five attachments, I am free to decide who, what, when and where!

Do you remember how a while back, in one of our conversations, I mentioned the Oracle of Delphi? I did it for a reason. You know the story, of course you do: Pythia, in the Temple of Apollo, predicting the future... highly on drugs by the way!

A month before the ceremony, the priestess had to go through a purification ritual that made the connection with God possible, involving bathing in the Castalian Spring and drinking pure water from Casotis. Then she started prophesying, whilst inhaling the steam coming from the rocks. But the clue is not the oracle, Paul; the pointer is the temple, because on a column of that temple, there was an inscription... a secret symbol, a letter: *"E"*, which is epsilon. That epsilon is the point in the circle, ordinary number with a fixed point in the middle. Just look at letter *"Hei"* in the Hebrew alphabet. You know that better than I do; the five dimensions, the five senses, the five levels of the soul... and the common name for God. And that *"E"* on the Temple of Apollo stands for *"know thyself"* (Socrates), everything in balance and making a pledge. So if we find God within, trust and surrender to that divine energy, there is hope and there is free will too. Is it, Paul?

HE SAID

What you ask is if we have free will or are our actions and our life in general pre-determined by a Divine Agency. I will expand my beliefs, but first I ask you Devi when you have ever done anything freely? I mean without going through a thought process, shall I do this or that. So that you actions are not immediate but only after consideration during which time freedom is lost.

The mind does not like immediate unconsidered response because thought and knowledge are not brought into play. Also whist you formulate an answer, I can write the rest of my reply to your question.

It is an illusion that mankind has free will; everything has a driving cause whether it be a physiological or physical reaction. When I apply the brake pedal and stop at a red light, that is not free will; it is an action caused by the knowledge that, if I do not stop, I may kill myself or if not that it may be I will get a driving violation.

As I think about it, the matter of determinism or free will, as physiological or physical is immaterial because we are moving on a path back to our Creator, who or whatever that may be. We are given guidelines or curb stones between which we can move with limited choice. So we have a degree of free will, but there is a boundary beyond which it has been decided we cannot pass.

Our journey from Malkuth, the kingdom in which we exist returning to Keter, and, then past the three veils, is guided. It may take many lives for our soul to pass along but gradually the curbstones are narrowed so our actions become more refined and pure. Whether we do live in the mind of a Divine Being or not the aim of our Creator, is to see us ultimately become one within the Cosmic Soul. So a hand guides the tiller of our life's progress.

SHE SAID

Have I done anything freely? I will answer Paul, but please define *"freely"* first.

HE SAID

I meant, because it was driven by you without at some time in the past something causing you to do what you did. It may have been years in the past that an action was caused by another action; there can be no reaction without an initial driving action and at times it is hard to spot. Or you may not wish to acknowledge it!

SHE SAID

Oh no, Paul, I am going to answer! I act on instinct and rarely have a strategy before I jump into something new. I know that you are logically building your next steps. Not my thought! There were things I had to do in the past based on one thing lead to another; there were options too I had to consider and there were my instinctual jumps. I moved locations frequently just because I decided to; not because the change was needed. And then, just like that, I decided that I want to play an instrument or many more. It was not because something drove me to music; it was I acting freely. Those are little examples. I could say more, but I believe that I made a point. However, I would really like to add something to the topic of fatalism rather than free will.

In the ancient world, there were sects that based their beliefs on fatalism. One of them was Ajivaka, whose followers believed that acting on free will is a waste of energy and time. Their lives were a product of determinism and passivity. All Astikas (schools) of Vedic philosophy believed exactly the opposite; free will therefore played a main role in their philosophy. They acknowledged that we, humans, act on our volition and that there was a God who made sure that each action has a consequence. And this is where the concept of karma interfered with each deed. Therefore, from the beginning of time, for most Hindus, we, humans, build our own destiny based on karma and with the help of the divine. *"Please stand by my Architect of Destiny and please take me to my Destination"* says a verse in Atharveda.

We talked so many times about destiny, also about free will, so I will leave these topics aside. But I am interested in your position about how much we are able to achieve in this life. What is it possible what is not?

HE SAID

"If you believe all is possible, then everything can be achieved". I guess you will not believe me, but I wrote these words before I came across Mark 9:23 in the King James Bible.

Strangely, or perhaps not, I had written a passage for our other book, the one of quotations. Yes, I know, it is supposed to contain quotes from the erudite or not so erudite, but now it contains one from the *"ignorare";* although in my defense I did take guidance from words by Shoghi Effendi[123]. Anyway, the basis of my words was how to achieve our dream. Obviously this is a dream of a spiritual nature, not how do I obtain a million dollar Lagonda Taraf.

For me, it is the intangible not the tangible that we should believe we can achieve, because we can. If by some alarming turn of events I find myself in the local high street, I find no peace or satisfaction, I achieve nothing but frustration, whereas if I sit on the grass and watch the spring come all by itself then I achieve a wondrous feeling of becoming closure to my Divine Unity.

SHE SAID

I sense that big cities with their tempting high streets are not for you. I understand that much about you, Paul. I now know by heart the metaphor of grass growing by itself too. Thank you for that because, if I am healed now, it is because of listening to your advice of observing the silence within me.

So what can be impossible for the Self? Let me please jump back to Atman and Brahman. We define Atman as the Self, the soul, but Paul, it is so much more than that. Atman is in fact the true Self. If I would refer to the Self only, I would use Jivatman as a proper word, which means the individual Self. Jivatman is a reflection of Atman that is in fact the Universal Soul equal to Brahman. So I am asking myself if there is anything higher than Brahman. We both know the answer, Paul. Brahman is absolute, infinite, pure consciousness; and so is Atman. Therefore, everything is possible for Atman. So, now that you know that you are that infinite, what are your true Self's desires?

HE SAID

Well, spiritual peace and, dare I say, an approach to my enlightenment I can long for and achieve. It has always been within me, I know it has, so I can achieve everything in this life. It will never be in my power to own the latest Apple watch, but it is in my power to move closer to the Cosmic Soul and find what I desire.

In answer to your question, Devi Harjeet, everything is possible and in our power, provided we do not lust for superiority over our neighbour but look for peace within.

As ever, if you wish to overwhelm, my words you have the right of reply but remember to achieve this you will have to believe you can!

SHE SAID

Believe I can? You are challenging me again. I have no option other than doing my best in satisfying my mentor with a proper answer. Everything is in our power as long as we aspire to live in the right world.

The Sages believed that there are fourteen Lokhas (worlds) that make up our Universe; also that there are many universes, just like ours, floating around in the space, all bigger than ours. *"There are innumerable universes besides this one, and although they are unlimitedly large, they move about like atoms in You. Therefore You are called unlimited"* (Bhagavata Purana 6.16.37).

Rig Veda talks about Yugas (cycles of time), in each Yuga, the Universe being destroyed and recreated. Would Pralayah (cataclysm) be what you refer to as big bang? I think it is.

Paul, *"Iha"* is the earthly realm, the here, the now! Hindu cosmology refers to three levels of the present; Bhur (dense), Bhuvah (subtle) and Svah (casual). Gayatri mantra, the most well know mantra in the whole Vedas starts with these three words. A translation of the Gayatri mantra would sound like this: *"We contemplate the glory of the light that illuminates the three worlds: dense, subtle and causal. I am that life-giving power, love, radiant enlightenment, and the divine grace of universal intelligence. We pray for that divine light to illuminate our minds."*

On a deep spiritual level, Bhur (earth, the physical plane), Bhuvah (sky, the astral plane), Svah (heaven, the mental plane), followed by the four higher levels, Mahas (above the mental plane), Janas (place of birth), Tapas (*"mansion of the blessed"*) and Satyam (*"abode the truth"*) are for Hindu philosophy the seven modes of being or the seven levels of consciousness.

So, again Paul, everything is possible if in the right state of mind and… the right world.

CHAPTER 6

CREATION AND DISSOLUTION

HE SAID

On his Emerald tablet[124], the Thrice Great Hermes Trismegistus wrote, *"As above; so below"*... as within, so without. As with the universe; so with the soul." If the antiquity is correct thirty-seven thousands years later, physicists started to give credence to Trismegistus' words.

Let us consider *"As above so below"* and use the formation of the universe against the structure of matter. As we look up into the sky, we observe stars and planets, all in motion. In between these densely packed masses of matter, there appears to be no thing but a yin and yang hold them in position. It is known as dark Matter and dark Energy. It is called *"dark"* because the cosmologists and theoretical physicists have no idea how this field of gravity and antigravity, attraction and repulsion works, so we have these spheres moving around in a substance of some sort. This is the *"above"*; now let's look at Trismegistus' *"below"*.

I know there are subatomic particles, but for my analogy let us look at the atom. It has a nucleus with protons and neutrons revolving around it. In between, there is space; this space makes up for 99.99 percent of the atom. Does this not remind you of the Universe's planets (protons), stars (neutrons) rotating in 95 percentage of undetermined something 99.9 percent in respect to the atom? Areas of the universe rotate around the location of their combined centre of mass with similarly the atom revolving around its nucleus.

So my dear Devi, let us now consider *"As with the Universe; so with the soul"* and where our Divine Unity lies within these lumps of matter swimming in seas of unknown composition. It is proven that the basis of our material world is non-material; even your love of the rebuttal cannot refute this fact! When a particle is not observed, it becomes a wave, spreads out. Imagine a large blanket wafting in the breeze. In simple terms, it is a wave of potentiality; the particle is potentially somewhere only re-appearing again when it is interacted with.

Somewhere within these particles that are not particles but waves, vast oceans of Yin and Yang where opposite forces may be complimentary and the few remaining percent that are matter, I propose that we can find our Divine Unity. I will call what I am trying to find my Divine Unity because although we insist on acting as separate individuals, how we love the words *"I"* and *"Me"*, the connectedness is there we have just lost touch with the undeniable truth. If as I suggest the divine essence is within everything, it must be in every atom because that is what all matter is structured from. So does my Divine Unity act in a manner similar to the particle? It is always there for us, but if we ignore it, it becomes a wave not apparent but potentially there. We call upon its assistance and instantly it is by our side showing us the way, giving us succor and guidance. The unmanifest becoming manifest... Dare I suggest that my hypothesis confirms Hermes Trismegistus' words *"As with the Universe; so with the soul"*? I await the *"She Said"* response with interest.

SHE SAID

As below, so above? Paul, you just quoted Yajurveda. *"Yatha pinde, tatha Brahmande"*. This verse denotes oneness with the Universe; the microcosmos being the macrocosmos. Isha Upanishad goes even deeper in saying something similar to *"As within, so without"*. And how right the Sages were in saying that! All five elements the Universe is made of, earth, water, air, fire and ether, reside in our bodies too.

But the story is even longer. The Rishis believed that the three worlds or planes of our Universe are present in the body too, in a system called the Cakra (Chakra)[125] system. The first three chakras, Muladhara (Root chakra), Svadhisthana (Sacral chakra) and Manipura (Solar Plexus chakra) form the Lower Triangle that corresponds to Adho loka, the lower planetary system, populated by animals. Moving upwards, Anahata (Heart chakra) corresponds to Bhu loka, the middle planets, where us, mortals, reside. Vishuddha (Throat chakra), Ajna (Third eye chakra) and Sahasrara (Crown chakra) form the Higher Triangle that is linked to Urdhva loka, the higher realm populated by Devas, angels and spirits.

I did not even ask you, Paul, if you are familiar with our energetic system, formed of thirty-three chakras... exactly how many vertebras in the spinal area are. I would call them energy organs. The Rishis worked with seven main chakras and explained them as being *"wheels"* of energy.

We, Kundalini yogis, base our Kryias (sequence of Asanas- postures) on these powerful energetic organs and learnt from our Sages how to unblock them and how to move the Shakti (energy) from one chakra to another. The Western world associated colours and even feelings to each chakra. However the Rishis represented them in geometrical forms, correlated them to physical organs rather than to emotions and assigned them numbers of petals based on how many Nadis (vessels of energy) cross each chakra. They explained that we are all born with a special energy called Kundalini Shakti that stays coiled up as a snake in the Muladhara chakra at the base of the spine.

Once agitated by performing a special yoga Kriya or in a Shaktipat ceremony, where a guru initiates the awakening, a miracle happens. The Upanishads have the answer: *"The sleeping Kundalini is to be awakened by agitating it, like hitting a snake with a stick; it then stands erect and enters the Sushumna nadi*[126] *(the central nadi), like a snake entering its burrow"*. The miracle continues by "Having pierces the six chakras, Kundalini Shakti merges with Shiva at the thousand petal lotus in the crown of the head (Sahasrara chakra). That is the supreme state. That is the cause of liberation".

You see, I started talking about the Cosmos in our body and ended up with the body in the Cosmos. I hope my question to you Paul will keep you challenged. Does the Universe have its own consciousness?

HE SAID

Some years before you were born Devi, a Nobel Prize was awarded to two physicists who proved that subatomic particles have intelligence. Such particles are smaller than an atom. The Universe is made up of these particles; ergo the Universe is intelligent. More recently studies in the manner in which the Universe is expanding have found that the fashion of this expansion is similar to a brain growing, with the electrical firing between brain cells mirrored by the shape of the expanding galaxies. In support of this simulations of natural growth dynamics have proven that these dynamics are the same for differing kinds of complex systems, whether it be the human brain, the Internet or the Universe as a whole.

So having considered your question from the viewpoint of the technologist, let us look at a spiritual consideration. Many thousands of years before that Nobel Prize was awarded, our ancestors believed that God is mind and that the Universe is a mental plane. Now, my dear, I will stretch your mind further. If we are within the mind of a Divine Being, is it possible that the Cosmic Soul is in fact a hologram and that the Divine Being shattered that hologram? Many traditions talk of a shattering, so the Being shattered the Cosmic Soul into many holographic images. This so he could experience what it is like to be an individual soul, to feel how emotions affect us, to see how we purify ourselves and to return to the Cosmic Soul and then experience the divine. This movement from Cosmic Soul to the base manifestation is shown within the Kabbalistic Tree of Life.

Do you have any structure within your Vedic philosophy upon which to test my hypothesis? A straight rejection is not acceptable you must prove that rejection.

SHE SAID

Everything that defines the Universe and us is Chaitanya (consciousness). Are we living in God's Chaitanya? One united consciousness only? I am not sure about that, but I certainly know that we have that divine Kundalini Shakti within us and that energy, of the size of a thumb, as the Vedas describe it, has its own consciousness, different from ours. *"In the Mulladhara chakra there is a yoni and that yoni there is a linga"* as per the Yoga Upanishad. *"Yoni"* means a divine energy and *"linga"*, a divine consciousness. So we have God's consciousness in us. Most of the Vedic scriptures refer to it, but I would quote this time Devi Bhagavatan[127], which is a main Purana for Hinduism and Jainism: *"I take refuge unto that highest Shakti Kundalini, of the nature of Supreme Consciousness"*. Thus, I would argue that if Kundalini Shakti has its own divine consciousness, the Universe should too.

Vedic scholars consider ten levels of consciousness starting with the physical and sensorial degrees and

171

evolving to the highest level that is the non-dual Atman-Brahman. There is nothing above that. To get there, the steps of evolution include emotions, rules, mind's map, reflexes, logic and psychic abilities. I also admit that the soul has its own consciousness on a subtle level as well as the spirit on a casual level. Sri Aurobindo[128], a famous philosopher and Vedic scholar described beautifully the evolution of consciousness using the Isha Upanishad model.

As a follower of Vedanta philosophy, I assimilated a concept called Vishaya- Chaitanya, which is in fact *"the object consciousness"* that refers to an object as a phase of consciousness rather than that object being conscious. Just a way of turning things around and creating an argument on polarities... But if I mentioned polarities, the question that pops into my mind is about the opposites... heaven and hell. What are your thoughts on the subject?

HE SAID

Yes, but the actualisation of the states is accomplished within your mind I suggest. To accept the concept of a heaven and a hell you have to believe in a God depicted as a benign old fellow and a Devil with hot breath and waving a pitchfork. These are wonderful figurers with which a society can be frightened into conforming. Do as you are told and each day you will be given a virgin, not gender specific, disobey and the man with a red hot poker will make your eyes water.

Once society started to structure itself, there came a need for the populace to be controlled. It was likely that the leader in the early days was from a religious order, so why not invoke divine pleasure or displeasure to ensure people fell into line. They would be aware that God's will should be followed and God's spokesman would be the priest, vicar, witchdoctor or whatever; so why not use the God and introduce an anti-God to cajole or threaten the populace with.

As you are aware Devi, my concept of God is very different to yours. My only thought is that the Divine is an unimaginable energy, my Aur. So the prospect of this source having good or evil capabilities is a nonstarter. If you look at many religions, they all have their own vision of heaven and hell which further strengthens my argument that the two are just figments for control. Take the word *"lust"*, in the Christian tradition; it is one of the seven deadly sins on the road to hell but for you, unless you indulge in lust, you can never know pure love, the road I assume to heaven. So to have two so opposing views causes the concept you ask about to collapse.

But heaven and hell do exist in your mind. As our soul progresses upwards toward reunification with the Cosmic Soul, it is slowly purified so the understanding of what is spiritually right or wrong sharpens and it is here that we experience positive or negative vibrations caused by our actions. Such vibrations enable our ego to establish joy or despair and it is here that what we describe as heaven or hell are activated. So my answer to your question is a yes and a no?

SHE SAID

I have to be perfectly honest with you. I don't

believe in heaven and hell. And this is not a fundamental belief in the Vedic philosophy either. There is a word for hell in Hinduism, which is Naraka, but it has nothing to do with the concept of hell as we know it.

You talked about vibrations caused by our positive and negative actions and this is closer to karma than many others definitions I have ever came across with.

Reincarnation and karma are concepts I believe in, rather than hell and heaven. They are related on the admission of the same thing: achieving Moksha (liberation) one must skip Samsara (cycle of reincarnations). Why would we reincarnate to pay off for karma if the guy with the pitchfork would exist? So thank God he doesn't!

Initially, karma was described in the early Vedic texts as a sacrificial action related to esoteric rituals. It was in the Upanishads where the term of karma was developed as a spiritual law of cause and effect. *"As it does so it becomes"* (Brihadaranyaka Upanishad 4.4.5).

Some of the Vedi schools of thoughts acknowledge three types of karma; others even four: Sanchita, which is a sum of all effects of all actions performed in each incarnation; Agami that is the amount of karma we create in this very moment; Prarabha, which is the portion of karma already in action and Kriyamana, representing the karma accumulated in this life. It may seem a bit complicated, but in fact it is not. We reincarnate, as many times as we need to base on the karma we have to clean up.

Don't let me blurb for longer! Can effect exist in the absence of a cause... or the other way around?

HE SAID

Your email of this morning had but two words *"cause and effect"*. So the effect was that I started to type this, caused by your rather brusque note. It is not possible to split these two apart. I challenge you, Devi, to tell me an effect that has no cause and transversely a cause that did not come from an effect. Everything acts as a law dictates. There are seven causal planes, the Astral, the Akashic and the Mental being, three of them, but all these will have to operate in accordance with the law. Ask yourself, are you a cause or an effect; recognise your thoughts and how to amend them to give a positive outcome.

When something does not work out as you plan, ask yourself why, what was the cause? Ask deeply - you know my old cause identification technique *"the five whys"* - use it. Often you will find it was because you reacted to the world around you and did not be your own woman establishing Devi's path. Do this and the empowerment you feel will be wonderful. You can say you, Devi, did it!

Response from your Vedic mind awaited, so I can say I have been a cause.

SHE SAID

I admit that there is always a cause that initiates an effect. One leads to another, is that not true? I would not go that far though in saying that every effect creates a new cause.

Evolution is based on cause-effect and the psychological levels of evolution manifest it. To prove my point, I would go back to Kapila and Samkhya school of

Vedic philosophy. He believed that our reality consists of twenty-four Tattva (principles), one developing from a previous one. For instance, Buddhi (intelligence) developed from Prakrti (primal substance) and caused Ahamkara, ego or self-consciousness to be created, which initiated Purusha, the Self, as an effect. All I am saying is that what was for Kapila a Mahat (great principle), for you and I may be just an option, not necessary the only one.

I noticed that you mentioned the principle of the five whys. I understand a *"why"* and I can even go further admitting another one; but five?

HE SAID

I had a feeling you will ask about the five whys so be prepared to be bored. At one time, I worked with automotive brand leader on new vehicle projects and we used this technique to help root cause analysis. I was introduced to it by the Quality Director, who had worked for a plant that built commercial vehicles in South Africa. They had problems with the body assembly lines, continual errors made by the operatives. They kept thinking, they had introduced process corrections, but the problems were still occurring. A full five why activity was undertaken, which on the asking of the fifth why identified that the workers lived in such poor surroundings with poor diets, that they were continually tired and so mistakes were made. Improvements in their home lives were made and no more build line problems.

Does Vedic Philosophy have a Sanskrit five why process?

SHE SAID

One would say that the five why's analysis confirms that not all the problems have one cause only, but I strongly disagree; and I will prove it my way! The only root cause of karma is Avidya (ignorance). By the way, Avidya is the top Kleshas (blockage) of spiritual development in *"Patanjali's Yoga Sutra"*, a two thousand years old text. Patanjali believed that, if Avidya was eradicated, the other four (Raha- attachment, Dvestra- hatred, Asmita- egoism and Abinivesah- fear of death) would not exist.

So here you have it. The five whys are not always necessary, but let's get back to the main topic, cosmology and atomism.

HE SAID

This is a question for you, Devi, but I will give you my thoughts first. I will use the Hermetic word correspondence for my question and ask how does your Vedic Philosophy view correspondence. I have alluded to the maxim of *"as above so below"* before, but let us now have a closer look. The laws of our reality are the same no matter which plane of existence we are working in.

Let me consider the two extremes of macrocosm and microcosm. In this, I shall use spiritual and scientific examples to show how the two disciplines are starting to reflect one another.

Superstring theory proposes that all the fundamental forces of nature arise from vibrations of tiny supersymmetric strings. You and I are used to four dimensions, length, width, depth and of course time. These superstrings have ten dimensions and exist in a field of energy; the Higgs boson particle[129] travels through this field and, when one particle collides with another, subatomic particles are created. As an analogy, imagine a saucepan of porridge bubbling on your stove. Every now and then, a tiny piece of porridge breaks clear of the surface and flies upwards, a subatomic particle. So, at the smallest known scale of the microcosm we have an energy field developing matter.

Now let us fly upwards to the extreme of the macrocosm and switch over to a spiritual concept. Keter, the Crown, through which our Creator manifests, stands at the head of the Kabbalistic Tree of Life.

Beyond Keter, in negative existence are three veils En Sof Aur, the limitless light, En Sof, the limitless and Ain, no thing or the absolute. Ain is a mirror of the Higgs field, for from Ain come all beings that have ever been or will ever be. So there is another energy field, but it is not possible to describe this one except to say from it all beings are created. We must remember though that whether macro or micro, the whole is encompassed by our Creator.

Perhaps the words of your morning mantra spring to mind *"may there be wholeness for all"*. I am not sure if you remember that many months ago, I described our wanderings as a game of tennis with thoughts being hit to and from over a net. If you do, I send these thoughts with a lot of topspin towards your racket.

SHE SAID

Since I was a little girl, science always fascinated

me. Let me now captivate you with the science of the Vedas. I will go back again to Vaisheshika school of Vedic philosophy, so very famous for the atomism theory, and its founder, sage Kanada, also known as Kaishiapa.

Kanada believed that Parmanu (atoms) are eternal and interact with each other forming Anu (molecules). He called the binary molecules Dwinuka. Kanada believed that atoms exist in states of rest and states of motion, according to the cycles of the Universe; at the moment of the dissolution of the Universe, atoms, being eternal, are passive rather than being annihilated. Therefore, when the Universe will go through dissolution, all matter will be divisible to the smallest particle, which is Parmanu that, being indivisible, will be motionless and passive. Kanada also argued that soul, space, time and ether are also eternal, but not atomic, so cannot be divided.

It is fascinating how thousands of years ago, without a microscope, a library and Google, this Sage was able to put together a whole theory about atoms and molecules. He said that atoms can interact in three ways: if one of them is in motion, if both are in motion or if one of them is in contact with another atom that was initially in contact with the second atom. He approximated the size of different molecules formed by non-identical atoms and his measurements were not far from what science agrees on now. But the most fascinating thing is that this Rishi came up with an algorithm on how the Universe was created, based on chemical reactions between atoms and molecules.

He then divided the atoms in four classes and said that each of them is an active ingredient of reality.

Kanada put together a book of atomism of ten chapters called Vaisheshik Darshan[130], mostly known as Kanada's Sutras. You would absolutely love it because it is a treatise of physics and chemistry, but it contains also chapters of epistemology and philosophy, because Kanada called himself a philosopher. And to be perfectly honest, his description of perception and human reasoning process is absolutely stunning.

CHAPTER 7

THE DARK NIGHT OF THE SOUL

HE SAID

You questioned me about the Dark Night of the Soul. There is a book entitled *"Yoga and the Dark Night of the Soul"* by Simon Haas; this is based on the teachings of the Bhagavad Gita. The Gita is your focus, Devi, so I will give you my thoughts on the original written in the sixteenth century by the Spanish mystic and poet St John of the Cross[131].

I quote from E. Allison Peers translation, *"Although this happy night brings darkness to the spirit, it does so only to give it light in everything; and that, although it humbles it and makes it miserable, it does so only to exalt it and to raise it up"*

St John's words narrate the journey of the soul to mystic union with God, or perhaps sacred love. The word *"darkness"* is used because the destination; God, is unknowable. I have seen it described as a **kind of** existential crisis, but I prefer the description that it is a detoxification, a clearing away of gross matter that your soul has gathered through maybe several life times. That little destructive voice in your head could be included here.

SHE SAID

I am going to interrupt you here if you allow me please, and start with the book you mentioned, *"Yoga and the Dark Night of the Soul"*, which I absolutely love. You are right in saying that it is based on Bhagavad Gita, so I will just put things into perspective with respect to that.

Gita, the sixth book of the epic poem Mahabharata, is a pure masterpiece, Paul. Written sometimes around 200BC, Gita is a main scripture for the Vedanta school, which I follow. The author is Sage Krishna Dvaipayana, mostly known as Sage Vyasa, who compiled the Vedas... another total masterpiece. Bhagavad Gita is a dialogue between prince Arjuna and Krishna, an avatar of Vishnu. I know you read the Gita and we talked often about the wisdom of its eighteen chapters.

Us, yogis, if we mention Jnana (knowledge) yoga, Bhakti yoga (yoga of devotion), Raja yoga (yoga of mental control), Shakti yoga (yoga of expression of power), Karma yoga (selfless yoga) or the Sovereign Path (yoga of Science) and the War Within (yoga of compassion), we refer to Bhagavad Gita.

"Yoga and the Dark Night of the Soul" follows the journey of the soul based on the teachings of the Gita. Beautiful book! But back to you, Paul, and your interpretation of the Dark Night of the Soul...

HE SAID

As with everything spiritual, I will give you my interpretation of St. John of the Cross' words. If I meet him in a future life and he disagrees, I hope he will not be *"cross"*. Yes I know *"Paul be serious"*.

If I use the Tree of Life as the return pathway from birth to death, I place the Dark Night at Da'at on the central pillar. Da'at is a turning point and it is here that you realise that your soul is cluttered with the mistaken wants of life. The belief that to be happy you need the large house, top of the range automobile, model husband or wife, the things that the glossy magazines instruct one are needed to be seen as successful. This lusting detaches you from your soul and it becomes a dried Kernel. So the spirit of Divine Wisdom is never felt.

In Da'at, you realise that your life has no sweetness, no pure true love and so without being aware, the soul is being prepared to be cleansed of the grossness that clogs it. A detoxification, but this is not a fifteen day green tea sanitization of the gut; it's a spiritual purification. In 1945, F. Scott Fitzgerald wrote "In a real dark night of the soul it is always three o'clock in the morning". He may have been right but I think not. I have known of people for whom the Dark Night has been a sudden harsh storm from within and without. This leaving them in emotional turmoil before they experience the innumerable blessings of a soul that has become purified is nearing restoration with its twin and then with the Cosmic Soul. My experience was very different and was not a sudden event but, my dear Devi, I hear you say *"I asked about a spiritual process not about you"* so no more.

When the Dark Night is past, you realise that, in purging your soul, the gross matter has gone and been replaced with thoughts of compassion with empathy for the unfortunate and love for the Divine Energy from which we manifested and of course the Ego is deflated. We then move to Binah, the Sephirot of understanding, and on to Chochma, wisdom. It is within this triad of Da'at, Binah and Chochma that we meet again with our twin soul, for whom we have been searching. Then of course we will truly be prepared to be enlightened.

SHE SAID

You know how I asked so many - too many - questions about your past and not without a reason. You mentioned the Dark Night of the Soul and the wholeness after the crisis and all I wanted to know was what was your expectation in life because there is no dark night of anything if Purusharta (aim in life or object of human pursuit) is not in perfect harmony with Rta, the order that makes the Universe possible. You talked about unhappiness and not understanding who you were and I pushed you even more because I knew that your Purushartas might have been based on Maya (illusion) rather than on Satya (soul's truth). Let me explain.

In Hindu philosophy, there are four Purushartas (Purusharta comes from Sanskrit Purusha, the original source of the universe): Dharma (moral values), Artha (economic values), Kama (lust or pleasure) and Moksha (liberation). We kind of build our lives around the *"good and bad"* and this is why I asked you what was good and what was bad for you. We live our lives the way our parents taught us; then we base them on money and lust without ever focusing on dissolution and liberation of our souls.

You talked about making people happy, but never about what would have made your soul happy, whole and complete. So, in the absence of awareness of time and space, objectivity and individuality, if you look back to your life, long periods of time might have been just stages of status quo... just because down the track somewhere by pleasing others and abiding to their rules, you lost yourself. You may have built up enough Ahamkara (fake self or ego) to keep your life going.... to nowhere really. And in that state of maybe confusion about who you were, Rta, the force that demands order in the universe, did what it does best: demanding order! How? By kicking in the Dark Night of your Soul, a time for reflection and transformation, a crisis based on sufferance, numbness and total helplessness.

So look back at the Avidya (ignorance) before the crisis and to hope of Moksha (freedom, liberation) in the present. There should be such a difference! And the same relates to everybody on this planet. The Dark Night of the Soul is a blessing really and its effects are aligning your spiritual journey with the destiny of your soul... if you believe in destiny. So what is that Dark Night? Just a rite of passage, a journey in the underworld; again if you believe in the ancient Egyptian mythology. And what is it next? Just wait patiently and enjoy what is on the way!

In esoteric astrology, the Dark Night of the Soul

may be, who knows, the return of Saturn. I believe that you would agree with that. There are three Saturn returns in one's Ashramas (stages of life): one in the Grihastha state, householder stage, when you were maybe twenty seven to thirty one years old; a second more dramatic one in Vanaprashtha, closer to retirement, around fifty five to fifty eight years old; and the last one in Sannyasa, the stage of wisdom, seventy five to eighty years old. Just look back to your life and remember the crisis you may have gone through in those stages in your life.

HE SAID

"You know how I asked so many – too many-questions"? Never too many, Devi. When I give you answers, I feel as if something buried in the earth has lifted into light and I am made to look at it. Say I was a statue that fallen over forgotten about and weeds and other plants had grown over it. Each time you ask and talk to me about things it is as if someone has spotted the statue and bit by bit is taking a brush and is polishing parts slowly returning them to a beauty that has not seen daylight perhaps for most of my life. I am writing this as I always write to you just letting the words rattle out no thought just emotion and belief. You say that my Purushartas might have been based on Maya rather than on Satya. In my ignorance, I suggest that there is no might about it.

I believe that every now and then, my soul tried to show itself the unhappy chaos of my life. I find strange that when I look back, it has always been an Eastern tradition that emerges; it was yoga at first and I have not told you, but in my early life I had a copy of the Upanishads and Gita. Then I read the Tao and other sacred books; perhaps the fallen statue tried to stand, but then the weeds regained control.

You asked when I felt happy. I have thought hard about this truly. I have only felt happy twice, when Matthew and Jacob were born. I used to be at peace when I was at the Lower Full Brook Hermitage amongst the monks, but then the weeds grabbed me again to keep my life going... *"to nowhere really"*. And after events that people would call coincident, but they were not, I believe my Maker was losing patience with me. *"Oh, Paul, I am trying so hard to guide you get on with it; I am becoming fed up with pushing you"*.

Then, the final part of my jigsaw fell into place. The statue was still buried, but I felt something was happened. I ignored it. It took a bit of work poking and prodding me.

You have just been through a difficult time, soon to be finished. I was so frightened, not because I thought you would die. I was frightened because you had so much fear. But, during this time, underneath I realised I was filled with joy. My whole being is singing with wonder of where you will be directed next and, as I read the words you sent me and read the Dark Night of the Soul, it is as if the gaps in my life are being filled in and I truly just sit and laugh and cry. It is wonderful.

SHE SAID

You focus on the mind, when in fact it is all about the body because, believe it or not, the body is a vessel of consciousness. Vedic philosophy is very specific about this. Nobody feels at a mental level; we do feel because our bodies desire those feelings and, to be perfectly honest, our bodies attract emotions; not our minds.

Yesterday we had a chat and I mentioned the four Pandas (levels) of consciousness in Vedic philosophy. In fact, all those are based on the doctrine of the Three Bodies... one mind, three bodies. Vedanta agrees with that, as well as Tantra. Vedanta states that to cross that bridge of the Dark Night of the Soul, Jiva (being) would have to go through three manifestations of bodies and three levels of consciousness to be able to achieve the highest state.

The first body is Stuhla Sarira, the gross body, that you could relate to the waking Panda of your own consciousness, described as *"Banish- Prajnya (outward-knowing), Sthula (gross) and Vaishvanara (universal)"*. This body holds the meaning of Jiva (being) and all the experiences of Jiva. This is where Ahamkara (Ego) feels more comfortable, in its element and this is where your mind finds answers from outward introspection.

The second body is Sukshma, the subtle body, that corresponds to the dreaming or unconscious Panda of consciousness, described as *"Antah- Prajnya (inward-knowing), Pravivikta (subtle) and Taijasa (burning)"*. This is a weird state really because whilst the mind starts questioning, Samskaras (conditioning) and witnessing the journey inward, the body lets feelings and desires rule and to be in charge. This is the Body of Kama (lust).

The third body is Karana Sarira, the casual body that corresponds to the deep sleep state of consciousness, described as *"hearing and learning about the Sarv' Eshvara (Lord of all), Sarva-jnya (the knower of all), Antar-yami (the inner controller), Yonih Sarvasya (the source of all) and Prabhav- Apyayau Hi Bhutanam (the origin and dissolution of created things)"*.

Can you relate to any of those manifestations of your own body? You should because you have been all of those. And I have been too.

HE SAID

You complained that I was slow to answer you but it took a while for me to work my way through the spaghetti of your mind.

You opened, by saying to focus on the mind when in fact it is about the body. I pondered on this sentence for a while, if the *"I"* is focusing on the mind, what is the *"I"* focusing with? For an entity cannot focus on itself using the same entity. Am I not focusing with my mind exploring thoughts, so my mind is being introspective?

You speak of one mind and three bodies, Hindu doctrine, but there is only the mind; we exist in our mind which lies external to this thing we call a body and the mind is universal and indeed, when I say our mind, it is because it is ours not yours, not mine but the all-encompassing Mind.

I agree with the thought of three bodies, Stuhla Sarira, Sukshma and Sarira, but am uncomfortable with this suggestion of stages or separations. Will you permit me to use the process of falling in love to explain what I mean? Two people are attracted towards each other, but for this to occur there must be something intangible pass between them or does this intangible lie dormant in the ether that surrounds us just waiting for the right moment to be needed? This is where the second body is activated, the subtle body. The feeling of oneness between the two grows almost imperceptibly until they are one and become your third body. For me, there are no stages in this process; it is like the flowering of my orchids, it is pure and just happens because it is meant to be. Overall, it is guided by our Divine Unity and we have no say in the matter.

I can place this journey of twin souls re-uniting, upon my template for all of life's activities, the Kabbalistic Tree of life. Stuhla Sarira sits within the lower four Sephiroth, Malkuth, Yesod, Hod and Netzach. Sukshma relates to Tiphareth, Gevurah and Hesed, whilst Da'at, Binah, Chochma are where Karana Sarira resides. Watching over this wondrous manifestation sits Keter at the head of the Tree gently showing the path.

You asked if I can relate to the manifestations you describe. Yes, I can, but can I explain, no, I cannot because the feeling was always there it just needed something to make me aware of it. I don't know when or how; it just occurred as naturally as the moon rises.

SHE SAID

I haven't complained, Paul about you being slow in answering. Not entirely, but I have to admit that I was curious about your reply. So it came with you talking about the feeling of falling in love. Therefore I feel obliged to respond with my thoughts about love in all shapes and forms, acknowledging though your disagreement with part of the Three Bodies' concept.

All the religions and mystical schools relate the concept of love mostly to God, whilst all ten Hindu philosophical schools talk about unconditional love at human level too. For them, there is Kama (lust), a product of the God Kama, accepted by Hinduism and Buddhism as well, and there is an elevated form of love they called Prema or Prem, which is pure spiritual love.

According to the Vedic scriptures, no human can achieve Prema if Kama wasn't consumed. Hindu gods have a human side to them and their relationships is as much sexual as spiritual. Just read about the love fling between Radhika, the Goddess of love and Krishna, an avatar of Vishnu, and you may blush. Yes, I know, you may bring up the Song of Songs from the Bible[132]... but that is nothing comparing to the physicality of the love relationship between Krishna and Radhika.

So, yes, Hindus believe that love is not pure love if it is not consumed at all three levels, physical, psychological and spiritual. So, if love is defined on levels of symbolism, I argue that it is a sacred symbol, a very meticulously designed code, eternal and infinite. What do you know about sacred symbols, Paul?

HE SAID

I imagine you are thinking of Sacred Geometry[133], Devi. *"Mathematics is the alphabet with which God has written the Universe"*; these are words said by the astronomer Galileo Galilei. In our life we are surrounded by sacred forms, not only in nature, but also in artists' work, philosophers' thinking and it is suggested that Mozart used the Golden Ratio[134] when writing his compositions. For myself the most wondrous form is the sacred spiral or the Fibonacci Sequence[135]. This form is fundamental in the pinecone, a snail's shell, it is also apparent in the human body in things as diverse as the ear and the umbilical cord. There is also the relationship of the Golden Ratio that occurs in the body; if we call the length of our hand *"one"*, the combined length of our hand and forearm is 1.618 and the ratio of upper arm to hand plus the forearm is also 1.618. If you get your tape rule out and check you will agree.

There is also in your shapes and forms of the Platonic' solids so named after Plato who hypothesised in, *"Timaeus"*[136], that the classic elements of Air, Earth, Fire and Water were made from these regular solids.

There are many other representations of Sacred Geometry, one of the oldest being the Flower of Life which is believed by some to represent a visual expression of consciousness and creation. It is believed that within the symbol of this flower is a blueprint of the Universe.

Closer to my belief is the Tree of Life symbol, although this geometric symbol is at the centre of the Kabbalistic tradition it first appeared over three thousand years ago in Egypt. The Tree depicts our divine unity with the universe and guides us how we can return to our spiritual home and become one with Cosmic Soul.

I hope this answers, in part your query but as you are aware I do not have the mental capacity to do more than wonder about the shapes and forms so I leave it to you to examine further so that I may learn.

One question; I would ask you to consider is, with this amazing synchronicity occurring all around as well as within us, does it strengthen the belief that we are living in the mind of a Divine being?

SHE SAID

I am pleased you mentioned the Flower of Life because I am going to refer to Yantras, which are mystical diagrams or symbols of the sacred geometry in the Universe. But before I start, just know that for the last thirty years, I wore a little Flower of Life pendant on my bracelet. I still do.

Yantras are present in Tantric traditions that are nothing else than esoteric heritage in Hinduism. According to some myths, most of the Yantric Sadhana (practice) was transmitted by Shiva himself.

As you know, the Vedas contain four main books of knowledge, but there is the Upa Vedas[137] that are complementary scriptures. Vastu, one of them, explains that Yantras are linear geometrical sacred patterns, designed to balance the five main elements of the Universe, earth, water, fire, air and ether and that they are the foundation of, let's call is Feng Shui.

Both Yantras and Mandalas are considered by Hindu traditions as being geometrical projections of the Cosmos. You may now wonder what makes them so different if they may look quite similar. Well, the Mandalas, which mean *"circles"* in Sanskrit, are mysterious concentric spiritual patterns and the main belief regarding them is that, by using the correct mantras, Devas would enter into the Mandalas. So, mantras again, Paul, because mantras are the vibrations of the Universe; therefore the audio correspondent of Mandalas. By the way, we refer to the Vedas having a number of Mandalas, but this is a different story. In this case, Mandalas are how many books there are in that Veda.

The geometry we find in the Universe is present in the microcosm too. I would almost want to say that there should be a universal code where everything fits in perfectly. Therefore I ask myself if love can fit in a mathematical formula as perhaps a cosmic geometrical symbol?

HE SAID

In despair, I ask, where do you think these questions up from Devi? Do you take a perverse delight in thinking *"this one will finish him off"*?

So what is a mathematical formula? I will quote from something you may well have written *"A mathematical formula is an equation expressing one variable as a combination of other variable(s) using algebraic operations such as add, subtract, multiply..."*

Cosmically geometrical shapes, now these I can visualize. I have written a little about them before. I will narrow my focus here and just consider Platonic solids sacred geometry. I do this because you seem to be asking can love be structured and exact. Of course it cannot. Each evening I walk along my local beach and I can observe couples walking arm in arm so very much in love. What is between them is love, soft gentle wrapped around them, I cannot envisage that such an intimate relationship having structured forms and sharp edges or the preciseness of a mathematical formula.

If I can be an observer of life, I see two people who have replaced pure love with geometric shapes. They walk two meters apart, not speaking but even in this case of love becoming a formulae 1+1 still equals 2.

Love is the medium, which binds people together or indeed people to tangible things they admire. As I write this, I look at my two orchid plants I love them and do you know I almost feel they love me. So Devi, love is not hard and sharp it is the ductile, malleable substance that binds and gives wonder.

SHE SAID

I will go back to Mandalas, if you don't mind, and their sacred symbolism. For Hinduism, Mandalas are mostly used to tune in meditation and what a great topic to contemplate on is love. Therefore there are Mandalas designed specifically for love. The way they differentiate from the rest is that the middle feature is always a symbol of love, either a heart, a rose, or the infinity symbol. All these are believe to relate to unconditional love.

And there is the Padma (lotus flower) as a central piece that symbolises the eternal open heart. In Hinduism, the lotus flower is everywhere, starting with the chakras, each having a number of lotus flower petals, and finishing with their own deities; Vishnu for example, who holds a lotus flower in his hand that gave him the name of Padmanabh (Lord of Lotus). But to be perfectly honest, there is more to this story. In most representations, Vishnu's wife, Lakshami, the Goddess of Love and Beauty, stands on a lotus flower and massages Vishnu's feet. So another love story, I guess...

My question to you, Paul, is a bit more complex. Is there a universal law of symbols and if there is, who needs to recognise them, God or us?

HE SAID

A strange question for you to ask me when your background is immersed in symbology... Who needs to recognise them, God or us? You well know that my view of God is that of a field of potential energy, so any symbolic form will emerge from that field for us to recognise. It comes from our source so it is known at the point of conception. What is generated at that point is inherent within it, so it is not there for recognition by the Creator. These forms are there for us to recognise and understand.

Elsewhere I have spoken of *"the survival of the fittest"* and the loss of *"soft skills"*. As the recognition of and understanding of sacred symbols did not help to *"put meat on the table",* this was one of the abilities that has drifted into the far corners of our conscious. The concept of *"if you do not use it you lose it"* applies here.

I will outline some of my sacred symbols and how they came into my life and below I expect you to give the correct interpretation for my increased comprehension.

Many years ago, I presented a paper discussing the Tau Cross[138], which was the sign placed upon the foreheads of the poor of Israel to save them from extinction. I have always connected it, due to the similarity in form, with the Ankh; the Ankh, which is often referred to as the key of life. Do you now see the connection with the Tau Devi? The Ankh[139] emerged from Ancient Egypt, the Tau from Norse mythology where it was the hammer of Thor. There are other suggestions but as my colouring and DNA confirms I am a Celt, I accept this as the correct source.

SHE SAID

I won't deny the significance of the Ankh in the ancient Egypt, but I would argue that this symbol has a special meaning for the Hindu customs too.

Wearing the Ankh ring on the ring finger of the right hand was and still is part of the ritual in many religious ceremonies. This ring, made of Dharba grass, is called Pavithram, which means *"purity"*. Please continue elaborating your point.

HE SAID

There are other symbols, which affect me in some way of yearning; perhaps it is as I suggest some dark corner of my consciousness removing a few cobwebs. I will merely list them with no comment except to say to me they have significance, they tell me of some forgotten sacred law.

Of course the Tree of Life is there, in its many forms, the Yin and Yang symbol, my early wonder and acceptance of Daoist philosophy emerges here. I can hear the synapses in your brain firing here as you burst to answer your question factually so will just mention the Lotus Flower with no further comment. As ever, over to you, my tormentor.

SHE SAID

Well, the Hindu iconography is vast. I already mentioned some of their symbols; therefore I will just say a few words about the unwritten ones, the Mudras, which are symbolic gestures, performed with some of the body parts, mostly with the fingers. There are three hundred ninety nine Mudras, divided in five categories: Hasta, performed with the fingers, Mara or head Mudras, Kaya that are performed with the whole body, Bandha or heart shaped and Adhara or perineal Mudras.

As I know you so well, I imagine that you are already shaking your head, asking yourself how many of those I actually master. Well, I won't disappoint you, Paul. I know them all because I use them in my daily yogic practice. They are extremely important because their role is to seal energy. Therefore anytime an Asana (posture) is performed, which involves a special Pranayama (breathing technique), a Mudra will follow to seal the intention. So here you have it, Paul, a different kind of symbolism in Hindu rituals.

But, I still want to go back to the topic of love, this time asking you what is love for the Baha'i faith you sympathise with, so I would appreciate at least a few lines on the topic.

HE SAID

Spiritual qualities such as love and knowledge grow and flourish within our minds and hearts. With knowledge love grows and for us true or pure understanding is enhanced by love.

I add a shortened quote from Abdu'l-Baha[140] *"in the world of existence there is indeed no greater power than the power of love. When the heart of man is aglow with the flame of love, he is ready to sacrifice all—even his life"*. Only a few short words in answer to you enquiry Devi, but I would suggest that no more is needed.

SHE SAID

In one of your emails today, you mentioned your friends, food and love. It is quite telepathic, because today I was reading my notes about the concept of love in the Vedas and Hinduism in general.

Thousands of years ago, the Rishis came up with a theory about love transiting at five different stages or levels and I am just wondering whether or not you would agree with that. So the Vedas say *"Only those who have love, would attain God"*. This is a main mantra in Sikhism by the way. You may have heard this too *"Love is Kumara (wisdom of the four Sages), love is Kanda (ritual)"*. In other words, love is beliefs and rituals too!

The first stage of love, according to our Rishis, is Kama... and the name says it all: craving for the other person or perhaps sexual desire. This is very different to Christianity and Judaism, where the fall of man happened because of Kama; in Hinduism, Kama is joy!

The second stage is Shringara, which in Sanskrit means romance, also understanding the gestures of the other person; followed by Maitri, which is nothing else than compassion.

The Sages said that there is no love in the absence of compassion and I am sure that you agree with that. Then, Bhakti or pure devotion... The Vedas are very specific about it, saying that interpersonal devotion should be at the same level as devotion for God. The last stage is Atma Prema or unconditional love... *"The river that flows in you, also flows in me"*[141].

The Rishis believed that there is no unconditional love until self-love is a fact. *"It is not for the love of all that all is dear; but for the love of the soul in the all that all is dear"*, Bridadaranyaka Upanishad. What is love for you, Paul?

HE SAID

There are many aspects to this. If one receives a picture from a woman they love, as they look at it, would feel three of them; psychological, physical and spiritual love. The love that was sent with the picture would generate a physiological feeling and, when expanding the picture and looking at the face of that woman, just washed, no makeup, would bring up spiritual love, unconditional love for a woman. But then, the animal love coming from deep inside would be present too; another form of deep emotion. All three aspects combine as pure white love, despite the wild exhausting physical action involved in the spiritual feeling of an unbelievable nature.

There are many other aspects of emotional love. I love my sons, I love my family and I love my old mate, Ken. I suppose this is protective love. When I look at their nature, I feel love for my Creator who made them. But overarching all the facets of love, I suggest must be the love for what we all have been given. We live in the love of a Creator who was wrapped us in a blanket of unconditional love within, which we excitedly explore. What is love for you?

SHE SAID

What is love? Well, I have been back to Europe in 2019 and traveling through all those countries, all I've done was attending exhibitions.... hours and hours in front of paintings! I've seen them all. But before that, four years ago, I travelled to Melbourne only to see Van Gogh at MoMa. So I will relate love to all those feelings I have had then.

So for me love can be sad (Van Gogh)... and exotic (Gaugain)... and beautiful (Degas)... and simply colorful (Cezanne)... and abstract (my dear Picasso!)... and smaller than expected (Dali)... and a monstrosity (Goya)... and truly handicapped (Toulouse Lautrec)... and romantic (Turner)... and idiotic (Pollock)... and accurate (Delacroix)... and mysterious (Caravaggio)... and minimalist (F. Stella)... and stubborn (Frida Kahlo)... and absolutely everything (da Vinci). Never this and almost that... up and down...this and that...

Have I experienced all these? Maybe I did, maybe I didn't... It's not relevant! I'm thinking though that maybe love is the mission of our souls. By the way, please let's go back to the essence of everything, the soul. I never asked you about the Kabbalah interpretation of the soul, so I do it now.

HE SAID

You ask that I talk about the soul and the Kabbalah Devi. The word Kabbalah means *"to receive"* and what we are looking to receive is an understanding of the power of the Universe, the source of manifestation and thus achieve an interface with the Energy I call the Divine Unity.

The twelfth Century Kabbalists employed various forms of meditation and prayer to induce mystical states of consciousness and initiate a process of psycho-spiritual transformation. Now please recollect that nineteenth Century Copper mixes and matches his beliefs so what I shall talk of will be my Kabbalah; not perhaps the Kabbalah of Isaac Luria, although I use his depiction of the Tree of Life, but still developed from meditation and spiritual examination.

You may think of the soul as some deep locus within your being, this is quite alien to Jewish mystical thinking. In Kabbalah, the soul transcends four realms these known as *"Olamot"*.

The soul flows into the lowest of these, Assiya and this is also the realm of consciousness, time and space. One way to visualise this is to imagine a garden stake, say a meter high. With four equally spaced discs on it, but remember the Spiritual Umbilical Cord may be infinite in length. The stake runs through the centre of the discs with an equal space between the uppermost disc and the top of the stake. It could be proposed that as our soul ascends the Olamot, the stake, is travelling through the higher realm of our subconscious. Scholars suggest that the soul has three parts, animal, spiritual and higher. You would laugh out loud if I compared myself to a scholar but, in my own stubborn way, I maintain we have one unified soul and that, as we grow spiritually, our soul changes its form. It grows in purity.

SHE SAID

The umbilical cord you mentioned is present in the Vedic philosophy as well as in Kundalini/ Laya Yoga. We, yogis, refer to the Silver Cord that starts in The Muladhara chakra, the Root chakra, and finishes in the Vishudha chakra, the Throat chakra. In order to raise Kundalini Shakti (energy), we follow what our Sages taught us, which is applying hydraulic Bandhas (locks). We use the same three locks they used, firstly the Mulabandha putting pressure and pushing the temperamental Shakti up to Manipura, the Solar Plexus chakra; then Uddiyana bandha that helps the energy rise towards the vocal cords and finally the Jallandhara bandha that sends Shakti towards the Ajna or the Eye of Shiva.

This is the point where the second umbilical cord starts. We, yogis, refer to it as the Kundalini Golden Cord. This makes the connection between the pineal gland, associated with Ajna or Third Eye chakra, and the pituitary gland in Sahasrara or Crown chakra area. This is where enlightenment starts. Can you relate to that, Paul?

HE SAID

On the lower plain, the earthly plain, our task is to explore our consciousness, become aware of what the state of earthly being is and in doing this we start to ascend the four realms. Ultimately achieving enlightenment... Before we can understand the nature of God, we must first understand the nature of our own being. As Socrates said *"To know thy self is the beginning of wisdom"*. Popular belief is that Enlightenment equates to seeing the light, a brilliant light. I cannot accept that, as enlightenment means being made aware, achieving an understanding. May I say, the *"Eureka Effect"*, as we comprehend whence we came and then journeyed, possibly, over many lifetimes back to the energy that is the Divine Unity.

SHE SAID

The soul is Atman, the real eternal Self. That says it all. The soul is deprived of ego and is everlasting. Vedanta school of philosophy refers to Atman as the first principle or the first cause of everything whatsoever.

Monism and dualism are the main concepts that differentiate the Hindu Astikas (schools of thought). You know how I mentioned that there are ten schools in total, six of them following the Vedas and four accepting other scriptures too? Of those six, Pursa Mimamsa focuses only on the interpretation of the Vedas whilst Nyasa and Vaisesika have very similar principles. However Vaisesika's focal point is on the metaphysics of substance and matter, atoms and their interaction.

In Vedanta, the limelight is the metaphysics of

Brahman and Atman mostly based on the Upanishads. However, Vedanta includes four branches, of which Dvaita believes in pure dualism, Dvaita Advaita (or Bheda Abheda) falls between dualism and qualified monism, Shudb Advaita falls between qualified monism and non-duality, whilst Kevala Advaita, mostly known as Advaita, believes in pure monism.

Even the non-Vedic schools of philosophy have different opinions with respect to monism versus dualism; therefore between Atman and Brahman. Trika Shaivism for instance approaches monistic idealism; Buddhism advocates neither dualism nor non-dualism, Saiva Shiddanta, a tantric theological school, follows dualism whilst Pasupata ranges from theistic dualism to yoga non-theism monism. So you see, there are various paths to God... One universal soul or more than one, Paul?

HE SAID

I suggest that our soul is the driver on our journey of return. It never lost contact with the Cosmic or Universal Soul, which was shattered by the Divine Unity. This shattering was a positive event to enable our earthly being to manifest itself. We are then tasked with purifying the now gross being as we return up wards on the Tree of Life, ultimately to reunite with the Cosmic Soul. Once the cosmic Soul is re-assembled it will move upward through the Veil and all will be made clear to us.

I am of the strong opinion that after the Cosmic Soul was shattered, a further break down occurred and the pieces of the Cosmic Soul broke in two. The two parts of this further deconstruction then followed the path or journey allocated. They gained differing understandings of creation, but eventually they will be reunited before moving on. Plato calls these two halves twin flames and suggests that they share the same personality traits, characteristics and appearance. I cannot concur. The two halves are forced together in the manner we may clasp our hands in front of us but they are opposite in personality traits, characteristics and appearance; I link them to the opposing poles of a magnet. You may suggest Yin and Yang. They come together with such a force that they can never be parted again. The final part of their journey will see many trials to test their strength so to ensure the final structure of the Cosmic Soul of which they will form part can never be fractured again.

As ever, Devi Harjeet, I await your comments and rebuttal's with nervous anticipation or is that nervous perspiration?

SHE SAID

Why do I have the feeling that you refer to the common path of twin souls? You mentioned Plato and you were so right. Plato explained the concept of twin souls so beautifully in *"Symposium*[142]*"*. He said that humans were created initially with four arms and four legs and a head with two faces. Zeus was afraid that they would have double power, so he split them in half and cursed them to spend their whole lives looking for each other.

Plato believed that a twin soul's purpose in life is to heal the other soul's luggage of memories, so I am absolutely thrilled that today again you were spot on. The advantage of being my mentor I suppose... Plato also believed that the energies of twin souls flow within their bodies in perfect symbiosis and form one aura only around both bodies.

As much as I wish, I cannot stop without mentioning Ardhnareshwar, the twin souls' concept in Vedic philosophy. Hindus believe that God's soul divided itself in two half souls: masculine God and feminine Goddess. Together the two souls are the highest avatar or incarnation of Shiva, called the Destroyer, the one who was always represented as half man and half woman. These twin souls in Hinduism are considered rays of Surya (Ra or the sun) whilst the atoms their half souls are made of are identical, belonging to the same sunrays. Once reunited, they represent wholeness.

We talked about the Dark Night of The Soul, love and twin souls, but we never discussed gender. I am waiting to hear your thoughts, which is always a challenge, dear mentor!

HE SAID

You asked about how I believe gender sits within the world. Let us consider the Sephiroth that sit at the top of the left and right hand pillars on the Tree of Life. On the left we find the side of severity structure, this side is feminine. On the right is the side of mercy, dynamic, the masculine. We find Chochma on this side and Binah on the feminine or left.

You will have heard me talk about the spark that

emerges from Chochma, as the beginning of life, and deposits a seed in the womb of Binah. In this way the Kabbalah projects the characterisation of Chochma as the male in relationship to the womb of Binah as the female. Binah then, due to its feminine nature, nurturers the Chochma seed or spark, until it has matured enough to pass to Da'at and thence bring into life the remaining seven Sephiroth. Do not forget I use Isaac Luria's depiction of the paths that lie on the Tree.

The Kabbalah also shows that both women and men have the properties of each other, women possessing latent male attributes and the male, latent feminine characteristics. This duality possessed by men and women being credited to Adam, the first person, who innately possessed both properties.

Male and female energies are apparent on the mental and spiritual planes as well as the physical. For creation to be successful it must have equilibrium of both. The Buddha called this equilibrium the *"Middle Way"*. If we can achieve this balance in body, mind and spirit we will find equilibrium in our lives. But as ever your Yogic philosophy may disagree.

SHE SAID

There is that beautiful concept of equality of gender in the Vedic philosophy, perhaps based on the duality of gender on earth as well as on higher planes of existence. Hindu gods were male and female or of both aspects, Brahman having both characteristics of male and female. You may have seen that representation of Shiva being half man and half woman. In fact, we all are a combination of Shiva (masculine energy) and Shakti (feminine energy).

Therefore, the distinction of gender in Vedic philosophy has its source in the way energy occurs in different genders rather than in the biological or sexual organs one possesses. Atman (Self) is genderless. Therefore, there is a three-fold aspect our perception of genders relates to, beautifully described in the Brihadaranyaka Upanishad. The first is Nam (name) that emerges from speech; the second is Rupa (form) that rises from what the eyes can see and the third is Karma (function or action) that stands up from the body itself. Therefore, the way we see a person is by Nam, Rupa and Karma, which in fact form the base of gender differences; not being able though to acknowledge their genderless soul, as well as their mind. Thus, there is no superiority or inferiority concepts based on gender... at least not in the Vedic philosophy.

There is however a verse that may be controversial for some, in the first Canto, 8:20 of Srimad Bhagavatam, that says: *"You Yourself descend to propagate the transcendental science of the devotional service unto the hearts of the advances transcendentalists and mental speculators, who are purified by being able to discriminate between matter and spirit. How, then, can we women know You perfectly?"*. This verse talks about more women than men being interested in spirituality, but it may be just right based on the fact that women may accept easier the superior aspect of life or be less prone to speculate on it.

But going back to the general concept of gender, I

am just wondering how can we humans define ourselves based on criteria that belongs to the body only, like gender for instance, when in fact all we are is conscious beings? Is this not a result of non-self recognition of our own consciousness, the *"I am"* and replacing it with *"I am this body"*?

HE SAID

We define ourselves based on the criteria that belong to the body only because once we go beyond that the description becomes more complex. We have awareness, we have a spirit, a soul and, of course, our physical presence. Now I know you are shouting what about the fact we are conscious? The previous four adjectives are about the individual; consciousness is fundamental, all matter is conscious to varying degrees. Awareness makes us aware; we are connected to consciousness.

You only say *"I am a woman"* because having a soul, having a spirit and being aware you are in a field of consciousness is implicit. We all have those faculties. Awareness, the spirit and physical being only exist between conception and death. After death, the soul maintains its progress toward the Cosmic Soul with consciousness being as is. The break in our connection to consciousness, as we are no longer aware, has no impact on the fundamentality of consciousness.

So if I describe my physical condition only it is because it enables the questioner to assemble a picture of me if we have not met before. If I said in answer to an enquiry, I have a spirit, a soul and am aware I exist in a field of consciousness it would do little to enable my interlocutor to recognise me as I arrived at the bus station.

SHE SAID

The soul has no gender; it is eternal, exactly as our consciousness is infinite. However, in desperation of fitting in a material world, we identify ourselves rather as the person than the soul. How limiting it is to have an infinite soul and consciousness and to recognize ourselves as a temporal body... It is our ego wanting to always be in control, create disharmony and disturb the consonance between the self and our divine nature.

HE SAID

This is classic thinking, quoting Sri Aurobindo and I long to hear your mind's interpretation.

"For all problems of existence are essentially problems of harmony. They arise from the perception of an unsolved discord and the instinct of an undiscovered agreement or unity. To rest content with an unsolved discord is possible for the practical and more animal part of man, but impossible for his fully awakened mind, and usually even his practical parts only escape from the general necessity either by shutting out the problem or by accepting a rough, utilitarian and unillumined compromise. For essentially, all Nature seeks a harmony".

SHE SAID

I love the fact that you brought up Sri Aurobindo, an Indian philosopher that had in my opinion a clear understanding of the Cosmos within us.

So I would ask you something Paul. What do you see or perceive? Do you see Sat (the truth) or Maya (illusion)? And what do you feel, Paul? Do you feel what you see or you feel an illusion you may be seeing? Because between the two there is *"an unsolved discord"* created by a natural instinct. The problem arising from the gap between the two shouldn't bother you at all because there can be harmony even in the problem itself... depending on the way you look at it. But normally, it shouldn't be any problem whatsoever unless you focus on seeing what is not real instead of perceiving the reality. But again, is illusion a dream or a reflection of the reality itself?

HE SAID

Your thoughts on Sri Aurobindo again? *"There seems to be no reason why Life should evolve out of material elements or Mind out of living form, unless we accept the Vedantic solution that Life is already involved in Matter and Mind in Life because in essence Matter is a form of veiled Life, Life a form of veiled Consciousness. And then there seems to be little objection to a farther step in the series and the admission that mental consciousness may itself be only a form and a veil of higher states which are beyond Mind."*

SHE SAID

I knew you would be challenging me on this because, when I am in pain, you are the one who knows that if my brain is focused on something else, the pain doesn't exist. Not even at 10pm... So I will ask you something. Do you agree that Prakriti (matter) is a form of energy? You should because even science considered that. The mind is nothing else than a series of thoughts; vibrations that penetrate ether, whilst consciousness is a form of energy too, exactly as matter is. Each form of development involves matter, because us, humans, as well as everything around us, are matter. But then, is consciousness also based on the development of matter? I asked but allow me to answer too. For our Rishis, Prakriti was a dependent and eternal aspect of Purusha (consciousness). The two are interconnected. The Vedas mention the withdraw of Prakriti from Purusha at the time of Bhasma (dissolution). Your thoughts?

HE SAID

Devi, you asked me if I agree that matter is a form of energy. I reply haughtily; of course, it's obvious it is, no need to discuss! But I hear you growling.

So now go back to the start of everything, the Big Bang; how I hate that phrase for at that time there would have been no observer to turn the vibration into a sound. Also looking at my Tree of Life, Chochma burst forth a spark of immense energy; in this case there was an observer, a receiver, Binah. Binah received the energy and started to make it manifest. So whether scientifically or spiritually all energy, vibration, matter was combined in a pinhead of unimaginable power, the power of the Creator of all things.

As this incredible burst of energy started to evolve,

it developed vibrations, sound waves that spread out; then particles formed. These started to combine into what we call matter. Something we can touch, so we call it solid matter. Oh how we are fooled! Solid matter... How can it be solid when 99% of its structure is empty space? But back to your query. If everything we can see, every plant, tree, animal, rock and on was at one point in the initial spark that the Divine caused to be burst forth, we must be all one, one energy but in different forms.

When I stand and talk to my tree and hold its branches I feel its energy. I stand back and look and it appears to be solid matter. It only appears solid because our brains tell us it is. Our brain builds our perception of the visual world, as it wants us to believe it is. So yes, energy and matter are one and the same but in differing forms.

You also asked if consciousness is based as well on the development of matter. I believe not. Consciousness is fundamental; it pervades everything. It comes from our Creator. Was it there before the spark from Chochma perhaps? If so, this raises the question is our consciousness the mind of the Creator? And are we living in our Creator's mind? Is this a *"rabbit hole"* we could descend at some time in the future?

Finally, you asked and I notice this is three questions in one! The Vedas mention the withdrawal of Prakriti from Purusha at the time of Bhasma (dissolution). If I understand the Vedas, yes, matter will withdraw from consciousness at some point and dissolution will take place. Look around you. Everything is cyclical; it may be a cycle of a nano-second or a billion years. Everything returns to

214

its beginning, so at some point the burst outward the Big bang must become the *"big sucking back in"*. How is that for an intellectual description? Also think of our climb upward on the Tree of life. Our life long task is to combine with the Cosmic Soul and meet out Divine Unity. Just a glorious cyclical event...

So Devi Harjeet, I hit your ball back over the net and await its return.

SHE SAID

I totally respect your opinion about consciousness not depending on the development of matter, but not everybody would. As always, it relates to one's perspective or perhaps one's perception.

In Samkhya school of Vedic philosophy, the mind is based on the evolution of matter. This is what we call the Cartesian mind. So here you have it, exactly the opposite of your argument. It is just another point of view, Paul, you don't agree with, as you already said. I mentioned Samkhya though because even if Purusha and Prakriti are accepted by most Vedic schools, they are mostly relevant for Samkhya.

You threw in another great question... as usual! Is our consciousness the mind of our Creator? I sympathise with Vedanta and, as you already know, Vedanta accepts absolute monism, Jiva (being) and Ishvara (the Cosmic soul) being one. Therefore, for Vedanta, Atman, the soul that exists in each being and Brahman, the Ultimate Reality, are identical.

For Advaita Vedanta followers, Atman and

Brahman are indistinguishable. So yes, Paul, we are living in the Creator's mind, which is our mind really. *"A god is entirely of the nature of the Self"* (Ribhu Gita 10.50). Remember though that Vedanta has four different branches, each of them seeing Brahman in a different way. Vishishtadvaita[143] Vedanta school for instance believes that Jiva is different from Ishvara.

I must come clean with an aspect about my beliefs that you probably already figured out. Very similar to Advaita Vedanta, Brahman is all that is real and the rest is Maya (illusion); also that there are two paths to achieve Moksha (liberation): Jnana (knowledge of the Supreme Reality) and Atma Vicara (self-knowledge or self-enquiry). This is what I believe in and this is why I focus on knowledge.

I would love to know your thoughts on how much this reality is an illusion. So what is true and what is Maya, Paul?

HE SAID

My dear friend, first let us consider the meaning of the two words you use. Maya is the power by which the Universe becomes manifest. It is the illusion or appearance of the phenomenal world whilst illusion is an instance of a wrong or misinterpreted perception of a sensory experience. So as the word *"illusion"* appears in the definition of Maya, let us use that word. A magician is also called an illusionist because he or she fools us into believing that what we see is actual. What I think I see is not the true state. Indeed reality is an illusion; it is not as it appears.

In both concepts, the Kabbalists Ein Sof and the Hindu Brahman, an underlying reality is suggested beyond our perception. This suggestion that our perceived reality is not actual reality is reinforced by the quantum world. I sit here writing on what I perceive is a solid oak table, but if I examine its structure and how atoms have combined to form it, I find that 99.9% of it is empty space.

Our brain interprets the sensory perceptions it receives and transforms these signals into what we think is reality. If animals, birds and some flora perceive a different reality in colours, sounds, vibrations, we have to accept that our brain does not compute all its received data into a true picture.

So my answer to your question, *"what is true and what is illusion or Maya?"* is I do not know, but I do know that, as I look out of my window and view what my brain tells me is out there, I am looking at an illusion.

SHE SAID

Let me make my point based on my Vedanta views. Maya (illusion) is one of the main aspects that differentiate Vedanta from other Vedic schools of philosophy. The way it works is very simple really. Brahman is perfection. We don't have to search or find Brahman because Atman is Brahman. Avidya (ignorance) is the reason why some are still searching for the absolute and pure Brahman. So the idea of Maya in this case is in the way we mix up reality with illusion; instead of identifying ourselves with Brahman, we feel obliged to associate ourselves with a body or a mind. Instead of seeing the simple and pure *"I am"*, our egoic minds add a persona to it *"I am this material and temporal body"*, and everything starts going wrong from there on. This is the biggest illusion. Is this body who I really am or is it consciousness that defines me?

We started with the Dark Night of the Soul and ended up talking about the soul itself. So, I propose to perhaps detach from the topic only to define the difference between soul and spirit.

HE SAID

For many, the word spirit is a metonym for God; *"the Holy Spirit is within"* but for myself the energy of my Divine Being is all-pervasive. It is as the ether, consciousness is within and without all matter. That is not my spirit because my spirit is unique to me. I will ignore your sardonic thought comment *"you can say that again"* and continue. There is a strange phrase *"hapax legomenon"*, which means *"it happens once"*. These unusual words match how I view my spirit. My spirit is the *"me"*, my personality; it is how I think and act and it is the ethereal part of Paul that will just dissipate when his body dies.

The soul that is within me will live on; it chose to be within me because the spirit that is *"me"* enabled it to continue its journey of return to become one with the Cosmic Soul. My spirit on the other hand is how the world views me. Please do not ask how my spirit was developed because, as I write this, I do not know. I imagine that as my character developed so did my spirit because as I suggest my spirit is the *"me"* in myself.

Devi, I hope this is not rambling because I am building my case as I go. To quote Abdu'l-Bahá the human spirit is constructed *"From known realities, that is to say, from the things which are known and visible"*. With great humility I would add that the society we live in also has an unrealised influence on our spirit.

SHE SAID

The Vedic texts don't focus on the spirit, Paul, because spirit is just a minor aspect of being; perhaps best described as personality or attributes of manifestation. The spirit perishes when we die and it will never be reborn in the exact same form because it is unique.

The soul however is immortal. The spirit refers to material and the soul to spiritual. The difference between the two is similar to the polarity described in the Gita: *"There are two classes of beings, the fallible and the infallible. In the material world every living entity is fallible, and in the spiritual world every living entity is called infallible"* (Bhagavad Gita 15.16).

HE SAID

The spirit was never methodically defined in classical rabbinic Judaism, although later the Holy Spirit was believed to be the manner in which God communicates with his prophets. Note that I speak of my spirit, not the Holy Spirit, which is a different concept.

To return briefly to Baha'i writings, the

PAUL COPPER & DEVI HARJEET KAUR

development of just systems of justice, technological innovation, and artistic endeavors are all assertions of the power of the human spirit.

So, my interlocutor, these are my thoughts. How do you explain the spirit within you?

SHE SAID

The closest I was able to understand the human spirit is defined in the Bhagavad Gita 18.41 as Swabhava[144], the essential law of one's nature, *"the material modes"* that differentiate people. The term is associated with Gunaih (mode of material nature), linked therefore with the three Gunas (attributes of matter). Swabhava is discussed by Advaita Vedanta philosophy in Avadhuta Gita[145], also called *"The song of the free soul"*, attributed to Dattatreya[146], who is considered a Lord of yoga.

But because you asked me about the spirit in me, I will say that this is what makes me who I am, a mortal human under the influence of the Gunas, tendencies based on my moods and experiences, unbalanced, like we all are, but hopeful and grateful that my soul is ever eternal and as infinite as the absolute is.

CHAPTER 8

VIBRATION

HE SAID

I am not sure, Devi, if you have ever considered the correspondence between the Tree of Life I use as a base structure and the words of Thrice Great Hermes, *"As above so below; as below so above"*. Both express the belief that we can consider our being from two directions. As I pondered upon this, I thought that I would ask for your thoughts on the Principle of Correspondence[147].

The Hermes aphorism I quoted above tells us that the images and thoughts we hold in our conscious will manifest their likeness in our outer world. Never forget that our outer world is a mirror of our inner world.

SHE SAID

So you are back to the Vedas again. *"Yatha pinde tatha brahmande"* is a verse from Yajurveda, the second Veda, estimated to be transmitted around two millenniums before Christ, but some historians argue than it may have been way earlier, perhaps around 5000BC. It is an amazing scripture that has two main parts: the Black Yajur or Krishna with thirty-two Upanishads and the White Yajur or Sukla with nineteen Upanishads. Yajurveda contains Yajurs or devotional parts and Vedas or knowledge. It is in the Vedas part that the famous *"As above so below"* is.

I would hate you to wonder which was first, the chicken or the egg, so I would just add that the tablet you refer to is dated 800BC to maybe 200BC so way after Yajurveda existed. But please feel free to make your point. I love the way your mind works.

HE SAID

I will now tread on your corns, to prove my case further and speak of Sathya Sai Baba[148] or should I say Sri Dattaguru, I am never sure. I understand that he can create physical objects by thinking and imaging what he wants to create. This is the same law Hermes spoke of it is just at a faster speed than our mental constructs can be assembled into reality. You have proved this to yourself in the recent months. You were diagnosed with cancer and you did not dwell upon it. You insisting I gave you philosophical challenges to work out so you dismissed the thought of cancer completely. This meant that you put your illness and the following treatment to the back of your mind and you defeated the cancer. I recall later how you told me that you saw people who gave into the condition taking many months to recover and also how your doctors were and still are amazed at the speed of your recovery.

At the centre of this principle is the belief that there are constant links between the spiritual, mental and physical planes and that each is affected by and has an effect upon the other. As I mention above, by having high energy in your spiritual life, you manifest physical wellbeing within your body.

So without realising it when I started to write, I can sit back a little smugly thinking that no matter what part of your Vedic philosophy you throw at me I have won this round. Just remember you are what you think.

SHE SAID

I am admitting you winning. I do that with veneration for my mentor, by the way.

Dhi (thought) is created by Buddhi, the activity in our minds. We can live in our minds or we can shift the focus to valuable points that help us evolve. It is all about Dama (self control) that it is achieved mostly through meditation. For me, in beating my cancer, it was mostly through Vidya (knowledge) and I am forever thankful for pushing my mind to limits of study and understanding. You gave me work to do and I knew I couldn't disappoint you... So, as more I worked, as more I forgot. To be perfectly honest, I never remembered the cancer as it wasn't there! *"He who knows success becomes success"* (Chandogya Upanishad 5.1.113).

I mentioned meditation, so I will quote Srimad Bhavagatam on a verse I really love: *"Unless one is fully observed in Krishna consciousness (Cosmic consciousness), material desires will come and go. That is the nature of the mind- thinking, feeling and willing"* (Srimad Bhagavatam 4:29.68). So for me, there was one choice only, Paul, and thank you for being always on my side. I knew that if I can control my thoughts and higher my spiritual vibration, I would be healed. As the logical person you are, you definitely have more to share on the topic of *"vibration"*.

HE SAID

In that study of the Hermetic Philosophy of Ancient Egypt, The Kybalion[149], you will find the words *"Nothing rests; everything moves; everything vibrates"*. As I sit here typing, that is a concept that is hard to understand. Everything vibrates? Everything? I wish I had known this as a teenager for I would have had an adequate answer to my schoolmaster's complaint that my written submissions were illegible: *"But Sir, my desk vibrates"*.

I understand the concept of vibration and that it occurs in all matter to a greater or lesser degree, but it took the quantum physicist's verification of the concept for it to sit comfortably on my shoulder. It is here that the notion of *"as above so below"* again is made clear. The atoms and electrons are vibrating with the electron rotating around the nucleus continually; 99% of the atom being empty. Look into the night sky and what you observe. 99% of what you look at is empty or it looks empty. For the Universe is nothing other than a large atom…

But back to levels of vibration; pure spirit is vibrating at the highest level. Indeed pure spirit is vibrating at such an infinite intensity that it appears motionless as the spokes of a rapidly spinning wheel. At the other pole are forms of matter whose vibrations are so low that they seem totally at rest or unmoving. There are millions of variations of vibration between these poles.

The vibration is also true on the mental or spiritual planes. I believe that I am on the return journey ascending the Sephiroth on my Tree of Life and, as I ascend, my spiritual vibration is increasing until it is at a rate that will enable my return to the Cosmic Soul. Of course, this may be in a lifetime yet to come.

I will read your response with interest for with your study and understanding of yoga and Vedic Philosophy, your vibration will be far above mine and so the view from a higher level will be interesting.

SHE SAID

"Pure spirit vibrates at the highest level"; how beautiful. Your sensitivity is mesmerising and I remember this being the first emotion I felt when I was introduced to you as my mentor.

The Vedas agree that everything in the Universe vibrates and define the sound *"Om"* as the cosmic vibration. Even if Rigveda mentions the Cosmic Akshara (imperishable syllable) only once, perhaps being considered too sacred to be even written down, the other Vedas refer to it several times. *"One should meditate on the syllable Om, which is Udgitha[150]. One should sing Udgitha by uttering Om"* (Changogya Upanishad 1.1.1). Udgitha means the Divine Song.

You may have heard of AUM, which is in fact identical to Om; their vibration is the same. We, yogis, refer to it as Pranava (controller of prana, the vital force) and its vibration is considered to be the frequency of God. I will quote Prashna Upanishad[151] 5:1.5-7: *"What world does he who meditates on Aum until the end of his life, win by that? If he meditates on the Supreme Being with the syllable Aum, he becomes one with the Light, he is led to the world of Brahman, who is higher than the highest life"*.

I remember learning from you, at some stage in my development, the symbolism of number three. Therefore I am now able to apply it to AUM, which having three letters symbolizes the three Gunas, three Sandhya (devotional practice based on the time of a day), three Agnis (god of fire, believed to have three tongues), the Trimurti, the trinity of gods Brahma, Vishnu and Shiva, the Trideva formed by the wives of the Trimurti aspects. So much more to talk about this subject, but let's keep it open forever.

The yogic tradition says that AUM was created by God as the ultimate Svara (sound) of the Universe itself. Thus each letter has a meaning: *"A"* is the beginning of life, *"U"* the middle and *"M"* the end. This doesn't refer to our lifetime; it is the life of the Universe.

Thoughts are vibration too as you well know it. The more positive they are, the higher their frequencies. So if everything vibrates at a certain frequency, God including, is vibration the cause of our existence?

HE SAID

You mention about the first time we met. Yes, I remember that day it was the eleventh, I think. You intrigued me, you as an academic, almost seemed to defy me saying I was your mentor. Despite you skepticism, something seemed to resonate between us. I now believe, I know, it was our vibrations realising they were in tune. You ask me about vibration and if it is the cause of our existence.

There was a Singularity; it's called the Big Bang, which you know I think as a ridiculous name. I say ridiculous because in fact the Singularity was a burst of energy or a vibration, but at that stage there was no receiver to record the vibration as a sound.

As the Universe grew, separation started as matter developed into different forms but it was still held the same initial oscillation although at differing frequencies. So we now have the Divine Being vibrating at such a level it may appear stationary and at the other end of the scale inanimate matter which appears not to vibrate at all. Do you see the never breakable link? The lowest level has with Creator with both appearing to be in the same state.

SHE SAID

Let me please define the Singularity you talked about, this time based on my own Vedic faith. For me, it is Hiranyagarbha[152], the Cosmic Womb or the *"golden egg"* where creation comes from, mentioned in the Vishavakarma Sukta[153] of the Rigveda. The same concept appears in many Upanishads under another name, The Soul of the Universe.

You talk about separation of matter and I totally agree with that. I would just add my part of the story according to the Vedic tradition, which is that dissociation was possible because of one of the five main elements in the Universe, Vayu, which is not just air in itself; it is the space that contains Akasha (ether). Vayu means, *"wind"*, but the Vedic philosophy associates it with consciousness, Brahman as the Universal Principle of the cosmos. Taittiriya Upanishad[154] is very specific about that: *"O, Vayu, you are directly perceivable Brahman."*

I mentioned a parallel between Vayu and consciousness for a reason. Sound as vibration is the vehicle to express consciousness, also the only element able to travel through ether. What about vibration between souls?

HE SAID

When two souls meet and realise that they are oscillating, vibrating, at the same wavelength, an immediate bond is formed. The soul's journey is to return to and become one with the Creator and, to do this, it may need a companion. This matching of vibratory rates or resonation is not just to be found in individual souls but within the ether that surrounds everything. When you intone OM or AUM you are starting a resonance that lies forever in the ether. I see it sitting in a field of probability and, as more people chant or intone, this field of probability grows and becomes more stable in its vibrations. As it becomes more stable, it affects more people who then perform their OM. The stability of the field of probability will increase as it starts to wrap itself around the universe and its peoples. The awful separation we now experience between peoples and nations will cease, as the probability field becomes a certainty.

As the cessation of this separation becomes more powerful more people will experience what you and I have and the return to the Cosmic Soul will increase from a trickle to an absolute torrent.

So yes, my now less prickly friend, vibration is the cause of our existence.

SHE SAID

You developed an algorithm of souls connecting to each other. Your hypothesis was vibration and you built up beautifully on that. What a lovely argument and what a clear conclusion: everything exists because of vibration! I was tempted to say I had nothing to add to that, but I knew you wouldn't accept that.

I talked about Vayu in the macrocosm, but we already agreed on the physical body being a copy of the Universe; therefore as the macrocosm so the microcosm.

The Vedic philosophy accepts the existence of five vital Vayu in the body, Prana Vayu, Apana Vayu, Wyana Vayu, Udana Vayu and Samana Vayu; all moving energy and allowing vibration and sound to travel inward, outward, upward and downwards. Yogis and Ayurveda work with all five- life would not be possible without them- but one in particular is very important, Udana Vayu. It starts in the throat and moves energy upward, regulating speech, therefore sound and vibration. As sounds penetrates ether, Udana Vayu is considered to be a miniature copy of the cosmic Akasha (ether).

You said that the bond between two people is made if their vibrations have identical frequencies. I would argue that the frequency is measured once their vibration, starting in Udana Vayu, reaches ether... and perhaps returning to Udana.

As more as we discover as more as we talk about vibrations. What about polarities, Paul? And as a thank you in advance for your reply, I am sending you some beautiful Mooji[155] music.

HE SAID

The principle of polarity? So, as I listen to the Mooji music you sent me, I will write.

Opposite things do not exist they only appear opposite. They are the same thing just varying in degree. Physical matter and spiritual energy are the same; they came as one from the Singularity I have spoken of. Now they vibrate at differing levels or rates but they are the same from the same source. Like and unlike, opposites that are identical but in different degrees... Everything is dual until we return to the Cosmic Soul. That is a Singularity because that is how it all started, do you not see...

SHE SAID

Yes, we agreed on matter being Shakti (energy) in another form. The creation itself is the union between them, Purusha, the Self, entering into Prakriti, matter. Perhaps this was the moment when all the impurities let Gunas (attributes of mater) influence us all. So how did that affect you?

HE SAID

I was a spark from Binah; I progressed through nine

further Sephirot to become Paul but Paul is still Binah I am just vibrating more slowly. As I work at purification, my vibration will grow until I find my twin soul, two will become one and the final vibration will return the one to the ultimate Singularity.

We should apply this principle of polarity in the way we view negativity, I suggest Devi. This will involve a certain amount of mental juggling, which for you is easy, for the rest of us, we can but try.

Whenever you feel a lower vibrational emotion is disrupting your thoughts, you will recognise it, you feel its disruption so reconstruct it into a positive one, a feeling of love perhaps. So next time I aggravate you, turn that negative vibration into a positive; one you may still hit me with your handbag but it will be with love and you will feel great.

You can blame the Mooji music for this!

SHE SAID

Nothing is easier for me than it is for the others; we are all in the same boat. Please know that I would never hit you with my handbag – even if it were tempting- because, as a yogi, I obey to Ahimsa, which is the principle of non-violence and equal love for all.

You are so right in suggesting the switch from negative to positive thoughts. I would call that *"the reversal of polarities"*. Contrast needs both sides though; good things often evolve from bad. I am not sure if it works the other way around. But because we talked about polarity, why not jumping to another principle? Is this

Universe based on symmetry?

HE SAID

The principle of rhythm? This has an affinity to polarity as between opposing poles there is a fundamental rhythm. Like the tide on my local beach, everything flows in and out; all things rise and fall. The Kybalion tells us *"the measure of the swing to the right is the measure of the swing to the left"*. Rhythm compensates.

Think about it Devi Harjeet; everything is in motion, we breathe in and we breathe out. Nature like ourselves has it seasons its rhythms. The Universe has a rhythm as do the cells in our body; to paraphrase the thrice great Hermes *"as above so below"*.

We are aware that nothing lasts forever, the mayfly lives for twenty-four hours, the Greenland shark for more than two hundred seventy years and our Universe, billions of years but they all have a rhythm. We should recognise how our emotional states ebb and flow and use this knowledge to minimise the internal pendulum swing and so make our being more stable and more peaceful. So my friend what does your Vedic thinking have to say?

SHE SAID

There are several words in Sanskrit for rhythm according to what action it refers to, but the ones I personally use are Vrtti, rhythm in meditation, and Karana, in music and dance, mostly used as a term in Melakarta (musical scales). So I will refer to Karana in Samaveda, which I call the *"Veda of music"*. Even its name says exactly that: *"saman"* means song and *"veda"* means knowledge.

The Samhita (text containing mantras and hymns) of the Samaveda is divided into two parts: Sama Yoni, that takes in order verses from Rigveda, the first chronological Veda; and Sama Gana, which contains mantras, reorganized with extended or extra syllables making them easy to be sung. In every Yajna (Vedic ritual), these over fifteen hundred mantras are sung in thousands of Shakkta (singing in different rhythms). So, just another adaptation to of rhythm...

But, what about the vibration of the state of mind, the truth for instance?

HE SAID

I know, oh, so well you will counter what I am about to write but I will write anyway. The classic suggestion of truth comes from Aristotle *"To say of what is that it is, or of what is not that it is not, is true"*. I do not do cheap jokes so will not say that's all Greek to me; but give you my thoughts.

We use the words *"it's true"*, without considering that generally the situation we refer to cannot be an absolute. It is an absolute truth that I will die or that you cannot have a round square, but if I speak to my granddaughter in England and say *"it's night here that's the truth"*, she will counter with, but it's also true that it is daytime there, in York.

So very often truth is dependent on a frame of reference. I could of course use the word perceive *"I perceive it is night here in New Zealand"* that would be accurate because night is what I am experiencing but strangely that wording sounds cumbersome.

SHE SAID

There is no such a thing as absolute truth, Paul, other than the true identity of God. Everything else is personal, based on how we perceive reality. My truth is mine and your truth is yours... However the meaning of truth in the Vedic texts is totally different. A proper translation from Sanskrit of Satya (truth) is *"the absolute truth that liberates"*. Are the Western world and the Vedic Hinduism totally opposites when t comes to rightness? I actually don't think so; I rather believe that we, Westerners, accommodated the truth that serves us.

HE SAID

Mathematics is one field where truths prevail. If a mathematical statement has no errors in calculation, it is held to be true. Is this because only mathematical symbols are used with no semantics, except when QED is placed after a proof? I have commented that there are occasions where truth is absolute, but generally truth is a personal opinion. No, that comment is too soft; my truth is a conviction not an opinion.

In a book from the Baha'i faith I came across these words, *"We must not look for truth in the deeds and actions of nations; we must investigate truth at its divine source"*. I realised that is where I hunt for truth, at my divine source. As strong as my belief in a Divine Creative force is, I have to concede that it is my truth and Devi, you can legitimately comment that my truth may not be absolute.

The secret aspect of the Torah, the Hebrew Bible, is called *"the way of truth"*. A Kabbalist will insist that this is intrinsically true because it is the truth of the Torah, which is so but this truth is only irrevocable within the field of Kabbalah. It cannot be absolute truth because a Hindu, Daoist or Buddhist would have differing beliefs. I look forward, my friend, to your comments regarding what is truth.

SHE SAID

I agree to disagree... with kindness and absolute respect for my mentor. Hindu, Taoist or Buddhist have different beliefs indeed, but their common focus is enlightenment and truth, God being the same for all those religions you mentioned, even if they call it on a different name.

I can quote hundreds of verses from the Vedas or Upanishads about truth; but I won't, because we both know that the absolute, unchangeable truth called Paramartika Satya is only Brahman, the highest Satyasa Satya (reality); the rest may be illusion or just fake reality. But what I will do is to take you through the levels of reality according to the Vedic writings.

Firstly, there is the Paramartika Satya, the truth of truth, I already mentioned. The next level is Tratibasika Satya that I would translate as the day dreaming state. And lastly, Vyavaharika Satya is the reality as we see it as humans; it seems real if the ego finds it real.

The truth is our perception of reality, no doubt. But what reality are we seeing, Paul? We know that we live in this material world, based on Vyavaharika Satya, when in fact as spiritual enlightened beings we were created with Paramartika Satya, the truth of truth, in our bones.

CHAPTER 9

DEATH

HE SAID

We have been discussing a difficult, but unavoidable fact recently so let us put a few thoughts into type... death...

There are many aspects and forms of death. You and I Devi, both believe in a Cosmic Soul, although we may call it by differing names. So why do we fear what is just another stage in this incredible voyage we are on? It's a bit selfish on my part because there would be a large hole in my life if you were not there to talk with each morning, afternoon and evening, nor any more carrot cake and home baked bread. But if I think about it, is it Devi and Paul's inner being or soul that converses, because if it is, that will never die so we will not be parted, except for the baking.

SHE SAID

Nothing lasts forever, Paul. But in saying that, soul never dies. It's eternal, so we move from one life to another, from one existence to another; therefore always around in a shape and form until we become enlightened enough to get back forever to the source.

HE SAID

Kabbalistic soul doctrine speaks of a four-fold process of separation from the physical realm, emotional cleansing and transcendent awareness with the soul returning to the Source of life, wherein the highest level of soul qualities merge with the divine. This fits perfectly with my interpretation of the return to Keter, the Sephirah that sits at the head of the Tree of Life. Of course you must remember, Devi. that to reach this stage the soul may have progressed through a number of previous lives as it strives for purification.

When we discussed La Mort, we recognised that there are differing forms. There is loneliness, which is sadly akin to death for many young and old people. By and large society has no time for the elderly, they produce nothing cannot cope with rapidly changing technology. So instead of venerating them for a lifetime of knowledge they isolate them. We are increasingly living behind closed doors, high fences are built around a property to protect *"what is mine"* so it is easy for a young person to become isolated and friendless. Then there is the situation of severe disablement. No matter how someone is loved there will be those who feel that they have been subjected to a living death. The increasing isolationism between nations and individuals can only increase these forms of death, which to my mind, when compared with physical form of the event, are indeed a *"fate worse than death"*.

Earlier we have talked about changing the world, correcting the wrong turn taken. If mankind is to survive, he/she must change and one function of this change is to develop a society that is comprehensive in its treatment of all its members so a *"fate worse than death"* will become long forgotten.

How does Vedic philosophy consider death in all its forms, my friend?

SHE SAID

Well, for the Vedic writings, Mrityu (death) is the end of the Triani Pada in one, the three bodies, divine, spiritual and gross. What happens with these three aspects of the human nature after death may sound to you like a story, but will I be accurate enough to keep you interested?

The Vedic philosophy states that after death, the gross body reunifies with Prakriti, matter, and becomes one with all atoms. Things get more complicated with regards to the soul, so please be prepared for my explanation. *"The soul is neither born, nor it ever dies; nor having once existed, does it ever ceased to be. The soul is without birth, eternal, immortal and ageless. It is not destroyed when the body is destroyed"* (Bhagavad Gita 2.20).

Where does the soul go after death, you may ask. Well, Atma, the soul, reunites with the Devas for purification. This process lasts for twelve days; karma already imprinted in it in the past lives not being affected. And this is where things are not as easy as they may look because, as described in the second chapter of Mahabharata, *"Substances offered as homa to Purnima become food of the Devas and those offered on Amavasya become food for the Pitris ".*

Homa is a funeral ritual involving fire, similar to the Western cremation. Purnima and Amavasya are lunar stages, the first one symbolizing full moon and the second one no moon at all or dark moon. Therefore, according to brightness versus darkness of the experiences imprinted in Atma in the latest life, the soul will have to be purified by the Devas or just rest with the Pitris, the spirits of all ancestors. In the twelve days of purification, the soul learns more about the Vedic knowledge, so that, when transmigrated to another existence on this planet, the baby is born with it.

I will develop further, but before I would love to hear about the four-fold process you mentioned earlier.

HE SAID

In the late 1800's, the image of the Grim Reaper became the personification of death as being something to be feared. This image has been presented in other forms, with people always clad in black for funerals and so the fear of death has been developed over the years.

As I have said before, we are on a wondrous journey of discovery and we can use the Sephirah to plot this journey until we ultimately return to the Cosmic Soul. For me if I were to lose you, I know I would be distraught but that would be because our relationship would change. No more early morning texts from you, or would the cell phone be replaced by the celestial's phone, I wonder? So I would be selfish because you would just have beaten me to the next stage but my being would hardly cope with that.

SHE SAID

If one of us was to go first, there will be no early mornings philosophical discussions, no more writing a book together... or maybe the chats will still go on. No more mentorship for me! Death is an unknown territory for us, but what we both know is that *"The soul is glorious, unborn, free from old age, immortal and fearless"* (Brihadaranyaka Upanishad 4.4.25). This verse gives us assuredness that death as we know it is not the end. But go on please with the four- fold process of dissociation.

HE SAID

So let us examine the joyous side and stop Copper from indulging in the maudlin. I have spoken of the four-fold process; as ever this is my interpretation of things so perhaps not the *"party line"*.

We live in the physical realm, the Sephirah of Malkuth or the kingdom. As our soul starts its journey of purifying, we move upwards on the Tree of Life. Our soul passes through Yesod, Hod, Netzach, Tiphareth, Gevurah and Hesed. These Sephiroth are the emotional cleansing stage of the four-fold process.

My soul is now within the Sephirah of Da'at or Knowledge. From Da'at the soul journeys through Binah, Understanding and Chochma, Wisdom. This is the transcendent awareness' part of the four-fold process. Within this upper triad of Sephiroth, we feel complete and finally are ready to stand before Keter, the Crown. We are now able to move to the final stage of returning to the Source of Life, which is the veil above Keter, Ein Sof. So there you have it, the fear of death dispelled.

SHE SAID

Fascinating how each system of beliefs finds its own interpretation of the big subjects in life! I will respond to your thoughts about death by going back to the soul's journey after death. I am sure that there is nothing in any school of philosophy other than the Vedic texts that treats this topic in such a depth.

The Vedic texts mention three paths the soul can travel on after the physical death of the body and mind. The first one is Dakshinayana, the path towards South that guides the soul to the moon, where the ancestral world is. Uttaranayana is the path of the soul toward North, where the immortal Brahman's world exists in Ra, the sun. There is a downward path too called Adhogati, where there is the realm of Yama, the Lord of Death and where the souls must go through a deep purification process. I would just say that those souls traveling to South or North have a kind of similar future reincarnation or not, whilst those meeting Yama would have to be reincarnated as worm or insects. I am not sure that I can prove all these, but at least it is an interesting point of view you would find as fascinating as I find your Tree of Life.

Chandogya Upanishad has some fascinating verses regarding how death occurs and more than likely how a human loses consciousness in the presence of death. One of them sounds like this: *"O Somya, as this person is dying, his speech merges into the mind, his mind into praṇa, his praṇa into fire, and then fire merges into Brahman, the Supreme Deity"* (Chandogya Upanishad 6.8.6). And how right it sounds. The process of dying cannot be stopped once Karmendrijas (speech) merging into Manas or Mana Vriti (mind) whilst the mind is deprived by Prana (vital energy that keeps us alive) afecting Udana Vayu (metabolism). I hope it doesn't sound macabre.

Before I would ask you what do you think it happens after death, I would go back to the essence of the soul and ask you whether or not you believe that the soul is eternal indeed.

HE SAID

As you were aware your question was asked at a poignant time for me and knowing your kindness, Devi, I think it may have been asked to help me organise my thoughts.

My neighbor had died suddenly. It was a difficult time for me anyway and her passing made my upset worse. As I looked at her car and garden I realised that I was being utterly selfish in feeling sorrow. This because I should not be considering my loss, but I should be happy to think that she had moved to the next stage of her and our journey.

I say my dear neighbor had moved on, but of course I mean her soul had moved on. In his book *"The Point in the Heart*[156]*"*, Michael Laitman suggests this point is a source of delight for the soul. The heart is the first organ to be formed in a fetus and this is where the soul lives until the physical body ends. So as Laitman says, the soul rejoices when it enters the heart. Our soul was created when the Cosmic Soul was shattered by the Divine Energy. This shattering is recorded in the Tao Te Ching, the *"mother of ten thousand things"*, the Kabbalah, the *"shattering of the Sephirot vessels"* and many other sacred laws. Once the soul is separated from the Cosmic Soul, it is split into two parts, mirrors of each other; these two parts are twin souls and are constantly yearning to reconnect.

The soul is shattered from the Cosmic Soul and then into two by the Divine Energy to enable it to discover the joys and despairs of a sentient being moving from its gross form back to purification as it prepares to re-unite with its Creator. Once purified, the soul can then experience the utter joy of again being reunited with its twin. The soul may journey through many lives as it seeks purification but once purified and joined with its twin it then returns to the Cosmic Soul forever. Once this is confirmed, there will be no more duality. The seemingly endless journey will be over.

So Devi, the soul is eternal and thank you for enabling me to rationalise over my neighbours passing. My grief is now joy for the soul that lived in her being able to move forward.

SHE SAID

I am so sorry for your loss, Paul. Your sadness saddens me.

You are very right in saying that the heart is where the soul lives… at least from the Vedic philosophy's perspective. Mundaka Upanishad states clearly that the atomic soul resides in the heart, but it also says that it can spread around the whole body. Just a matter of enlightenment, I guess.

We talked on the phone at some stage about when the soul enters the body and I remember very well that we kind of believed in the same things. So I am thinking that I will just make light by quoting Srimad Bhagavatam 3.31.11 and it is up to you whether or not to believe what this verse says. I do! *"The personality of Godhead said: Under the supervision of the Supreme Lord and according to the results of his work (past deeds), the living entity, the soul, is made to enter into the womb of a woman through a particle of male Virya (semen) to assure a particular type of body"*.

So the soul enters in the first moment of conception; it enters in the body it decided over to according to the past lives deeds or karma. In the next verses, the Bhagavata Purana speaks about how the soul and the body of an embryo connect and what happens during the life in the womb. Fascinating verses I would love to discuss more at a future time.

I want to leave you with a verse I truly love, something that will put your mind on fire. It is a very important statement for Vedanta school of philosophy and it says: *"Avidya (ignorance) is regarding the transient as eternal, the impure as pure, the pain giving as joy giving, and the non-Atman as Atman"* (Yogasutra 2.5). Therefore we have to differentiate what is worldly and what is eternal... and the soul is just that, an immortal instrument of pure consciousness. So if the soul is everlasting, why are people afraid of death?

HE SAID

In Western culture, the word *"death"* evokes a characterisation that has been implanted in our memories for several centuries. Since the Middle Ages, a skeletal figure in a black hooded robe wielding a scythe with which to separate the living from their soul is how death is depicted. In the 1800's this figure was given a name, the Grim Reaper. In my beloved Wales, the Angau drives a deathly wagon with a creaking axel, piled high with rotting bodies. So no wonder we fear death. We have moved on a little, my local Angau now drives a shiny black Jaguar hearse that purrs not creaks, but the hooded skeleton is still deep within my psyche as the driver. The word strikes fear in our hearts for we consider it as unfathomable and inevitable. But what is death?

Surely the mystery of death is connected to the mystery of birth for they are both stages on the progression of a soul towards one united with the Cosmos. We seem to consider birth and death as the two bookends of life because we measure everything by our five senses. But Devi, we have other less tangible senses and we must involve these to enable us to transcend and develop the logical assurance that death is just a stage and should be seen as an opportunity for the soul to move upward.

SHE SAID

I actually believe that humans are afraid of unknown and of losing control rather than of death in itself. We are afraid full stop. Is there anything after death and, if there is, how would we fit in the new realm? These are questions that I am sure we all struggled with. My mother used to say that nobody returned after death to describe the afterlife. They may have been or not, but deep down we all know the truth. We were born with it in us; we were given the opportunity to surrender to it, but we still keep searching for answers. I couldn't affirm that faith is the solution for overcoming Bhaya (fear), but I know that it can help.

Therefore, based on Vedanta's philosophy, I would argue that death is just a state of deep sleep, in which we may be conscious of nothing to be conscious about. Would this statement be enough to reassure us that there is a shape or form of existence after death? Well, for me it is. But just because I want to be more specific in my answer, I would focus on fear in general.

Our Rishis said that fear is part of the Vritti (mental activity). They identified every process of the mind being part of perception, produced by sensory organs, cognition, a product of Buddhi (intellect) and emotions or feelings. Vedanta school of philosophy is clear about us, being the observer of Vritti, and in charge of them. Therefore fear can be managed if Raga (attachment) is not associated with it. The Sages described the cause of fear being Avidya (ignorance), which also creates blindness about reality. They described the veil of ignorance that stops us from accepting our true divine nature and association to the immortal Self.

I mentioned many times the Rishis, but according to Bhagavad Gita *"he who is free from attachment, fear and anger is called a sage of stable mind"*. What I believe that stops us achieving that wisdom is our attachment to people, possessions and life in general, when in fact without all these, we would accept that it wasn't only in our control to be born and it definitely is not in our power to avoid death.

HE SAID

Devi, you commented, *"My mother used to say that nobody returned after death to describe the afterlife"*. I found her statement intriguing. I have known a few people who speak of previous lives. They will only talk briefly saying that there were this or that person. I have never pressed and thought they must discuss details only with their physic medium or a group of similar returnees. Your mothers comment made me realise that they talk of a previous life or lives going back perhaps hundreds of years but never the interim period between lives. Of course when they say *"I"*, they had a previous life they mean their soul did, or do they is it possible they were the same person but with a different soul.

I can see an Alice beckoning me down another rabbit hole. So are these people who recall previous lives only aware between conception and death, if so how are they suspended between lives. As I write, it strikes me that my suggestion of differing souls is a non-starter because there is a memory involved. Does the soul have a memory of previous existences? Help me out please.

SHE SAID

To be perfectly honest, I am not sure what my mother referred to, but definitely not to past life regression.

This is more my area of expertise, not hers, because past life regression is part of my work as a hypnotherapist. So I will try to make a little light here.

Regressing somebody to a past life is as straightforward process, as it is regressing them to the period spent in the womb. During the years, I have the privilege to witness past life memories of thousands of clients remembering memories from hundreds of years ago. It is perhaps the easiest job a hypnotherapist does because the memories belong to the client only. However, during the process, there is a regression to what you call *"the interim period between lives"* and what I would refer to as *"life between lives"*. So, this is not a new territory either, Paul, many people recalling memories from that realm too.

If you remember, I already quoted Vedic texts in regards to the soul journey in between lives. Bhagavat Gita refers to two paths, one towards the sun for souls that are enlightened enough to break the cycle of Samsara (reincarnation) and a path towards the moon for souls that have to return to a human existence.

For a pertinent explanation, I have to go back to the soul that is infinite and eternal and that travels through each incarnation. As I mentioned previously, the Vedic texts refer to the soul residing in the heart, so within our body, not lingering somewhere in the atmosphere as some would believe. So, you were right connecting the *"I"* to the soul because *"I am"* refers to Atman, the Self. Our egos though deny our divine existence by attaching a body to the soul and referring to ourselves as *"I am a man or a woman"*. Therefore, I believe that your enquiry was more about if the soul is the one that remembers. Well, yes and no. There is another factor involved, the mind, mostly the subconscious part.

Going back to what my mother used to say, I kind of believe that she referred to people who would have come back right after death to tell us what happens in the afterlife, but this was covered as well by the near-death experiences. Their testimonials are quite similar, which may prove that their experiences were almost identical too. I personally, don't doubt reincarnation or the capacity of our minds to remember more than what is stated in psychoanalytical manuals.

HE SAID

Going back to somebody describing the afterlife, I have a friend who has many tapes and printed words from Jach Pursel, who channels a nonphysical entity called Lazaris. Lazaris describes himself as a *"spark of consciousness beyond our physical and causal plane"*. He advises the listener on how to reach the next evolutionary step. But, again no comments on the afterlife... So your dear mother is quite correct we may have contact with something beyond but no detail. Can Vedic philosophy help a mind filled with loose Lego bricks?

SHE SAID

I don't have enough knowledge about the person you mentioned to make a pertinent statement, but what I would say is that we are all sparks of consciousness, not just him. So, I would base my answer on exactly that consciousness.

We are all Sakshi, witnesses of this reality. We witness our Vritti (mental activity), materialized in thoughts, emotions, words, and experiences. Our bodies are objects that perceive reality though sensorial organs. Vedanta names this as the Drik Drishya concept. Drik is the *"seer"*, us, the observer, and Drishya is the *"seen"*, the object of observation. Objects are separate from us, the Drik, and so is the body that is just an object attached to us in a human existence. Whatever happens in our mind, all the Vrittis, perception, feelings and cognition, is known to us through consciousness.

Atma (or Atman) though is the unborn and uncreated Self that is Sat (truth), Cit (consciousness) and Ananda (inner source of bliss, happiness). Therefore, consciousness is unlimited too. We cannot possess or lose consciousness because we are consciousness and we are part of the divine Cosmic Consciousness. However the veil of ignorance we constantly build is the source of the illusion described as the body being identical to the soul.

Therefore, going back to your friend, based on the fact that consciousness is infinite, I cannot disagree that somebody is able to channel, but I would with the fact that this phenomena is based on a spark of consciousness. We are all conscious beings and consciousness is present in every aspect of our lives.

HE SAID

Let us now conjecture about the end of the Universe as though we had the confirmed facts. Perhaps as it is part of a series and I should say the death of this Universe.

To do this I would wish to consider one of the similarities between the structure of the cosmos or Universe, the macrocosm and the human being, the microcosm, or as Thrice Great Hermes puts it *"as above so below"*. Every part of our being and the world around us is cyclical. Most days I watch the sunrise and, guess what, the next morning there it is again. A cycle of twenty-four hours... The tide comes and goes twice in the lunar day. Cycle of twenty hours and fifty minutes; Saturn's orbital period is a cycle of 29.5 years and finally the length of the astrological cycle 25,860 years; cycles of differing periods, but all going around and around. As I are looking at the ending of the Universe I will ask you, Devi, to report on any none cyclic activity in the microcosm from Vedic literature. This, to complete the recurrent certainties...

SHE SAID

The Vedic philosophy mentions our Universe as being Anadi (beginningless) and Ananta (endless). All this means is that once it exists, it will be going though cycles of creation and dissolution. Brahmanda (the world) exists because of Brahma (God).

It may surprise you, Paul, saying that the Universe itself is embodied in a feminine entity, which is Saraswathi (or Shatarupa), the Goddess of awareness and knowledge. Rigveda refers to her as the River Saraswathi, which in fact is the river or the wave of awareness. So Brahma is the source of the macrocosm and Saraswathi is the source of microcosm.

As we are born and die, so is Brahma, but as I have mentioned before, its years are different to our years. Again, the microcosm and macrocosm is created and dissolved as many times as is required. The Universe is born and reincarnated exactly as we humans are! Is this just a form of reincarnation of the macrocosm? Please pick this idea and develop it based on your beliefs.

HE SAID

The Universe was formed and I repeat myself here, from a vast surge of energy called the Singularity. Since this event 13.8 billion years ago, the Universe continues to move outward, now expanding exponentially.

Scientists ask if the Universe end in a Big Crunch[157], rip, freeze or decay. My super brain (sic) tells me that as everything within the Universe is cyclical, the Universe itself must be cyclical so the end must be the opposite of the singularity or Big Bang, hence the Big Crunch as it collapses into the pin head of unimaginably dense matter again that burst forth over 13 billion years ago. This could be a cycle of an unimaginable period of time but it will still be a cycle of birth and death.

No doubt my hypothesis will end in a big crunch from your Vedic standpoint.

SHE SAID

I talked about Yugas (cycles of time) when we discussed time. This time though I will quote Linga Purana[158], a text part of Mahapuranas. *"The period duration of Prakrita creation is said to be a day of Brahma.*

The lord effects creation during day time and dissolution during the night".

Just to be clear. A Kalpa (one day of Brahma) is 4.32 billion human years, which means that after this period, the Universe is dissipated; during a Pralaya (one night of Brahma) the creation doesn't exist and another creation starts with a new Kalpa. *"During Brahma's night, the creatures perish; at the end of the night they are created again".*

It is said that each Kalpa (each day of Brahma) is ruled by a Manu (ruler) and each Kalpa has fourteen Manvataras (cycle of time lasting three hundred six million years). Vishnu Purana mentions Vaivasvata, known as Sraddhadeva or Satyavrata, being the current Manu; Brahma Purana 1:10-13 talks about the seven Sages that appear in this particular period of time and the three groups of Devas (Sutapas, Amitabhas and Sukhas) around, each consisting of twenty Devas.

I will go just a bit deeper in the concept of Yuga. The Vedic philosophy accentuates that each creation has seventy sets of four Yugas or generations. The first Yuga is Sarya Yuga, known as the *"Golden age"*, a time of truth and understanding; followed by Treta Yuga, a time of trinity, because three avatars of Vishnu are always present in this time. Dvapara Yuga is the cycle of compassion and truthfulness and Kali Yuga is the world age of discomfort, ruled by the demon Kali. So all these four cycles repeat all over again in the time when energies are active and disappear when creation is not manifested.

I don't want to go in more details because it may

sound complicated, but all I would ask you is to keep an open mind. What if this is as true as I believe it is?

From the Universe back to us, humans... Is life a gift we have to accept or we can give up anytime we want?

HE SAID

Devi, you asked that I speak about psychogenic death or giving up on life. It is ironic - is it not? - that in our society, where there is so much available, this condition should still occur. Is the root cause that one of the success measures of our society depends upon the individuals' ability to gain material wealth? Even when we have goods around us we continually look around and are depressed when our neighbor gains the latest *"must have"*, which we have missing.

In the late eighties, stock market crash, Black Monday, persons took their own lives. Why? Because they lost money and money was more important than life. Do you recall the opening words of Don Henley's song *"In a New York Minute"*? This tells how quickly a life filled with joy can change. Often, not because of the loss of a loved one which is intangible, but because of the loss of a tangible asset or balance sheet...

May I say that this distortion of values is engendered from childhood? At school, we are taught to turn the free spirit of the young child into an efficiency machine, where ultimately mammon will rule. So diminishment in our wealth is equal to a drop in the all-important standing in society and for a few the decisions to end their lives.

SHE SAID

Your words today are sad... Do you think that some people give up on life because of the pressure the society puts on them? Bigger, faster, more, more, more... It is exactly how I lived my life for many years. You, my mentor, put a stop on that and I am forever grateful for that!

I would add a few words about Dukha (suffering), because I believe that this is the cause of living in a somnambulism state. The Upanishads identify two mental processes that initiate Dukha: attachments and Avidya (ignorance). Attachments are in fact Trsna, desires and greed. This makes me think that perhaps for many years I based my life on Trsna. Avidya is not allowing ourselves to see the bigger picture: our unconditional divine nature.

HE SAID

The above words were to bring me to a topic that you asked for my thoughts on, namely suicide. In this country, New Zealand, suicide sounds like a forbidden word, so to a family who suffers this dreadful event shame is felt. I may be unfair but I blame organised religion for this ostracising of those who suffer.

In 1880, the Jewish population in Iraq suffered from mass anti-Semitic persecution; to escape this tortured life many of the Jewish populace ended their lives. How did the Iraqi Rabbinate fight against this, by fighting the persecution of their congregation, oh no, they turned upon their own *"flock"* with a decree: those who commit suicide will have no part in the-world-to-come. I may stand correction Devi but where in the Bible, Talmud or Midrash is suicide viewed as a heinous sin. I would wish to think that sixty-one years later taking one's own life rather than facing the German gas chamber was viewed more compassionately.

In fairness to my criticism, in 1990's John Paul II did approve a softening of the Catholic view by accepting physiological disturbance could be seen as a mitigating consideration. Sadly it seems Jewish Law still forbids suicide. How does the Church of England advice compare, this prior to an event. The advice from a local vicar was *"pull yourself together"*.

I spoke of financial loss being a cause for ending life, but consider other causes. Is it possible to feel the utter despair of life's events being the cause of such blackness that there seems no point in going on? There are organisations that one can turn to, but just imagine standing upon a bridge wanting to just drop into the traffic below. To say that at such a time the Samaritans telephone number pops into the mind is a little unrealistic.

I think I am plunging to the depths so let's turn a hundred and eighty degrees and say how can the driven isolationism of the world's population be corrected. I think we are back to the wrong turn taken by the mankind are we not. So Devi, how will Vedic thought lift us from this gloom?

SHE SAID

Well, Paul, I may surprise you again. In the ancient Vedic time, there were quite a few suicides of very important people, some even Sages. The Adi Parva of

Mahabharata[159] talks about Sage Vashishta's attempt of suicide in Sutlej River. He was one the Brahmarshi (main Rishi), also one of the Saptashishis (one of the seven most important Sages); he is accredited with Mandala seven of the Rigveda, Vishnu Purana and Agni Purana.

In Bhagavad Gita 12:18, Krishna said *"one who is equipoised in honor and dishonor.... Is dear to me"*. I am not saying that Krishna's message to Arjuna was that suicide is good or bad; I am just trying to make a point about how fair Vedic philosophy was treating the subject.

At some stage I came across a verse in Garuda Purana[160] that mentions the spirit of a person who committed suicide as being a ghost and I remember debating with some people on that topic. However, I would say now what I said then. The term ghost means gone earlier than the right time. Not good, not bad...

Suicide is a huge and very sad subject... Every death is sad, Paul. What is your faith saying about hope in the afterlife?

HE SAID

Devi Harjeet, you asked me to consider reincarnation or for you Samsara and me, Gilgul. I have talked with you before about how everything is cyclical, this whether we speak of the macrocosm or the microcosm. Gilgul fits perfectly here because the Hebrew word translates as cycle or wheel and reincarnation is a cycle. We have also considered the possibility that mankind took a wrong turning. We pondered on this trying to identify when and reached no conclusion. I have given this further thought and considered is the wrong turning associated with Lau Tzu's term the *"Mother of 10,000 Things"* or the cosmic catastrophe that caused the *"shattering of the vessels"*, which occurred at the point of creation. Yes, I know, if this is the case, I have to consider my Divine Beings part in a breaking up. I know how impatient you are but bear with me whist I construct.

If I go back to Copper's philosophy, this breaking up equates to the Cosmic Soul being broken with individual souls further broken into two parts, twins. The task our souls have been given is a journey or path that requires rectification to achieve returning to the state of purity in which the Cosmic Soul resides. I felt this gradual rectification occurs during the time a soul resides in a being following the birth – life – death cycle. Yes, another cycle.

There is a conception that the progress from one life cycle to another on the path to reunification can be an up and down affair, depending upon the virtue or not of the being the soul resides in. I cannot accept this, as Einstein said to Max Born[161] *"God does not play dice"*, so the souls return does not depend upon chance. The soul decides which being to attach itself to at the point of conception so each time the soul will reside in a being that will enable the purification process to be enhanced. Yes, this may take many life times but ultimately the soul will reach the level of perfection that will enable the Creator to introduce it to the being in which its twin resides. So the twin souls will merge, this being discovered during the life cycle of the two separate beings and so preparing the now united soul to look ahead to enlightenment. Remember I have already given you my words on enlightenment.

But before I close, let me return to the cycle of reincarnation. Of course, we have to break out from this cycle but I see this as a spiral effect going around in circles but moving upwards so eventually the peak of the spiral is reached and the purified, united soul breaks free from the cycle of reincarnation and is united with the Creator and enlightenment occurs.

What you have read is my philosophy, without doubt it will be in conflict with many erudite thinkers but it is mine. So I will wrap my words up in a phrase well known to you and I Devi, *"So mote it be"*.

SHE SAID

The Halliwell Manuscript or the Regius Poem? Amen to that, Paul!

You linked your argument to the Kabbalah's views on twin souls. I will however look at the soul only. Have you ever thought about why the soul decides over one body and not another one? I would applaud you if your answer were Occam's Razor, you so often mention, because this is exactly what happens. The soul attaches to the body, the family, the country that gives the simplest solution in achieving a certain destiny through learning a particular lesson.

I personally talked heaps about Moksha (freedom) achieved when Samsara (cycle of reincarnations) is not needed anymore. So I would pick one of your ideas and develop it further. Twin souls! You talked about the merge of the souls in the twin souls' scenario, so I would just give you an example of the opposites who attract each other. So what better illustration than Shiva and Parvati?

Shiva, as you know is one of the aspects of Trimurti (trinity of Brahma the Creator, Vishnu the Preserver and Shiva the Destroyer). Shiva is in charge with transforming and destroying the Universe. So, if he is an aspect of God, he has no body; is immortal and divine. Parvati on the other hand, was a princess, a human, and the daughter of king Himavan[162]. They met as twin souls and complemented each other, deity and human, because what gelled them was the commune energy they both possessed. The myth says that because they couldn't have children- remember that Shiva is nonhuman- whilst he was often away, Parvati conceived children by breathing the united soul of them.

Shiva is a form of Shakti, energy, which we yogis use in our practices. In fact our bodies are a union of Shiva, as a masculine principle, and Shakti, feminine aspect of life. Therefore, our bodies are nothing else that a merger of the twin soul connection of the two, Shiva the consciousness and Shakti, the energy. One cannot exist in the absence of the other one! Being that, we are continuously aiming to balance our feminine and masculine aspects, trying to merge two different polarities actually, exactly as unlike Shiva and Parvati were. By the way, he, the destroyer, was the only one who was able to put up with her grumpy personality, because when Parvati was angry, - and boy, she was!- he was able to calm her down. Pure magic! At the end of the day, it is all about our own image we see in another person… and that brings me to another question. Is self-image reality or illusion?

HE SAID

You know I am a lover of Zen kaons, don't you Devi, and your question brings one to my mind. *"What was your real face before your parents were born"?* I think at first I must dig around to find the illusions caused by our egoic mind regarding the nature of our real self.

From an early age, self-perception is formed not by the self but by one's family, society and for me more disturbingly the education system. We are told this is the way it is, we believe and so our face to the world, our egoic nature, is formed. For me, one person stood out against this, perhaps I did not realise it at the time, but he taught me to let my mind fly. To inquire endlessly, accept nothing. Johnny Way was my English tutor and he introduced his students to a wonderful thing, unrestrained thinking. I think Mr. Way shaped my life for I have never been able to accept conventions because society says that convention is the norm, concordats have to be challenged. Society does not appreciate this but never mind that, what I think is my interpretation so the face I have is mine. The older I get, the stronger this resolve becomes.

As you know Devi, for many years, I have enjoyed aspects of the Baha'i Faith, this because the teachings of the Báb and Baha'u'llah have not been distorted. I remind you of this so you understand why I quote from the Baha'i Scriptures *"Consume the egotistical veils with the fire of oneness".* From this, you will understand that left uncontrolled, our ego can separate us from nature, our maker and our genuine self.

We need to recognise that the ego constructs to

satisfy itself and that the construct is an illusion. In most cases the ego is seen to be the basis of our self-esteem, it needs others to compare itself against and strives to elevate itself above them. The ego tells its *"owner"* when you have enough power you will be secure, do not share with anyone, I am so much better than they are, and so on. These lies are believed easily and give satisfaction and protection, but also cause separation from others. Look around Devi, is this separation the curse of modern society?

SHE SAID

To answer, I have to go back to metempsychosis, the transmigration of souls. It is just fair in a chapter dedicated to death, because at the end of the day, your whole dialogue was about the death of a fake image.

Reincarnation and Punarjanman (rebirth) is debated in the Vedas and Upanishads and very clearly described in Jaiminiya Upanishad Brahmana[163] 3:28.4: *"If being in heaven one might wish: 'May I be born here again?' then one will be born again in the family one desires, be it in a Brahmin family or in a Kṣatriya family. As to this Śātyāyani spoke: "This world is full of disease. And we also speak about yonder world and exert ourselves to reach it. Why throw away yonder world and try to return here? In this heavenly world (about which we are speaking now) one should be".*

So why do we continuously come back to this planet? Well, in my opinion reincarnation is just a chance we give ourselves to make spiritual progress. The Vedic knowledge tells us that this advancement is based on admitting that Atman is in fact Brahman.

So lately a question pops to my mind. If transmigration of souls is a fact, at least for one like me, is transmigration of mind possible? Is it within reach to train our minds to see in the mirror the real image of us? In my opinion the clue is in two Vedic mantras: Asmi (I am) and Soham (I am Thou). The soul is so simple, Paul; our souls identify with *"I am"* only, acknowledging its divine nature in *"I am Thou"*. However, what our ego sees is *"I am that person, of that age, doing this for a living, having that house, that car"*... and this is a fake image of our Self. We will never get to the seed of our identity unless we train our minds to let go of the body whilst acknowledging the soul only. This process is based on spiritual evolvement, the ability to separate ourselves from materialism whilst still living in a material world.

Self-imagine is an action of our mind. If the mind is still, there is no action and there is no image... other than Soham.

HE SAID

I know these are supposed to be my words and please Devi, do not moan, but I will quote again, this time from the Kabbalist Rav HaLevi Epstein[164], who in the 1917 spoke these words *"In order for a group to be able to reveal great Light, it's important that no one individual views him- or herself as more important than anyone else. The smaller the ego, the greater the Light"*. I add the smaller the ego, the closer we become to our own real self.

I think you and I agree that our souls are on a

journey of return to our Cosmic Soul. For this journey to be completed, we need to change our ego from one of self-aggrandisement to one of contemplating on the nature of our Creator and to having compassion for our fellow man.

Remember we are all fellow travelers, not the disunited beings our ego suggests we must be. In doing this we will become acquainted with our true or real self and find ourselves closer to our twin souls and hence closer to the Divine Energy from which we sprang and their duality will become unity.

SHE SAID

You are back to the sacred hieros gamos[165] of twin souls. You are again right because this relationship of pure, unconditional love may the key in ending Samsara. I am imagining this scenario: life after life learning lessons, passing teachings to others and still not enough. So a Punarjanman (rebirth) is necessary... and another one... in an endless cycle of awareness and enlightenment; struggle after another one, until we can double the strength in a spiritual union with another soul and suddenly all can be over. Just like that.

I always wondered why we are not able to recognise a twin soul if their mission is that huge, helping us to skip the cycle of Samsara. The answer is given by Krishna: *"Arjuna, both you and I were born many times in the past. You do not remember those births, but I remember them all".* It is our human nature that stops us remembering a past life... and souls we interacted with in other lives. Therefore we need a celestial power to help us recall,

Krishna or even a Deva or Devi!

CHAPTER 10

MAGIC

HE SAID

If I speak of the Principle of Mentalism (the Kybalion), will you give me your Vedic thoughts?

As you may have noticed from my previous words, I am starting to believe that the Universe is mental, so that all we observe is in our mind. Whether you consider the Big Bang or the spark of energy that shot forth from Chochma toward Binah, in either case it was pure energy that was released. This energy was the spirit of the Originator perhaps it was the Originator. As the spirit or energy condensed it became the matter from which all else evolved.

The process that you are using to read and consider my suggestion is of a twofold form it is simply creating the same thing twice; you read and formulate and answer you then change the incorporeal into the real by writing in some form. It is a simple movement one form to another, for myself the manifestation of our Universe should have been such. If *"All is Mind"*, it is three words that confirm what we see is what our mind tells us to see.

If what I suggest is accepted, it answers many queries we have. I understand that people who are close experience thought transfer. Albert Einstein spoke of *"spooky action at a distance"*, the instant reaction between two previously entangled particles. The lovers' thought transfer in a different form or is it different? If the energy that condensed into matter is what we call ether of dark energy, we are surrounded by it, we are surrounded by the mind of our Originator, so thoughts between people and objects that have a link would be instantaneous. This would answer the puzzle as to why the Institute of Noetic Sciences' random number generators change in unison when a dramatic event catches the attention of peoples across the world. The concentrated unified thought cause a ripple or wave to spread through the ether that surrounds every particle of matter in our universe and so causes a non-random effect in the generators.

SHE SAID

As you started this topic, I could very easily write about hypnosis, At the end of the day, this is my job, but I am keeping true to myself and fair to your request and, as a yogi, I prefer to develop mind control as one of the areas in Mentalism.

My yogi guru used to say, *"when the mind is our slave, we are on top of the world, but when our minds are our masters, we become monsters"*. The Manas (mind) is very complex and controlling it takes time, knowledge and skills. The mind experiences, not the body. The Yoga Vasistha text, attributed to Valmiki, the author of Ramayana, argues that Manas' main component is intelligence that is totally different to self-knowledge. Buddhi (intelligence) is instinctual.... as instinctual as Ahamkara (ego) is. So ego is the aspect that we can control for the mind to become a perfect vessel of consciousness, acting as a bridge between the physical body and the soul. Vedanta believes that the path to govern our own minds is through meditation. This concept is described mostly in the Yoga Upanishads, part of Atharveda.

In your opinion, can we control the mind and, if we can, how?

HE SAID

You ask specifically can we control our mind irrespective of a great energy that holds and directs our universal mind. You have this strange ability to see into me and so this question at this time has great relevance for me. As you found out this morning, but I believe you already knew, I have had difficult thoughts for several days. It was if there were two of me, one trying to totally disrupt my mental peace and one defending it. Let us call them ego ONE and ego TWO. For a number of days, ego ONE held sway. The most ridiculous scenarios were developed in my mind, totally bizarre and I knew they were but could not stop them. Then ego TWO spoke up saying do something about this. Slowly ego TWO broke through, it and I formed a plan and the nonsense in my mind was stopped.

This may sound a strange story, two egos with me

standing, watching them. But it happened. In the coming weeks I will try to understand this process because there is only my egoic mind and I do not stand and watch the goings on I am part of them.

So yes, we can control our minds; ultimately I did, with help but I started the process of correction so I controlled my mind. Although I await a visit from Freud's super-ego saying if you want a laugh, Sigmund come and look at this. I wonder how on earth you will reply to this, Devi?

SHE SAID

You are right, Paul. There is only one self-ego and the easiest way to quiet it is through Dhyana (meditation). These days meditation is very trendy; therefore a whole industry was created around it, one that in some cases promotes masters of fakeness, when in fact things are so simple.

People refer to conscious and subconscious and forget the main key in awareness, the superconscious mind, a powerful tool that can be used to tap into a realm beyond reality. I would refer to it as ether, but I am aware that there are more like me acknowledging the universal dark energy in our minds. However, if I am right and the superconscious mind is the ether in our mind, then thoughts as vibrations would naturally penetrate it creating a wave of positive changes. And if I were right again, then meditation would quiet down the negative energetic vibrations of our thoughts. I however define meditation as a date with my own soul. *"Having made the conjunction with the mind, one should meditate on the Atman (soul) through his own Atman"*. (Yoga Upanishads 1:31)

I mentioned a while back that there are thirty-eight Yoga Upanishads, twenty of them being dedicated to Kundalini Yoga, a name the ancient secret Laya yoga was invested with. The Vedic vision on Dhyana, sometimes referred as Adhidhyana, expressed in most Upanishads, Sutras, Brahmasutras, Dharmasutras, Bhagavad Gita, is based on two things only: Pranayama, breath control, and Dharana, focus; therefore Samadhi (oneness with the object of meditation) can be reached. So, I would argue that to achieve oneness, one must start with focusing the superconscious mind on the flow of the five vital Vayu (winds) that move energy in and out of body. This is not a supernatural process, nor a paranormal ability.

Do you believe that extramundane powers, like intuition and mediumship for instance are in fact natural abilities?

HE SAID

I am so tempted to just say yes, and return this to you Devi, but as I hope to live a short while longer, I will give you my thoughts. They are supernatural if we accept that the Divine Being is within us and ergo we are supernatural. If not, just accept they are powers we have, in the large part, ignored and so they have become dormant. My comments must be a little general because there are some individuals who still have these powers in abundance. As I have told you, I have a close friend who has the ability to spot if I do not wash behind my ears in the morning.

But a little more seriously although, I was not joking! I believe that we had what we now call supernatural powers but for most of the population they were not needed. The powers we needed were the ability to gather food, be able to prepare a shelter, procreate for the continuance of the species and perhaps most important the ability to observe danger and react immediately.

These enabled survival. *"Survival of the fittest"* ("Principles of Biology", Herbert Spencer) evolved from Darwin's Evolutionary Theory, he refined requirements even further than I. He commented *"Survival of the form that will leave the most copies of itself in successive generations"* (*"On the origin of species"*, Charles Darwin). The individual, whose skills lay in the form of telekinesis, levitation, precognition, and extrasensory perception, was of little use in the hunter-gatherer communities. *"The way you can levitate is so cool, dad but the hut needs a roof and what have you caught for dinner".*

So such skills were not needed for survival. A few members of the society gave spiritual learning and so retained what we now call supernatural powers, the Shaman, the ancient Japanese Miko, the Bush Aborigine and others. So these are my thoughts for acceptance, rejection or amendment my dear.

SHE SAID

I cannot deny that some people have special skills. I haven't decided though if they possess supernatural powers or they just know how to use abilities we may all have since birth. I witnessed people Laghima (levitating) when I was a teenager, too young to even be tipsy... I've seen people stopping their breathing for more than what I thought it was normal. I personally seen many times the unseen, but I will keep that to myself and hope that everyone would experience it in their own way!

I believe that we all have Sarama (intuition), an amazing ability perhaps created by the activity of the right side of the brain, which is logical, analytical and rational. Exactly as you are, Paul, so I don't doubt that you are more prone than many others to be an intuitive guy.

The Vedic texts associate intuition with Buddhi, the higher intelligence. The Rishis believed that Sarama is the act of finding the path to the Absolute Truth. If their supposition is right, intuition is a natural ability rather than a supernatural gift. What about miraculous powers? Well, Srimad Bhagavatam describes Mahima, the power to expand the body size and also talks about Anima, the property of a body becoming minuscule and Prapti, the ability to get anything from anywhere. Bhagavata Purana mentions too Dura Darsana, a mental capacity we now call remote viewing and Para Citta Adhi Abhijnata or mind reading. All these are mostly related to enlightened people, mostly yogis, who can attain a high level of mind control. Therefore, the level of awareness would, for me at least, be crucial rather than the belief of being special from birth.

Because you are so logical, I am wondering whether or not you believe that predicting the future is possible. So I will let you think about that with your analytical mind. So is precognition possible?

HE SAID

Devi, my thoughts on precognition? I am sorry, not many, but I will tell you the few and you will reply and I will work from your writing.

What I will say is that logic says that precognition, the metaphysical knowledge of future events must be available. I have talked about us being on a path, I feel sure that as I now ascend the Kabbalist Tree of Life from Malkuth to Keter. This is the route of our path, so the future events upon that path must be laid out. In the mind of a Divine Being perhaps…

I have told you that a while ago I was, by some intervention, advised about what I would be faced with and what I was told came to pass and rather dramatically so is that precognition. Strangely or maybe not, I felt that I was crossing the Abys that lies below the upper triad of Sephiroth before I was told' what to expect' again was that precognition.

Many, many years ago, I was shown a building rather like the interior of the Albert Hall in London. The building was filled with papers and books. I was puzzled, what was that about I asked myself. Some weeks later I found out about the Akashic Library was that precognition. In late 2019, I was told by an acquaintance not to book any travel in 2020. Now that was precognition.

So you see, my dear, my thoughts are bouncing about, so please write about you experiences, so I can clarify my mind and perhaps add more to our discussion on this subject.

SHE SAID

Maybe seeing that library was precognition or perhaps clairvoyance. Either way, I wouldn't be surprised at all because I know that a mind like yours could have both abilities.

Rigveda and Samaveda mention seeing the future In a Swapnawastha (dream state). There are also verses about this phenomenon in the Upanishads.

Do you remember Kanada, I talked so much about in one of my previous emails? He defined gloriously dream cognition as a combination of memories, images and visions from the past, binding with the ego and mind. So, a kind of mixture really... However, I cannot deny the ability to predict the future. Some people astral travel; why would others not be able to see what is there to come? So I would ask you, Paul, what are the dreams? Do they have any significance to you?

HE SAID

For a while, Devi, you have been asking about my thoughts on dreams and do they lead to reality. To your request Copper cocked a deaf *"un"*. I have not heard this phrase since I left England so I thought I would find out the 'compasses' of its use. I find that it is British intransitive slang, so my linguistic skills expand for not only can I speak Brummie dialect but also intransitive slang. Oh, the phrase means *"I turned a deaf ear"*.

The reason I was so reticent was because I realised I seem to have stopped dreaming beyond just a fragmentary image. That's not totally true because I do have a dream that you and I are sitting on the grass side by side. We do not speak, but just sit there. It is there and then gone. Until the last few months, I had dreams just jumbles of things, factories I knew, motorbikes, people but rarely a subject that left me wondering. As far as I can remember, just things with illogical connections...

SHE SAID

We just sat... and wrote a book! As a little girl, I dreamt about a world of love, compassion and kindness... I still dream about it!

Dreams are huge topics in the Vedic writings and are seen as prophetic windows to the future mostly based on messages from departed souls. There is a whole chapter called *"Dreams, omens and Shri Rama (seventh avatar of Vishnu)"* in Agni Purana, which is a conversation between Agnidev (God of fire) and Sage Vashishtha. This particular chapter though is based on Sita and Laxmana's nightmares, whilst being in exile, and the explanation given to their dreams by Lord Rama. I know it is not related to our topic about dreams, but I would like to explain who those characters where. Sita was Rama's wife and Laxmana was married to Sita's sister, Urmila. When Rama was sent to exile, Laxmana left Urmila and joined Rama and Sita in exile.

There are many verses about dreams and their symbolism in Rigveda, the oldest of the Vedas, as well as in the other three Vedas. But, in fact, the best explanation of the dreaming phenomena is in Mandukya Upanishad, part of Mandukia Karika, compiled by Sage Gaudapada[166], because this Upanishads focuses on the three stages of consciousness, corresponding to the Doctrine of the Three Bodies. According to it, there are three Koshas (layers) that cover the soul and three Sharinas (bodies) emanating from Brahman, corresponding to three levels of consciousness: Jagrat (state of awekeness), Svapna (state of dreaming) and Susupti (state of deep dreaming). Very similar to what neuroscience agreed on thousands of years after the Sages revealed it. The tricky part though is that the Rishis added another state of consciousness, Turiya, which is pure and infinite consciousness, almost identical to what we call now transcendence.

But if you don't mind, I will bring up Acharya Kanada again, who had quite a unique interpretation of why we dream, one that is aligned with what science believes nowadays. Kanada, the founder of Vaisheshika school of philosophy, explained that dreams are created by the consciousness generated by the self and mind, in line with subconscious memories of past experiences. Knowing that this statement was made by somebody who lived thousands of years ago makes me excited. But, back to you Paul, and your dreams.

HE SAID

Now I ask your opinion, my friend, as my meditations started to take me places and as my mind started to be clarified regarding spiritual activity did this negate my need to dream. Twelve months ago, was I searching in my sleep but now many questions have been answered is there no need for dreaming, is my work done during meditation?

There is an ancient Sephardic Kabbalistic tradition which suggests that our dreaming mind can be made manifest in daytime awareness and this enables us to achieve a different consciousness. It is a little more complex than this but this is the basis. As you are aware, during the last months my mental perception has and is changing so I ask you is my conscious awareness now at a stable level where it is constant for twenty-four hours a day.

If this is so the second part of your question has been answered. As you may have realised, from our discussions, since childhood I have looked, dreamed of finding the truth concerning this life. I am now having it unfolded before me. So yes, Devi Harjeet, our dreams do lead to reality. We just have to find someone to take our hand.

SHE SAID

To complete what you have said, I must go back to Rishi Kanada, whose name means *"atom eater"*. He believed that dreams are the liquid substance of our own consciousness that happen when the knowledge arising from the mind is under the influence of a *"defect of sleep"*. Kanada described dreams separated from Viparyaya (illusions) because the external sensorial organs do not produce them. The real cause of dreams, according to him, is: Samskara (*"latent impression of inhibited desire"*), Dhatudosa (*"defect of humor and affection of body"*) and Adrsta (*"unseen factor of merit and demerit"*).

I will comment quickly before you are even able to

disagree with this. Datudosa has its root in *"Dhatu"* that means organs preserving the body: Asrk (blood), Mamsa (flesh), Mima (fat), Vasa (brain), Asthi (bones), Majja (bone marrow) and Ocukra (semen). Kanada believed that these organs can be affected negatively by Vata (wind in the body), Slesma (phlegm) and Pitta (bile) and dreams are in fact what he called *"defect of humor and affection of body"*, which is actually the influence of winds in the body, bile and phlegm on the protective organs of the body. In the same way, the unseen factor of merit and demerit is nothing else than the object of a dream where a subject dreams about things they have seen or never seen before.

Let me just mention the fact that Kanada talked about dreams as being determinable non- isolated phenomena, where Adrsha (the seen- unseen cause) relates a particular dream to an individual history. His theory about dreams is fascinating and very much agreed on by today's neuroscience. And if Freud agreed, everybody should!

CHAPTER 11

A WORLD OF ORDER

HE SAID

Devi, we are considering the relationships between persons and also relationships between nations, which at day one was unity or oneness, so how and when has humanity taken a wrong turning toward separation?

This is a question I have been asking for a long time. I have looked back through the ages to see if I could come up with an answer but have yet to draw a conclusion. So let you and I explore.

First, of all we should confirm that humanity has indeed got it wrong. Technology is changing our lives rapidly, the ability to communicate worldwide in an instant, the access to endless information, at the press of a few keys, is phenomenal. Virtual reality enables us to attend meetings, visit friends and family without leaving our fireside. But it is not reality and the Oxford English Dictionary tells me virtual is *"near enough"*. For me near enough is not good enough.

The rich and powerful nations struggle for superiority whilst the poor nations slip further behind and tear themselves apart with internal conflicts and famine. Whether the nation is rich or poor, the populace becomes the whipping boy for the political leaders and the animal kingdom and nature are exploited for personal gain. The mantra of those driving this destruction is *"I want it now"* despite the implications. So yes, Devi, we have got things terribly wrong.

Returning to my opening thoughts, when did we go wrong? Was it when Newtonian physics split religion and scientific thinking or was it much earlier? As you are aware Devi, the words I write come as I write with no or little prior thought so will you let me make a fanciful hypothesis.

SHE SAID

Your concern is mine too. Our selfish attitude towards fellow human, flora and fauna is destroying the planet. In our fight for accumulating more money, assets and knowledge we forgot about traditional virtues that worked for our ancestors. But what am I saying, Paul? The hunger for domination started thousands of years ago; wars, battles and injustice were around ever since the history was recorded. Therefore, as much as I would love to put a day to the first event that turned us from loving and kind human beings to indifferent and cold people, I could not pinpoint it. But what I am aware of is the fact that our impersonal and lately virtual relationships based on the Internet only created an even bigger separation between us; and with it, we disconnected even more from our souls. Our divine nature is hardly noticeable and our relation with God is minimal.

Perhaps this is why I love the Vedic texts. They talk about the union with God, the Universe and about oneness with all mankind. These magical writings encourage me to look my dog Hendrix in his eyes and acknowledge our common nature, to respect everything and everybody. So there is a way back to our meaning and we would have to witness even more the nature's revenge if we decide to ignore it.

HE SAID

There was an event, the big bang, singularity or whatever but I will call it Creation. A Divine Energy caused an occurrence and the Universe was generated along with this event consciousness and the Cosmic Soul were formed. Perhaps the Creator was playful and caused the Cosmic Soul to splinter and fragmented things further breaking the splinters into two further parts. Dare I say that our mischievous Creator gave the twice fragmented parts of the Comic Soul too much freedom not realising that the beings created would develop egotistical natures. This breaking was done so that the Creator could watch the pure souls find their twin and then journey home, but our Creator did not realise that the purity of the soul would be soiled and this caused the ego to develop. So did it go wrong from the start? Elsewhere I think I posed the question; do we exist in the mind of a creator if we do all this could just be a mind game.

I have seen you wrinkle your nose like that before,

Devi, so you do not accept my hypothesis. Whether my fanciful proposal is true or not it matters, not because the bottom line is only one form of life is destroying our world and it is the human being. We are made of nature and, if we destroy it, we are no thing for nature will just take over. The signs of this reclamation are becoming more and more evident.

Gloomy thought perhaps but now let me give you my thoughts on how the situation will be turned around. Of course I will read your comments on what I have written first.

SHE SAID

I believe that you are right again in saying that we were given too much freedom, which none of us knew how to use. That makes me remember two words in Sanskrit that are relevant to the freedom we were invested with. The first is Daksha, which means *"strength"*, as well as *"to hurt"*; or being that strong that you can hurt others. The second word is Sveccha or living a freedom where consequences are inexistent. This is the highest freedom in any yoga, where reality manifests as God's will. Therefore, I am wondering if we are living a freedom that has no bad side effects or we are free only to hurt others?

I believe that the real pandemic of our century is Nirmamatva (indifference). We don't care about anything whatsoever other than our own desires and, in the rush of having more, we forget to ask ourselves *"how much is too much"*. We pass by the homeless whilst eating burgers, ignoring that their bellies may have been empty for a few days and we close our curtains to don't see our neighbor struggling to lift something too heavy. It is not that we don't see the reality. We are not blind, but we don't want to see.

This double nature we allow to take over our lives makes up apathetic, anxious, fearful and depressed, because deep down we know that there is no happiness in seeing people around us struggle. So we got to the point where we compromised Manasika (mental happiness) and Adhiatmyka (spiritual happiness) and swapped it for Bhautika (happiness given by comfort in life). Can we actually change, Paul?

HE SAID

Not being able to say when mankind went wrong, I made a fanciful suggestion, Devi. Now, I will suggest how things can and must be corrected without fancy. The first thing the human being must accept is that we are not the most important things on this planet. We are just contained in an undivided whole. We plunder the planet, its minerals, flora, fauna, we modify animal and marine life into a convenient form for our insatiable appetites. We lock them in cages, feed them chemicals and then eat them. We happily accept that slave labour will be used to make inexpensive goods. The opulent want more and more when logic says if the well-off had less and less we could ensure fair shares for all the nearly eight billion people who are our neighbours.

As we write our words, the world is suffering from a warming of the planet with its peoples dying in thousands due to a pandemic. If someone looked at this situation from the outside, they may think the way forward is one of unity, stop the sectarianism, stop the separation become a whole, work together. Manic self-interest can only destroy. Think about the pandemic; it would have started with one person being infected and now it is worldwide, that is how interlinked we are.

SHE SAID

I don't want to sound too blunt in saying that yoga was just one of the reasons I turned long time ago to vegetarianism; and I don't want to be perceived as too pedantic in affirming that the other reason was my compassion for animals. There is enough food growing in trees and in the soil, so I could not be that hypocritical to preach love and be part of killing animals.

You asked how did humanity get it so wrong. Turn the television on and all you can see is crime, blood, violence and torture. Our path to disaster is present in every detail of our lives. We drive our cars with anger, we are jealous when one succeeds, we fill the beaches with our rubbish, we kill animals, we destroy beautiful landscapes to build more and more retail shopping centers and sometimes we forget that we are human. We are too busy to remember that everybody around us is part of the same big planetary family. When and why we forgot what Rig Veda says, *"The entire world is a family"*?

I too live in this era of plastic, rudeness and indifference, Paul, but am aware that things have to change in order to save us and the planet. And the change has to start with us…

HE SAID

I do not believe that I am hopelessly optimistic when I say I feel the vibrations for change are becoming stronger for they are. I may not see the ultimate change, but I hope you will and your and my children also. I say this because the change in thinking that is paramount will be slow and there may be some hard lessons to be learned on the journey.

There is an ancient Chinese saying *"A journey of a thousand miles begins with a single step"*. The first step is one of regaining a tranquil mind. The eighteenth century philosopher Jean-Jacques Rousseau said that man is not born once but twice. At the first birth, he comes into existence; at the second into life. He may not have been speaking of what I am, but we need to become reborn into the second life that lies deep within our very being.

I will let you consider and reply to my thoughts Devi and then I will develop my thinking about the change needed using the Kabbalistic Tree of Life as the process guide.

SHE SAID

Born twice? The Dharmasastras, which are texts about Dharma (moral virtues) call this rite of passage, Dvija, whilst in the Mahabharata it is mentioned at Dvijottama. Both refer to Upasana as the initiation into spirituality, a ceremony of being twice born. Srimat Bhagavatam (canto 3) says *"Human beings must be twice born. A child is first born of a good father and mother, and then he is born again of the spiritual master and the Vedas. The first mother and father bring about his birth into the world; then the spiritual master and the Vedas become his second father and mother"*. A guru, a spiritual master, always played a primordial role in the Vedic society. How can I thank you for being that for me?

I believe that spirituality is the way out of the disaster we brought the world to. In the absence of a model, we cannot change. We wouldn't know how; but once one is reassured about our divine nature, the change can happen. I am not sure though if the society would dare to leave behind a materialistic lifestyle just to achieve spiritual freedom, but on a second thought, it may give it a good shot. I blend in my spirituality in making changes… first, within myself, hoping that others will follow. There are many people going through the same process of purification and enlightenment right now. The light is getting brighter and our earthly spiritual family is getting bigger. Can you relate to that?

HE SAID

I have given you my thoughts, some creative, some factual, so now I will propose my thoughts on how mankind turns to the East. If you will permit me, I will use the Tree of Life to plot my course.

You will recall Devi, that the path upward and downward on the Tree is through ten Sephiroth, arranged in three columns; the Sephiroth being the attributes through which our Creator makes manifest the physical and metaphysical realms. It is also used as a pathway returning to the Cosmic Soul. The column on the left has three Sephiroth, from the top moving down, Binah (understanding), Gevurah (judgement) and Hod (reverberation). The column on the right holds Chochma (wisdom), Hesed (mercy) and Netzach (eternally repeating). The central column is slightly more complex as it potentially holds five Sephirah. At the head is Keter (the crown) below Keter is Da'at (knowledge). Da'at is also known as the invisible Sephirot and is often not shown. I believe Keter is unknowable, so I place Da'at at the head of my central column although Keter remains in place. Below Da'at lies Tiphareth (beauty), and then comes Yesod (foundation) with at the foot of the Tree Malkuth (kingdom).

I propose that my journey of correction will be a return upwards from the current spiritually chaotic world to the unity mankind should have with nature and amongst ourselves. My proposed journey will start at Malkuth, move up to Yesod and then go left to right, rather like a lightning flash until I reach Chochma. I am calling this my journey of correction, but it is more than that. We spoke of mankind taking a wrong turning at some point, my journey is my proposal for a journey that mankind can take. I use the locations on the Tree as stages at which we change our current state of destroying our planet to ultimately being in harmony with nature and our Creator. This change is in our mental condition from *"I"* matter to one of *"we"* matter that being part of nature. It will be a slow process, so I suggest stages taking things slowly. It will not be completed in a generation, but as what I suggest will change the consciousness the transition from generation to generation will be seamless

I hope this is clear, so if you are sitting comfortably, I will begin.

SHE SAID

Letting behind a comfortable dual nature may not be that easy, but change will follow its way once we understand that we are all as divine as our God is. Oneness in everything and in all is the most precious concept happiness arises from. We are all one and we have one God only! *"The truth is one; Sages call it by various names"* (Rigveda 1.164.46). *"Ek Ong Kar, Sat Nam"*, there is only one reality, the eternal truth.

In the absence of unity with fellow human and with the Absolute Creator, we suffer. We live an illusion that this is the happiness we aspire to, but as we get older, and we strip off our layers of ignorance, we realise that there is another way... the only way!

In my opinion, only change can lead us from Dukha (sufferance) to Ananda (total bliss). It starts with introspection and self-enquiry and, whilst going through the process, our own Vritti (mental activity) changes. We suddenly perceive the world as it is and we instantly learn to love each member of our planet Earth family. And then we discover God within ourselves and there is nothing more beautiful than acknowledging our divine nature.

More and more people, like us, are awakened... and their enlightenment lights up the world. They all started with one question only: *"Who am I?"*.

HE SAID

I have given you my thoughts Devi on our current condition and as you have asked will suggest how a correction could be made. Please do not think I am on a giant ego trip; these are just one being out of eight billion beings' thoughts.

I said that I would use the ten Sephiroth as my stepping-stones so let us consider Malkuth, the kingdom as the first stone. This is where we are today, much of what I will say will be a summation of my earlier thoughts or could I say a conclusion. The world is largely driven by avarice; the rich nations make it clear that they will not soften their power whether it be fiscal or political. This is reflected by the individual members of that nation. Those who have wealth and power are reluctant to release any part of those things they value so highly to the less fortunate members of society. Note I do not say their society because, for them, there are the haves who inhabit their society; the rest inhabit a society they most likely have no concept of and want no contact with.

Yes, I am making generalizations, but the rationale in my conclusion will become clearer as we go directly upward to Yesod, the foundation. Here are seen the first glimmers of a harmonising principle that will be expanded as we move on. There are signs that humanities destruction of the planet is causing concerns among small groups of its inhabitants. Wave functions play a vital part in our existence indeed; there are theoretical thinkers who suggest that the basis of the Universe is just one wave function, but let us step back from that to you and I, Devi. We are both members of groups who are generating positive thought waves regarding the correction we speak of. These are very different in format; you speak to world groupings of possibly thousands of people, whereas my groups are much smaller, but the outcome is similar.

You will recall me talking about the random number generators that are placed around the world, all reacting to a world event that causes the peoples of most nations to take notice. So a common thought pattern can be measured as it travels through the ether that surrounds all matter. Is this consciousness, I wonder? So at Yesod we are making the foundations for a worldwide change in conscious awareness.

SHE SAID

You talk about Yesod, the only avenue of change from one condition to another. I talk about the Kundalini energy, always there for us to use in the switch from material to spiritual. How beautiful that, besides different beliefs and faiths, we are all identical, worshipping the same God. The diversity of our beliefs brings us all together. One God, one only; call it what names you wish, still one... Multitudes of souls, starting to look within and discovering It! Is this not reassuring that humanity started getting the power back?

There is a long way ahead and we may not be around to witness the return to the real values of humanity, but there is hope that one day our successors will live on a better planet, in harmony and synergy with the nature. That is the Earth our Rishis talked about!

HE SAID

Some while ago you introduced me to a Sikh[167] mantra that I have grown to love, so several times in the day I intone *"Ek Ong Kar, Sat Nam"*, *"One Creator, Truth is his name"*. This brings peace inside, but more importantly, the sound waves that come from the words enter the consciousness that surrounds all beings, ethereal or otherwise. You may say what difference will that make to the consciousness of the world. As one person, the change is only within me, but what if a billion people uttered similar words that would be the foundation for a change.

I will now move up the Kabbalistic Tree across to the left where we will find Hod (vibrating). Before I write more, I will draw breath and allow you to comment on what I have written so far.

SHE SAID

The Earth is awakening and people are looking for the truth. Many realised that there is so much more to this life other than money and assets. Happiness comes from within and this joy can help us move to that level of bliss our Sages talked about.

Yes, I have my Rishis on my side and you may have wondered why do I give them credit. Ten thousand years before Christ stepped on this planet, my Sages knew how the Earth looks: *"Shape of earth is like an oblong spheroid"* (Rigveda 30.4.5); *"Earth is flattened at the poles"* (Manukandeya Purana 54.12). They talked about the gravitational force that holds in their orbits the planets and satellites: *"Through establishing the all illuminating powerful sun, you maintain control over all cosmic bodies through mutual forces"* (RigVeda 8.12.30). In Vishnu Purana, they described the rotation of our planet: *"Earth rotates in two ways: first it rotates on its axis, secondly, it revolves around Sun. Days and nights are distinguished when moves on its axis. Seasons change when it revolves around Sun"*.

The same Sages identified the tectonic plates and their geographical position. They were thousands of years ahead modern science in talking about Shiv Linga, the Big Bang; about the ozone in the protective layers of the Universe, about the low and high tides, about the gravitational force and the forces of motion. So these are my Sages I trust! And these Rishis had foreseen the harmony of this planet once people will awaken to the Absolute Reality. Oneness in all and everything!

HE SAID

My dear friend, everything is connected. Much of what we have discussed earlier suggests that a connectedness exists and I will add new thoughts to our previous words.

We, as individual beings, are connected to each other and the source of nature. As you read my words, your heart is beating, as mine is and as the hearts of humanity are. There is a connection here because, as the heart beats, it drives hemoglobin around our body; this molecule contains an even smaller molecule called Heme A or Heme B. Heme B is an atom of iron so we all have this atom of iron in our hemoglobin; it is there to keep us alive. Iron was formed by stars forming, exploding and reforming after the singularity and so the iron generated by the stars enabled mankind to become alive. So here we have an immediate link between the burst of energy that was the commencement and every being. Yes, we are connected.

I will drive you to utter boredom as I say yet again, everything in our Universe came from a pinhead of energy. So if we started from that we must be connected.

SHE SAID

Everything is connected indeed! Paramanu (atoms) don't exist separately; they connect in Atum (molecules). Paramatma (Cosmic soul) exists in us all as well as in the whole Universe. The Vedic writings are very specific about the similarities of the attributes of matter in the human body and in everything around us.

The Vedas speak about heat and energy part of Agni (fire), light because of Surya (sun) and lightening based on Apsara (clouds and water). Let me surprise you though. The Vedas mentioned electricity because of Indra (thunderbolt), thousands of years before science acknowledged it; also about Citra (different polarities) and Sakhya (attraction). All in us and all in the Universe! Their entire philosophy is based on the dual characteristics of matter: positive versus negative, day versus night and evil versus good, all described as Agni versus Soma.

In Vedic mythology, there is a little story about Agni and Soma, which I am sure you will enjoy. Agni, the God of fire, was married to both goddess Svaha and to Soma, the male God of the Moon. Let's consider the unions equally Pavitra (pure) and Pavamana (purifier) because Agni represents energy whilst Soma is the mater. In other words, the perfect union between the fire of the sun and the coolness of the moon... Their relationship is described as *"I am both eternal heat and the matter being offered into it"* (Rigveda 3:26.7).

I mentioned the marriage between Agni and Soma to make a point that everything in the Universe and within us is a combination of energy and matter as a form of energy; also to prove how non-judgmental the Vedic philosophy is. What humanity struggled to accept for centuries, a same gender union, was so obvious and discussed so openly in the Vedas. Should I remind you again how much I love the Vedic philosophy?

HE SAID

Now let us consider esoteric oneness. Every morning on waking you chant a mantra that contains the words *"sarvesham purnam bhavatu*[168]*"*. I speak the same mantra but use the words in English *"may there be wholeness for all"*. So we are recognising that a return to the wholeness, the oneness of the peoples of the planet is an urgency and we ask our Creator to help us achieve this.

We have already talked about the cyclic nature of life and matter, upon this cycle there is a starting point and indeed this start point is also an end point. At this begin and end point there is no duality; all is unity. Please close your eyes and imagine this circle at the top there is a point, a dot, call it what you will, now above this point there are three veils, these are veils of pure abstraction and essential unity. We do not have the intellect to even muse on this, it is the wellspring of being but as we return to the cycle we can explore. Perhaps the first question asked is how long does the cycle take from beginning to end. Remember we are talking of esoteric thinking, not cosmologic calculation. So my answer is it is unknown for it will only be complete when the Cosmic Soul is fully unified. This may shock you but I know what your finely ordered mind will say a hundred years of Brahma or 311.04 trillion human years, my eyes water at the specificity.

As the cycle is completed and unity is re-established, the vast and indescribable burst of energy will occur again and duality will return. May I suggest that we are living in a word of multi-duality as mankind decides that the *"I"* or *"me"* is vastly more important than *"us"* or *"our"*? There is a phrase that is attributed to the Greek storyteller Aesop in his fable *"The Four Oxen and the Lion"*, with great humility I suggest that we ignore it at our peril *"united we stand, divided we fall"*. I have described elsewhere the manner in which the individual soul returns to the Cosmic Soul and will not wish to repeat myself.

SHE SAID

I will repeat myself in saying that duality of matter stays in positive versus negative. And I'll go even further and argue that the concord of those two is what makes us one. So if we are all the same, interrelated in every way, why do people judge? Who is who in an environment of oneness?

I will be going back to the Vedic views, which are so tolerant and don't fit things into small boxes with tight lids on top, and back to the gods that are all gods, even if their genders are different... or extremely contrasting. The Vedic schools of thoughts never paid attention to what makes beings unlike; it did on what connects them.

I talked about Agni, marrying Soma, a male, but what about transgender Gods? Well, Krishna was an avatar or incarnation of Vishnu and in order to marry Aravan, the son of Arjun, he became Mohini. The story is beautiful. Before his death, Aravan wished never to die unmarried, so because there were no women around, Krishna became Mohini and married him. Then the androgynous Shiva, half man, half woman calling himself Ardhanarishvara; or the hermaphroditic Laskimi- Narayan, the god formed by the union of masculine Vishnu and feminine Lakshmi. Or the daughter of king Drupala who was born as a girl called Shikhandini and rose as a man after swapping gender and calling himself warrior Shikhandi.

There is another story in Mahabharata about the royal dynasty of Chandra- vamsa, established by the children of Ila and Budh. And it goes like this. Rishi Briahspati[169] cursed his unborn child, Budh, to be born neither male, nor female when he found out that his wife Tara with her lover Chandra conceived the baby. Later, Ila, who was cursed herself to switch genders every lunar month, married Budh.

So we are all one, Paul, besides our genders or gender preference… or anything else that may seem to separate us. Because let's be honest here, in the macrocosm, the planets have no genders! Therefore I ask myself first whether or not us, humble humans, can change the world by changing people's small minds?

HE SAID

With apologies to Henry Ford *"If you always think what you've always thought, nothing will ever change"*, to change the world, you must first change the thinking of the population because it is our thoughts that have driven us to where we are today. To cause the thought patterns to change we need a ninety-degree rotation. Stage, one is change yourself. You may say, my dear, if one person changes this will affect nothing! Being in the mood to quote again this time verbatim from the Columbian Orator, circa 1795, *"Large streams from little fountains flow, Tall oaks from little acorns grow"*.

I suggest that as each person changes, this will resonate within the ether that surrounds us and eventually this change will become so powerful that the thinking of all the beings inhabiting the world will find a correction.

To effect this change, will be a four-stage process based upon, silence, contemplation, meditation, and compassion. These are the change agents. Your thoughts, my friend, before I write further.

SHE SAID

Beautiful, Paul! Tranformation is imminent;

otherwise we will tear down the whole planet in the same speed we destroy ourselves. The change starts with planting the seeds of love, compassion, and empathy, because we are all in this together. And it starts with being aware that this Universe doesn't belong to us: it is the legacy we leave to our children. *"Ether, air, fire, water, earth, planets, all creatures, directions, trees and plants, rivers and seas, they are all organs of God's body. Remembering this, a devotee respects all species."* (Srimad Bhagavatam Mahapura 2:2.41). Respect, what a powerful word!

I am not sure if you are familiar with Manusmriti, Paul. This is an ancient legal Hindu text, divided in twelve Adhyas (lessons), describing the moral duties of all four Vastas (caste) of the society, including the Brahmins, which were the highest class. The beauty of this writings is that it brings up the concept of reaching Brahman, the higher state of consciousness, by recognizing the equal state of all creation: *"He who thus recognizes in his individual Atman (soul) the universal soul that exists in all beings, becomes equal-minded towards all, and enters the highest state, Brahman"* (Manusmriti 12.125).

Therefore, I believe that the change you were talking about it should start with admitting that I am you and you are me. So please contemplate in silence on the oneness of our souls in this big family called Earth!

HE SAID

In response to my thoughts on changing the world you, my beloved friend, have said *"I am you and you are me. So please contemplate in silence on the oneness of our souls"*. These words cause joy to well up inside me. So yes, Devi Harjeet, I will now give you my thoughts on how silence will enable us to contemplate on a correction to the wrong turn the beings who inhabit this world have taken.

I had suggested that the process for correction is in four parts. The first activity being silence the stilling of the mind. Remember that, what I will talk about, as an activity for the individual will also become an activity for the Universe. I will remind you about this as we start each stage.

What is silence? The absence of noise you may suggest, but noise needs a receiver for it to turn a wave, which is silent energy, into sound. Therefore I argue that the absence of noise is the absence of sound. Remember elsewhere when I spoke of the tree falling in a forest. When the singularity occurred, the Big Bang there was no receiver so the most violent burst of energy there was, was silent. You may say, Devi, that physist John Cramer[170] has recorded a sound from that event, but remember he had to introduce an observer over thirteen billion years after it occurred.

The Universe expanded and matter started to form. Ultimately human life occurred but the matter that life came from was silent so our first task is to still the mind. Stop the continual inane chatter that goes on, my monkey on a chain, which we need to rein in. Chinese astrology tells that the monkey is known to be very clever and talented and can outwit opponents. So do not think the quietening of our *"monkey mind"* will be easy but it must be done to progress along our process of changing the world.

Rabban Shimon ben Gamaliel[171], who died in 70CE taught that there is nothing better for a person that silence. So with Gamaliel in mind, we can start the work of silencing our minds in preparation for the next stage of the process towards changing the world, which is contemplation.

SHE SAID

Let's then contemplate the oneness of all and, in that moment of silence, discover the need to accept that what differentiate us, brings us together.

Manua (silence) is a state required in the interspace, the state of Shiva, the supreme consciousness and, according to Dhyanabindu Upanishad[172], a text of only one hundred and six verses included in the Samadeva, *"Silence is the highest place"*. I adhere to Vedanta philosophy; therefore I agree with that and with another concept in Vedanda that states Manua as the language of God.

The Vedic texts treat silence as pure awareness, highest consciousness and Atman (soul) being Manua in itself. Therefore, according to the Vedic philosophy, the states of Turiya (pure consciousness) and Samandhi (transcendence) start with the practice of silence. However the control of speech is not forced silence; it has to come from the desire within us to evolve and ultimately transcend. Mandukia Upanishad has some beautiful verses about Manua and develops the idea that the essence of consciousness is manifested at the soul level in peace, silence and non-dualism. *"The Self is silence of the Universe"*. How perfect this sounds…

So, I argue that if Satya (truth) is a quality of speech and language; silence should be too. And with this, we enter in another territory, very familiar to me actually, Manua yoga, the silence union. So I would propose an insight into contemplation before we are able to approach transcendence.

HE SAID

For many years I have plotted my journey back toward my maker, using the Kabbalistic Tree. I have the thought arising that I am at Da'at, knowledge. The knowledge that seems to be pouring into me is that I am becoming more and more spiritually aware. I am emerging from the dark night and my soul is not alone. As I write this, the intensity of my feelings has been increasing for the last two hundred and ninety five days and daily my internal joy is growing in intensity. Perhaps Devi, we may explore this further or perhaps not for as you have found I can be somewhat insular.

Now back to the correction. As we work through my proposed process to change or correct the wrong turning that has been taken the work becomes more intense. We have quietened the mind, silence, focus on wellbeing, peace, happiness and wholeness, contemplation and now we must spend time in meditation.

For myself, meditation can be accomplished anywhere although perhaps not on the motorbike. I have two favourites early morning or evening by the sea, no people around then or in my room with my candles and incense. For me meditation is intensely personal, as with other things. What I will comment upon is what I believe meditating upon wellbeing, peace, happiness and wholeness will achieve, note I say *"will"* because for me there is no doubt about the power of my mind so the power of a thousand or more minds is unimaginable. The positive energy from our mind will merge with the Cosmic Consciousness and change will be inevitable.

Never forget that it is the quality of our thoughts that create the quality of our life. So if we project our positive need for mankind to change, en masse, it will combine with other positive energies and a change will occur. Vedic philosophical comments please, my dear friend.

SHE SAID

With the topic of meditation, we now both stepped into my territory, which, dear mentor, I declare that I am very pleased about! I would start with the fact that Vedic Dhyana (meditation) is associated with Saraswati, the Goddess of music, art, poetry and learning and the wife of Brahma. Exactly as the main Hindu gods, Brahma, Vishnu and Shiva form the Trimuri, the three main goddesses, Saraswati, Lakshmi (Goddess of wealth and fortune) and Parvati (Goddess of fertility, Shiva's wife) construct Tridevi. The role of the Trimuri and Tridevi is to maintain the Universe.

For the Vedic texts, Dharana is the initial state of meditation, Dhyana or Upasana is the next step and

Samadhi is the phase of transcendence. As you can imagine, all the Vedic and non-Vedic texts discuss meditation, all identifying it with the state of separation from reality, transcendence and Moksha (liberation). This is the state of Samadhi, desired by all yogis, and described in Maitri Upanishad as Sadhana (six fold yoga). This ancient technique is based on Pranayama (breath control), Pratyahra (detachment from senses), Dhyana (meditation), Dharna (concentration), Tarak (self-enquiry) and Samadhi (total absorption). Only a Paramahamsa (Supreme Swan or enlightened individual) is able to go through the whole process and rise above everything perceived by senses.

The Rishis, practicing the ancient and secret Laya yoga, believed that Dhyana starts with the focus on Kundalini Shakti, which is the only way of purifying the thoughts; Bhagavat Gita identifies Dhyana Yoga as being a union of Bhakti (devotion) and Jnana (knowledge): *"A person is said to be established in self realisation and is called a yogi when is fully satisfied by virtue of acquired knowledge and realization"*. (Bhagavad Gita 6:8)

I could talk forever about meditation, Paul, because I practiced it for decades. I have my own way of transcending that it may not suit others. I personally have a place where I meditate and I wouldn't change it for the world. Same time of a day, same place! I believe that in meditation I have a date with my own soul, so, I respect my soul and I respect myself. I practice what the Rishis used to by purifying my body first and... I dress up, exactly as I would dress up for a perfect date with a perfect man.

The places I was able to travel in meditation are

difficult to be explained, but what I can say is that with each day, I mastered more the process of dissociating myself from what seems to be the reality of the moment... and with each day, I realized that the world is Maya (illusion) indeed.

You know what? It is your turn to point to an element required for our change, so which would it be?

HE SAID

You asked me to pick an element. You give me a hard time, so perhaps this is quid pro quo for I know how you dislike *"simplicity"*.

Lao Tzu said, *"Simplicity is the ultimate sophistication"*. This I propose is true; many times you have heard me speak of Occam's Razor, when there are many hypothesis the simplest is the best. As we have developed knowledge, our language has increased in complexity and as thought likes to be used it drives us to consider more tangled theorems because how do we do this? By using thought and this is a process that is exponential, complexity breeds complexity.

There is one area where simple thought still holds sway in my mind; it is that of the nature of our spirit and for me the study of this. When I look at the writings of the Ancients, they are clear no ambiguity, yes, you may have to ponder on a Zen kaon for a while but this is simple matter. You find a tree sit-down and think. You do not need a MacOS X with an OS 9 subsystem to do. To do this, just a clear mind that lets you watch the thoughts as they drift by.

When I look at most religions they also have been

overtaken by the drive to make life more complex. The words of the differing Masters are torn apart, persons who consider themselves as learned make even the simplest parable difficult to understand by complexities that were never intended.

So, before my diatribe on complexity becomes complex in itself, I give you these thoughts. Simplicity is unpretentious it has inherent modesty not attempting to impress. Leonardo da Vinci did not have a formal education; he was mostly self-educated. It was his experience of the quintessence of life that caused him to use the words I opened with *"Simplicity is the ultimate sophistication"*.

SHE SAID

Is this theme my punishment? I admit that I am complex, but under all the layers created by my own ego, I am simpler than you think. But before I start building on the topic you have chosen for me –thank you, dear mentor!- I would disagree with something you said.

You're right somehow in saying that da Vinci had no proper formal education, but you see, he had an extensive apprenticeship in Verrochio's very famous painting and sculpting workshop, so he learnt chemistry by mastering the skill of combining oxides for making oil paint; then geometry to be able to calculate volumes and areas of panting and sculptures. Did I mention anatomy and biology? On top of all that, he had the gift, the determination and … class. Because, Paul, class has nothing to do with the social level of the family one was born into. And now I got to where I wanted to, class, that goes perfectly with my very special complex simplicity"

The Vedic texts are simple... and complicated too. Simple for the one who keeps an open mind and complicated in relation to other ancient writings. Inclusive rather than exclusive... To prove my point, I will quote one verse only that explains the whole existence of humanity: *"Brahman is know when it is realized in every state of mind, for by such knowledge one attains immortality. By Atman one obtains strength, by knowledge, immortality"* (Kena Upanishad 2:4). Is this not the definition of simplicity?

Are we concerned about each other, Paul, and if we are not, how can we learn compassion for the fellow beings?

HE SAID

We have spoken about building the strength of the process from silence through contemplation to the power of focused meditate so let us now look at compassion. We have discussed this before, but not in this way. Just to recap we have established silence, the quiet mind contemplated on peace, wholeness, wellbeing and happiness, in any order, for all beings to give us focus. We then used meditation to send waves of positive energy into the consciousness that surrounds and is within all matter.

Now we must project compassion toward all beings, so they will feel the energy flow we have engendered and so establish their own positive energy waves. In effect, we have looked beyond all beings sending waves of correction outward so now me must look in towards all matter so it become motivated to follow our path.

What is compassion? First it should become the way we live. I will draw from the Kabbalah beliefs for more thoughts. Compassion contains a quality that is of an emotional and spiritual nature, spiritual writings tell that it is a virtue that should be nurtured in the manner a mother causes her new born to blossom. Unlike pity, there is no thought of condescension; it is not sympathy because sympathy is a response not a way of life. Compassion means being completely with someone no matter what. We form an emotional link with all beings this link made without judgment and is not dependent upon condition.

So minute-by-minute as we complete our daily tasks we should feel compassion flow from us. As it flows outward it causes compassion amongst all beings so compassion will be felt for the Universe.

We are created from the divine and, as we develop compassion, we will move nearer to the Divine. As we become compassionate, this movement will correct the thinking that is destroying Mother Ghia. You see Devi, by developing our spiritual process, I believe that cosmic consciousness can be made so powerful that the thought waves will pass from all beings and that we will see or be shown the error of our ways.

SHE SAID

The Vedic philosophy has a very special approach to Daya (compassion). The Rishis defined two different types of compassion for people: one refers to people whose bad acts was the cause of their suffering and the other to people who suffer without any reason. What is also different to other schools of thought is the fact that, Daya is the base of Ahimsa, which is the concept of non- violence and equal love to all. Ahimsa refers to all beings, humans and animals.

Ahimsa, alongside Satya (truthfulness) is first mentioned in Rigveda 10.22.25 in a hymn dedicated to Indra, the Deva of lightening and storms. From thereon, each Upanishad treats Ahimsa at the same level as Satya. A verse from Mahabharata says that: *"Ahimsa is the highest truth and Ahimsa is the greatest teaching"*.

But going back to Daya (compassion), in Sasnkrit the word comes from the root *"Da"* that means gift. If it is a gift from God or our gift to other people, it is up to you to decide, Paul. I have already made up my mind when I started practicing yoga; because for yoga, Daya is one of the Yamas (restrains), part of the eight limbs of yoga[173]. It needs time to learn compassion… and it needs patience.

HE SAID

What does patience mean to you Devi and do you practice it in your life? Patience is the Buddhist virtue that overcomes anger so may I suggest that from a spiritual perspective we need to eliminate anger from our minds by eradicating the manner in which we conceive the things and people who cause us anger. Sit and consider when impatience has brought you satisfaction or peace, it will not move things forward it just causes mental and thus physical disharmonies.

One manner, in which we can bring patience to the forefront of our lives is by contemplative meditation in which we slow the mad chatter in our mind and just sit and watch what the Divine places before us. Patience is not an easy virtue to attain. Everywhere we look in this world we see demands that we move faster, react faster, there is little time to practice patience.

If you listen to people talking they have no time to listen to what is being said for they are formulating their reply some time before the speaker has uttered their last word. Watch a Krisnamurti and David Bohm dialogue and you will see patience and consideration of the words spoken. There is no rush to reply but when they do it is awesome.

A long time ago, I found these words in a Daily Kabbalah lesson discussing the need to have patience to find the inner light. *"A thousand enter the classroom, but only one exits into the light"*.

You need much patience for the upper light to work on you and give you new qualities. When it is said *"Do anything but leave"* patience is what it speaks of. So my dear, next time you are at the back of a queue in your local shop just relax your mind you will find peace and the assistant will be please not to have yet another angst filled face glaring over the counter.

SHE SAID

You, more than others, know that I have no patience, none at all. I am fast, independent and stubborn. I had to be in order to survive in a life like mine. I have never had the privilege and the time to wait for things to happen, so, I had to constantly fight for each and every thing.

I know the Vedic writings very well; I read them many times, I studied them and I learnt by heart several texts. I have no doubts whatsoever that they all define Pariksaha (patience) as a high virtue. I just wish I could affirm that I have this gift... but I don't. My illness helped me change lately though and there is a small hope of being less restless. But until I will be in the position to master patience, I will keep preaching it, based on my dear Vedic literature.

Pariksaha is one of the main topics in Sandilya Upanishad[174], part of the Atharveda. Being one of the twenty Yoga Upanishads, this text is a main writing for Ashtanga yogis. It is in this Upanishad that the ten sources of patience are revealed. Ahimha (non violence), Satya (truth) and Asteya (non stealing) are the root causes for other virtues too. To these are added, Daya (kindness), Arjava (non deceiving), Kshama (forgiveness), Dhriti (calmness), Mitahara (moderation), Saucha (purifying the mind and body) and Brachmacharya (abstinence).

I am sure that, when you read the ten sources of patience, you would understand once and forever why I have no patience... because some don't match my personality.

I don't know if you ever heard that saying *"having Mahavishnu's patience"*. According to Gaudiya, one of the branches of Vaisnavism school of Hindu philosophy, Mahavishnu refers to three fundamental features: Brahman (invisible aspect), Paramatma (beyond human understanding) and Sarvatma (reincarnating in the aim of perfection). So that saying means to have the patience of understanding everything that is beyond human comprehension.

HE SAID

What does compassion mean to you? According to Buddhist scriptures, compassion is the *"quivering of the pure heart"* when we have allowed ourselves to be touched by the pain of life. I find it impossible to expand upon these words.

I have long thought that the Golden Rule should govern our lives but that for so many people it does not exist in their lexicon. The words of my Golden Rule do not quite match the classic meaning but are *"Do unto others as they want to be treated"* rather than *"how I want to be treated"*. I say this because, having spent many Christmases among the homeless, it was them I wanted to feel happy not me. When I saw a person who had nothing smile, it was so wonderful and when a person who was so fearful of society that they just stood in the shadows building up the courage to come and speak the feeling I got when they talked to me cannot be described.

One theoretical perspective of compassion says that it is simply a variation of love or sadness and not a true emotion so was it my feelings of isolation that I was attempting to remedy by *"doing unto others as they wanted"* in which case my motive was selfish not compassionate. I have never been able to conclude this internal dilemma. Perhaps you can, my dear.

SHE SAID

There are several words in Sanskrit for compassion, but the one I use is Karuna that relates to a system of conduct, rather than to a feeling. The Vedas advocate for compassion for the whole Vasudaika Kutumbam (universal family), in which all creatures, human or not, are equal. This concept of all living beings forming one and only universal family is used in all branches of yoga. Don't you find that beautiful?

Padma Purana also refers to the universal family and the need of compassion for each member of this large brood by using another Sanskrit name for compassion, Daya, which in fact means kindness. I just realised that I have never referred before to Padma Purana, one of the eighteen Mahapuranas. This work has five Khandas (books) and it cannot be attributed to one author only because it was written during many years by many Sages.

I am afraid that I cannot help with your dilemma, not even if I would pray to Krishna, the God of compassion; but what I can do is practice compassion selflessly... which I do as you know.

We started talking about the change that has to come from within and we both see it through our own system of beliefs. Through my study of the union, my yoga, I endeavour to change my perspective in life and get closer to understanding the cosmic truth. Chanting the Vedic mantras and meditating help me dissociate from a reality that is not necessarily perfect. Communicating with my

Rishies assists me in accepting that I cannot change the world if I don't change myself. I know that the world took a wrong turn, but have I done anything to stop it?

HE SAID

So at last, I will return to my proposed course of correction. If you recall Devi, we reached the Sephirah Hod on our journey, proposing a process for changing mankind's current destructive state of mind and how to correct the wrong turn taken. Just to recap, I am the Tree of Life. I started at Malkuth, where I gave my understanding of the current condition of mankind. The process then progressed to Yesod, starting to develop ideas about how our thought or intention waves can slowly combine within consciousness. The progression is now to the left on the tree and upward again to Hod.

Hod is known as vibration or reverberation. Here, the positive thought waves from the individual beings will begin to merge and the necessary change in the world's conscious awareness will move toward one of unity. At Hod, the waves emanating from man's positive thought will unify and a spiritual vibration will begin. Some words from the Book of Zechariah crossed my mind as I thought about how I suggest change is accomplished *"not by might or power but by Spirit"*.

In Hod, the united thought waves will combine to become vibrations and so we progress across the Tree to Netzach, known as eternally repeating. So at Netzach the vibrations repeat and increase in intensity. From Netzach, the process progresses upward and towards the left but first, in the centre of the tree we enter Tiphareth, beauty. It is here that the beauty of the change the vibrations are driving is felt; the beauty of respecting humanity and nature. Working with nature, not exploiting it, recognising all beings are equal and that this equality must be respected. There is the beauty of a wonderful realisation of unity in the Sephirah of Tiphareth. The process of correction now carries on upward and to the left entering Gevurah the Sephirah of judgement. I feel sure you will wish to comment on my thoughts Devi so again I pause.

SHE SAID

You talk about vibration that originate the change in us. I would refer to it as the origin of sound and ultimately word.

As I have said previously, AUM is the Bija mantra that created all sounds in the Universe. *"Bija"* means seed; therefore AUM is the source of vibration just becoming sound; the cosmic tremor of God that manifests in the whole Universe as it does in us. Vibration is the unmanifested state of Brahman that is evidenced in the sacred sound AUM. Every other sound started with it and all will finish with it too.

If every word has its roots in the vibration of AUM, I am wondering how was it possible to lower the vibration of some words? We speak with anger and hate and we pronounce words of very low frequencies. We forgot that *"silence is the language of God"* as beautifully Vedanta school of philosophy defines Manua (silence), so we even lowered the vibration of silence. We speak when we shouldn't and we keep silence when we must speak up. We turned the words upside down and, with them, we confused ourselves.

However, we agreed that there is hope. We can still become kind, loving and respectful people; we can still speak with humbleness and compassion. There is hope... It starts though with the return to AUM, the cosmic vibration created by God as a first sound, a sound of unity, of oneness with the whole Universe. It also begins with changing our thoughts that generate words and letting our divine nature be in charge.

HE SAID

Gevurah is the Sephirah of judgement; this may sound severe but it is disconcertment. The process I am attempting to propose is a drastic change in the mind-set of man so it must be balanced. Thought must be centered with extremes pulled to the centre. The aim of my proposal is to give a unity of mankind with the nature that spawned him, as the Creator envisaged. It is therefore important that the pendulum does not go from one extreme to the other. The judgement of Gevurah will ensure this balance between the being and the surrounding world.

At Gevurah, it is understood that we must live in harmony with nature and that this harmony is a balance. The mind-set of man will have taken or almost have taken a complete reappraisal so Gevurah will, as I say, ensure a centering. From judgement, we move right to mercy the Sephirah of Hesed. Hesed is where inner emotion rises. At his point, we have realised that our direction was one of error, but over time this error has been corrected and now is not the time for recriminations against our forefathers or indeed ourselves; we should give us and them understanding and mercy. I suggested that Gevurah was the stage for ensuring balance but this must also be looked for in Hesed. By this stage, the balance between the creature and nature must be made secure because the next stages of the process, or progression up the Tree of Life, will be a spiritual reunion with the Creator.

Above and to the left of Hesed is Da'at, the Sephirah of knowledge and consciousness. Da'at sits on the centerline of the Tree as Tiphareth does. As we enter Da'at, we will start to understand that the change made in man's thinking regarding nature, cannot be complete without the total acceptance of love of the Creator. This knowledge will enable a move up and left to the Sephirah of Binah, understanding. Here we will understand how the creature, nature and the Creator are one.

The old saying *"united we stand, divided we fall"* fits perfectly here, with the knowledge that a glorious harmony has been created, the process has one final move to the right, to the Sephirah Chochma, wisdom. Our journey has been one of perfecting corrections and gaining wisdom, and it is now found that that wisdom has forever been held in Chochma.

SHE SAID

You talk about knowledge, understanding and wisdom; three beautiful words. Sanskrit unites them all in one word only that has a meaning of all three, Prajna. For me, this is a reassurance that my Rishis, the ancient real scientists and philosophers, came to the same conclusion your Kabbalah did. Prajna is the way within. However, my excitement has another cause that starts with the same word. In Sanskrit, Prajna has another meaning too; it defines the state of deep sleep. Are we living in a state of deep sleep, Paul?

In our desire of owning more, being more and showing off more, are we moving from North to South and West to East in a somnambulist state? Prajna allowed that and Prajna is the salvation though acknowledging that you and I and everybody else must live according to our divine nature, understanding each other and being wise in regards to the future.

It can be done and, even in this slumber, there is hope because the sleep can be as deep as it is, consciousness is still awake; us being conscious of nothing to be conscious about. So perhaps we should take a step back, contemplate in silence and allow our thoughts to generate the right vibration needed for the big change.

HE SAID

My dear friend Devi Harjeet, you and I have looked at many spiritual aspects of life, perhaps some have been almost in despair, but our conclusion is that humanity has a joyous future if it will embrace nature with love and respect. What are your thoughts?

SHE SAID

You, my forever mentor and best friend, are letting

me, the student, to have the last word. This is honoring and encouraging for my future studies.

This planet is an amazing place, but less beautiful than it can be. What was balance at the beginning of time is now a state of chaos we all got used to. We show superiority over nature by destroying as much of it as it is in our power; without any guilt, we kill animals and we justify our crimes on five star meals. Compassion, love and kindness are these days just words we use now and then. In our rush for more, more, more, we turn a blind eye to our fellow humans' sufferance, forgetting that they are we and we are they. But, no matter how low we would go, we are still conscious beings and one day, perhaps today, one by one, we will be made aware that a change has to start.

This change is described in the most beautiful mantra, Gayatry mantra, created in Rigveda 3.62.10 by the venerated Sage Maharshi Vishvamitra. This mantra is dedicated to the ever-bright sun: *"We meditate on the most adored supreme lord, whose effulgence illuminates all realms. May this divine light illumine our intellect"*. The realms Rishi Vishvamitra referred to are the three worlds mentioned by the Vedas, Bhur, Bhuva and Swah, the three symbolical journeys we should be taken though in order to achieve Ananda (bliss). Our awakening will start when we will decide to leave behind the physicality of Bhur, the realm of material life and step into the interspace of the mental plane Bhuva, where thoughts are purified. Our third symbolical journey to the spiritual realm of the Cosmic Soul is where pure consciousness is the only way. There is hope...

REFERENCES

1. Knight Templers were also known as the Order of Solomon's Temple. They were a Catholic military order founded in 1119 and based in Jerusalem. Pope Clement V disbanded the order in 1312. (Page 8)

2. Tao te Ching is a short philosophical text relating to Daoism. It is credited to the 6th century BCE sage Lao Tzu. (Page 10)

3. Lao Tzu, was an ancient Chinese philosopher and writer. He lived between 6th and 4th century BCE. Actual dates of birth and death are unknown. (Page 10)

4. Occam's Razor, or the law of parsimony is somewhat inaccurately paraphrased as *"the simplest explanation is usually the best"*. (Page 10)

5. Kabbalah is an esoteric method, discipline and school of thought in Jewish mysticism. (Page 11)

6. Tree of Life represents the interconnected nature of all things, a bonding between the physical and spiritual realms (Page 11)

7. Sephiroth is one of the manifestations that allow God to manifest in the physical and metaphysical universes (Page 12)

8. Adam HaRishon, the supreme essence of mankind; the soul of Adam HaRishon, contained within it all subsequent souls. (Page 12)

9. Vedanda (means *"The end of Vedas"*) is a school of Vedic philosophy, mostly based on knowledge and liberation highlighted in the Upanishads. (Page 17)

10. Advaita Vedanta (means *"non-duality"*), originally known as Purushavada or Mayavada, is a Vedanta branch. It bases its philosophy on non-dual Atman/ Brahman. (Page 18)

11. Geneva Bible precedes the King James Bible by 51 years and is the most significant English translation of the Bible. (Page 19)

12. Veda Vyasa (Krshna Dvaipayana), also called Parasharia and Satyavateya, was the son of princess Satyavati and Sage Parashara (author or Vishnu Purana). Vyasa compiled the four

Vedas. As per the Vedic tradition, he is still alive, living in the celestial Adi Badarinatha in the Himalayans. (Page 20)

13. Ugrasrara Sauti was the narrator of Mahabharata, Shiva Purana, Bhagavata Purana, Padma Purana, Brahmavaivarta Purana and disciple of Veda Vyasa. He was the son of Lomaharshana, also disciple of Vyasa. (Page 21)

14. Kulapati is a ritual in the sacred forest of Naimisha, where the Puranas were read (Page 21)

15. Mahapuranas include the 18 major Puranas (Agni Puran, Brahma Mahapuran, Brhmanda Puran, Brahmavaivarta Puran, Garuda Puran, Kurma Puran, Linga Puran, Matsya Puran, Markandeya Puran, Naradeeya Puran, Padma Puran, Shiva Puran, Skanda Puran, Vamana Puran, Varaha Puran, Vayu Puran and Vishnu Puran). (Page 21)

16. Sage Badarayana was the compiler of Brahma Sutra, main text in Vedanta philosophy. Vedic tradition identifies him with Veda Vyasa. (Page 22)

17. Krishna, God of protection, compassion and love, is a major deity in Hinduism, worshiped as an avatar of Vishnu. (Page 22)

18. Sanskrit is a classical language in South Asia. It is considered the sacred Hindu language with roots in the Proto-Indo- European languages. (Page 22)

19. En Sof Aur is a term used in Kabbalah to summarise the manifest universe as it emanates from Consciousness. (Page 23)

20. Katha Upanishad, also known as Kathaka Upanishad, composed before 800BC, is part of the Krisha Yajurveda. It contains 2 chapters of 3 sections. (Page 25)

21. Swami Ambikananda, full name Swami Ambikananda Saraswati, is a Hindu monk and teacher of Vedanta philosophy and yoga. (Page 25)

22. Vajasravasa was a major Sage, identified with Rishi Gautama, founder of Vamadeva family, mentioned in the Rigveda. (Page 25)

23. *"Cabala Primer"*, written by Henrietta Bernstein, is an introduction to English Cabala. (Page 26)

24. *"Practical Kabbalah"*, written by Rabbi Laibl Wolf, is a guide to Jewish Wisdom for everyday Life (Page 26)

25. Dark Night of the Soul is a spiritual journey in the union of the soul with God (Page 28)

26. Atah, Malkuth ve-Geburah, ve-Gedulah, Le Olam, Amen, the words used in the Kabbalistic ritual of the Celtic Cross, Atah (thou art), Malkuth (the Kingdom), ve-Geburah (and the Power), ve-Gedulah (and the Glory), le Olam (forever), Amen. (Page 29)

27. Shat Kriya (*"Shat"* means *"six"*) is a six step yogic cleaning technique, aiming to get rid of toxins. (Page 30)

28. Trataka is a yogic meditation technique, which involve gazing at an object. (Page 30)

29. Neti is a nasal cleansing technique in yoga. It uses water in Jala Neti or a string in Sutra Neti. (Page 30)

30. Kapalabhati is a yogic breathing practice that involves passive inhales and alternate, short, explosive exhales. (Page 30)

31. Dhauti is a yogic purification of the esophagus and stomach, which can involve a cloth. (Page 30)

32. Nauli is a yogic technique using the abdominal muscles involving sucking up the content of the stomach and agitating it. (Page 30)

33. Kriya is an ancient meditation practice that involves a sequence of breathing control exercises. (Page 30)

34. *"So mote it be"* is a ritual phrase meaning *"so may it be"*, *"so it is required"* or *"so must it be"*. (Page 31)

35. Letter Tav, is the last letter of the Hebrew word *"emet"* which means *"truth"*. (Page 31)

36. Atharveda or the *"Veda of magical formulas"*, is the second Veda, including 6000 mantras and 730 hymns in 20 books. (Page 34)

37. Mundaka Upanishad part of Atharveda, contains 64 verses in a form of mantras in its 3 parts, each with 2 sections. (Page 34)

38. Isha Upanishad, the shortest Upanishad containing 17 verses, in the last part of Skuhla Atharveda. (Page 34)

39. Nelson Bible Dictionary is the most comprehensive and up-to-date Bible dictionary available. (Page 35)

40. Taittariya Upanishad is a primary Upanishad, compiled as 3 chapters in the Taittariya Aranyaka of Yajurveda. It is attributed to disciples of Sage Vaishampayana (Page 36)

41. Isaac Luria, 1534 – 1572, commonly known as *"Ha'Ari"* (*"the holy Ari"*) was a Rabbi and mystic in the community of Safed in the Galilee region of the Ottoman Empire. (Page 36)

42. Tree of Return is the title given to the Luria diagrammatic form of the tree of life. Simply it enables the shattered soul to return upwards for reunification with the Divine. (Page 36)

43. Thomas Young, 1773 – 1829 was a British polymath who made notable contributions in the fields of vision, musical harmony and Egyptology. (Page 38)

44. St. Augustine, 354 – 439 also known as Augustine of Hippo, was a theologian, philosopher and a Bishop in Roman North Africa. (Page 39)

45. Trimurti is the Trinity of Brahma- the Creator, Vishnu- the Preserver and Shiva- the Destroyer. (Page 41)

46. Bertrand Russell (1872 – 1970) was an academic he worked philosophy and logic. (Page 41)

47. Daniel Dennett, born in 1942, is an American philosopher. He is an atheist and secularist and a member of the Secular Coalition for America advisory board. (Page 41)

48. Christopher Hitchens, 1949 – 2011, was an English-American socio-political critic. He was in direct opposition to the belief in a deity. (Page 41)

49. Hermes Trismegistus, is a legendary Hellenistic figure considered to be a combination of the Greek God Hermes and the Egyptian God Thoth. It is believed he *"wrote"* the Emerald Tablet. (Page 42)

50. Aitareya Upanishad is a principal Upanishad incorporating 3 chapters in the Aitareya Aranyaka of the Rigveda. It contains 3 chapters of 33 verses. (Page 42)

51. Rigveda (*"Rc"* means *"praise"* and *"vedah"* means *"knowledge"*) is the first chronological Veda that contains 10 books, 10,028 hymns and 10600 verses (Page 42)

52. Mandukya Upanishad (*"Manduka"* means *"spiritual distress"*) is the shortest Upanishad consisting of 12 verses. It is part of Rigveda. (Page 42)

53. Chandogya Upanishad (*"Chanda"* means *"poetic meter"*) contains 8 chapters in the Chandogya Brahmana of Samadeva. (Page 43)

54. Samaveda (*"Saman"* means *"song"*) includes 1549 verses. (Page 43)

55. Brihadaranyaka Upanishad in the Shatapatha Brahmana of the Shuhla Yajurveda, accredited to Sage Yajnavalkya, is one of the oldest Upanishad, containing 6 chapters. (Page 43)

56. Yajurveda (*"Yajus"* means *"worship"*) is divided in 2 parts: Dark or Krishna Yajurveda (*"unclear arranged verses"*) and White or Shukla Yajurveda (*"well arranged verses"*). (Page 43)

57. Ha'Ari, see reference 41. (Page 44)

58. Gautama Buddha, 563 BCE – 480 BCE, approx. popularly known as the Buddha, he was s teacher and spiritual leader and is regarded as the founder of Buddhism. (Page 45)

59. Dvaita Vedanta (*"Dvaita"* means "dulism"), also known as Bhedavada, Tattvavada, Bimbapratibimbavada, Purnabrahmavada, Svatantra- Advitiya- Brahmavada. (Page 46)

60. Akshar Purushotam Vedanta is a dualistic branch in Vedanta philosophy.It makes a clear distinction between Para Brahman and Purushotam Narayan (Supreme God). (Page 46)

61. Aesop, a slave and story teller believed to have lived in ancient Greece between 620 and 564 BCE. (Page 47)

62. Super String Field theory, is the theory that fundamental particles are not similar to dots but are in fact tiny strings. (Page 49)

63. Puranas are symbolic texts on variety of topics as cosmology, gods, medicine, astronomy, etc. They are divided in: one Mahapurana containing 18 principal Puranas, 17 Mukhya (major) Puranas and 18 Upa (minor) Puranas. (Page 51)

64. Vaisheshika is one of the 6 Vedic schools of philosophy, founded by Kanada Kashyapa around the 6 Century BC. It accepts 4 sources of knowledge and it bases its beliefs on naturalism and atomism. (Page 56)

65. Nyasa (means *"justice"*) is a Vedic school of philosophy based on the theory of logic focusing on the Nyasa Sutras composed by Aksapada Gautama. (Page 56)

66. Hubble Law of expansion, is the observation that galaxies are moving away from the earth at speeds that are proportional to their distance of separation and that the further away they are the faster they are moving. (Page 57)

67. Karl Popper, 1902 – 1994, was an Austrian-British academic considered as the 20th century's most influential philosopher of science. (Page 57)

68. Donald Hoffman, born in 1955, is an American cognitive psychologist. He argues that conscious beings have not evolved to perceive the world as it actually is. (Page 57)

69. The law of conservation of mass, states that for a closed system the mass within the system will remain constant. (Page 58)

70. Stoics are followers of the Hellenistic philosophy, school of thought founded in the third Century BC in Athens by Zeno of

Citium. (Page 60)

71. Heraclitus was an ancient Greek philosopher, known as the *"weeping philosopher"*. (Page 60)

72. Lord Buddha see reference 58. (Page 61)

73. Cordovero Tree of Emanation. Moses be Jacob Cordovero 1522 – 1570, was a central figure in the development of Kabbalah. His depiction of the Tree represents a series of divine emanations of God's creation. (Page 62)

74. *"The secret doctrine of the Kabbalah"*, written by Leonora Leet, uses teachings extending over thousands of years to clarify concepts of quantum cosmology and physics. (Page 62)

75. John Milton, 1608 – 1674, was an English poet and intellectual. He advocated for the abolition of the Church of England and the execution of Charles I. (Page 62)

76. *"Paradise lost"* is an epic poem by Milton (see reference 75) it was published in 1667. It can be seen as a personal view of Christianity or a universal political statement. (Page 62)

77. Newtonian physics is simple and coherent but denies human values, creativity and evolution. (Page 62)

78. Ayin, is the third veil that lies above Keter on the Tree of Life. It signifies Negative Existence. (Page 65)

79. Talmud is the central writing of Rabbinic Judaism (Rabbism) containing the Mishnah (oral Torah) and the Gemara (Rabbinic analisys of Mishnah). (Page 66)

80. Zohar, is a masterpiece of Western religious thought. It uncovers the hidden meanings behind the world of appearances. (Page 67)

81. Caduceus or the symbol of Hermes (two snakes winding around) is the symbol of medicine. (Page 67)

82. Quran is the central religious text in Islam, believed to be a revelation of Allah; it is organized in 114 chapters. (Page 67)

83. Laya yoga (*"Laya"* means *"dissolve"*) is a form of yoga achieving the merge with the Supreme Consciousness. It works for Sahasrara (Crown chakra) downward to the Muladdara chakra (Root chakra). It is referred to Kundalini yoga, the yoga of awareness. (Page 67)

84. Yamas are ethical rules in yoga philosophy, as given in the Vedas and Yoga Sutras. The Yamas are: Ahimsa (non- harming), Satya (truthfulness), Asteya (non- stealing), Brahmacharya (moderating the senses) and Aparigraha (non- possessiveness). (Page 69)

85. The Age of Reason, late 17th – 1815, it was a period of rigorous scientific, religious, philosophical and political debate. (Page 72)

86. Sage Kapila was the founder of Samkhya dualistic school of Vedic philosophy and the author of Samkhya Sutras. He is mentioned in the Rigveda, Puranas, some Upanishads and Dharmasutras. (Page 73)

87. Thomas Young's Double Split experiment provided solid evidence that light was a wave not a particle. See also ref. 43 (Page 75)

88. Purusha and Prakriti are two different aspects of Ishvara (God). Purusha (meaning *"eastern dawn"*) is the soul, whilst Prakriti (meaning *"is which gives shapes or form"*) is the Creative Consciousness. They are both indestructible and eternal aspects. (Page 77)

89. Jainism, also known as Jain Dharma, is an ancient transtheistic religion in India based on the idea that the Universe was not created and cannot be destroyed and the celestial beings are reincarnated as humans are. (Page 79)

90. Svetasvara Upanishad, part of Yajurveda, contains 113 mantras divided in 6 chapters (Page 83)

91. Katha Upanishad (*"Katha"* means *"distress"*), part of the Krishna Yajurveda, has 2 chapters, each divided in 3 sections. (Page 83)

92. Wisdom Keepers are representatives of indigenous peoples and wisdom traditions from around the world. They have developed ancestral practices that enable them to live with joy without harming our earth. (Page 87)

93. Vishnu Purana is one of the 18 Mahapuranas, containing 7,000 verses. (Page 88)

94. Dwadasakshari mantra (*"Om Namo Bhagavate Vasudevaya"*) is known as the *"12 sylable mantra"*, dedicated to both Vishnu and Lord Krishna. (Page 88)

95. St. Thomas Aquinas, 1225 – 1274, he was an Italian Dominican friar an immensely influential philosopher and Doctor of the Church. (Page 89)

96. Devas (Means *"heavenly"* or *"divine"*), also referred to as Suras, are deities in Hinduism (deva for gods and devi for goddesses). (Page 92)

97. Sage Kashyap was the most ancient Sage and one of the 7 Rishi of Rigveda. (Page 94)

98. Ashtavakra Samhita, also known as Ashtavakra Gita is a treatise in Advaita Vedanta, attributed to Sage Astavakra. (Page 99)

99. Maitri Upanishad, also known as Maitrayaniya Upanishad, part of the Yajurveda, consisting of 7 Prapathakas (lessons). (Page 99)

100. Paingala Upanishad, attached to Shukla Yajurveda, is one of the 22 Samanya (general) Upanishad, containing 4 chapters. (Page 99)

101. *"Autobiography of a yogi"* is an autobiographical work of Paramahansa Yogananda, published in 1946. (Page 100)

102. Turyia Jnana or the knowledge of the absolute truth takes one to Turyiatita, the state of Moksha. (Page 101)

103. Moksha Gita, also known as *"The Song of Salvation"* is an essential work in Vedanta. (Page 105)

104. Pol Pot, 1925 – 1998, he was Prime Minister of Cambodia 1975 – 1979 during which time over 1.5 million citizens died of starvation, execution and disease. (Page 106)

105. Lhamo Thondup, 1935-, the 14th Dalai Lama. (Page 106)

106. *"Thus Spoke Zarathustra"*, written by Friedrich Nietzsche, is a philosophical novel in four parts published in 1883. (Page 111)

107. Ram Das (Richard Albert 1931- 2019) was an American spiritual author and psychologist. (Page 117)

108. Patanjali Sutras (*"Yoga Sutras of Patanjali"*), one of the main texts in yoga philosophy, was compiled by Sage Patanjali around 500BC. (Page 127)

109. Rishi Shankara was a philosopher who consolidated the teachings of Advaita Vedanta school of philosophy. Drik Drishya Vivaka is a text in Advaita Vedanta attributed to Vidyaranya Swami. (Page 134)

110. Prashasta Pada was an ancient Indian philosopher, author of *"Collection of Properties of Matter"*. (Page 137)

111. Nirvana Shatakam (*"Nirvana"* means *"Moksha"* and *"Shakatam"* means *"six"*) is a Shanti (peace) mantra written by Adi Shankaracharya. (Page 137)

112. Current Standard Model of Cosmology assumes the universe was created from pure energy and is now 5% ordinary matter, 27% dark matter and 68% dark energy. (Page 138)

113. Keynes, John Maynard, 1883 – 1946, was an English economist whose ideas changed the theory of economic policies of governments. (Page 138)

114. Copenhagen Interpretation, devised 1925/7, is an aim to explain how the mathematical theory of quantum mechanics agrees with reality. (Page 138)

115. Heisenberg's Uncertainty Principle states that it is not possible to certainly know the position and momentum of a particle at the same time. (Page 138)

116. Surya Siddhanta (means *"Sun treatise"*) is a Hindu treatise in astronomy consisting of 14 chapters. (Page 140)

117. Cartesian dualism based on dualism mind and body (mind can exist outside the body). (Page 142)

118. Bohm- Krisnamurti; the two met over twenty-five years to dialogue topics such as the nature of consciousness and the condition of humanity. (Page 144)

119. Kanada, also known as Uluka, Kashyapa and Kanabhuk, was the founder of Vaisheshika school of Vedic philosophy. He is the author of Vaisheshika Sutras. (Page 151)

120. Vaiseika Sutras is an atomistic text written by Sage Kanada, based on 9 constituents of reality: four classes of atoms, time, space, akasha, mind souls and direction. (Page 152)

121. Plato's' cave is an allegory used to show that what we see and hear may not be the truth of that which is before us. (Page 155)

122. Meher Baba, 1894 – 1969 was an Indian spiritual master who claimed to be his era's Avatar in human form. (Page 158)

123. Shoghi Effendi, 1897 – 1957, was the grandson and successor of 'Abdu'l-Bahá (see 149) appointed to the role of Guardian of the Baha'i Faith. (Page 162)

124. Emerald Tablet dates back to 36,000 BCE. The author is Thoth, it is a compact and cryptic Hermetic text. (Page 166)

125. Chakra (*"cakra"* means *"wheel"*) are 33 energy centers situated in the body and outside the body. There are seven major chakras (Muladhara, Svadishana, Manipura, Anahata, Vishuddha, Ajna and Sahasrara), 21 minor chakras and 5 advanced chakras (outside the body) (Page 168)

126. Sushumna, also known as Sukha mana (*"Sukha"* means *"joyful"* and *"mana"* means *"mind"*) is the central nadi (energy vessel) running along the spine. (Page 169)

127. Devi Bhagavatam (*"devi"* means *"goddess"* and *"Bhagavata"* means *"devotee of the blessed Devi"*), also known as Bhagavata Purana and Srimad Devi Bhagavatam, contains 12 Skandhas (cantos" with 318 Adhyayas (chapters). (Page 171)

128. Sri Aurobindo (1872- 1950) was an Indian philosopher, yogi and poet. His main works are *"Synthesis of Yoga"* and *"The Life Divine"*. (Page 172)

129. The Higgs bosom particle is a particle associated with the Higgs energy field this transmits mass to the things that travel through it. (Page 178)

130. Vaisheshik Darsham is one of the six Vedic schools of philosophy based on naturalism and atomism. See 64. (Page 180)

131. St. John of Cross, 1542 – 1591, was a Spanish Catholic priest and mystic. (Page 181)

132. "Song of Songs", also known as *"Song of Solomon"*, is one of the books in the Bible. (Page 191)

133. Sacred Geometry ascribes sacred and symbolic meanings to geometric proportions and shapes. (Page 191)

134. Golden Ratio is a mathematical ratio commonly found in nature. (Page 192)

135. Fibonacci Sequence is based on the rule that each number is the sum of the two proceeding numbers. (Page 192)

136. "Timaeus" is one of Plato's dialogues, mostly based on Timaeus of Locri's monologue. (Page 192)

137. Upa Vedas (meaning *"Applied Vedas"*) are 4 technical disciplines: Ayurveda (Medicine) associated with Atharveda, Dhanurveda (Archery) associated with Rigveda, Gandharvaveda (Music and Dance) associated with Samaveda and Shapatyaveda (Architecture) associated with Yajurveda. (Page 193)

138. Tau Cross, is a T shaped cross with the ends expanded to cause it to look like the Greek letter tau. (Page 197)

139. Ankh, or key of life, is an ancient Egyptian hieroglyphic symbol. In Egyptian art it represents the word for life. (Page 197)

140. Abdu'I-Baha, 1844 – 1921, was the eldest son of Baha'u'llah, he served as head of the Baha'i Faith from 1892 until 1921. (Page 199)

141. "The river that flows in you, also flows in me" is a quote by Kabir Das, a 15th Century mystic poet. (Page 200)

142. *"Symposium"* is a philosophical text by Plato, written in the 3rd Century BC. (Page 206)

143. Vishshtadvaita Vedanta (Meaning "Advaita with uniqueness") is a branch of Vedanta philosophym, based on diversity bringing unity. The main adherent was Ramanuja. (Page 216)

144. Swabhava (means *"own becoming"*) is the essence of all thngs, concept popular in Advaita Vedanta philosophy. In yoga philosophy, Swabhava is Brahman. (Page 220)

145. Avadhuta Gita (*"Song of a free soul"*) is a text, attributed to Dattatreya, based on the rules of Advaita and Dvaita Vedanta. (Page 220)

146. Dattatreya was a monk, considered the *"Lord of yoga"*. (Page 220)

147. Principle of Correspondence is the conditions under which quantum and classical physics agree. (Page 221)

148. Sathya Sai Baba, 1926 – 2011 was Indian guru and philanthropist, believed that he was the reincarnation of Shirdi Sai Baba (Page 222)

149. Kybalion, written by *"Three Initiates"* and published in 1908. It is a study of the Hermetic Philosophy of Ancient Egypt and Greece. (Page 224)

150. Udgitha is the name of the mystical syllable AUM. (Page 225)

151. Prasha Upanishad is a Mukhya (primary) Upanishad in the Atharveda containing 6 Prashna (questions). (Page 226)

152. Hiranya garbha is the source of creation of the Universe, the

"Golden Womb" or the *"Primeval Womb"*. (Page 227)

153. Vishavakarma Sukta of Rigveda states that Vishavakarma is the indirect form of the Absolute reality, later developed as Brahman in the Upanishads. (Page 227)

154. Taittiriya Upanishad is a primary Upanishad in Yajurveda, containing the seventh, eight and ninth chapters of Taittiriya Aranyaka . (Page 228)

155. Mooji (Anthony Paul Moo Young, born in 1954) is a contemporary spiritual teacher. (Page 230)

156. "The point in the heart", is inserted into our selfish hearts as a gift from above. It is the desire to take pleasure in all that is around us. (Page 243)

157. Big Crunch is a hypothetical proposal that the ultimate fate of our Universe will be the expansion eventually reversing and the Universe collapsing (Page 253)

158. Linga Purana is one of the 18 Mahapuranas, being a main text in Shaivism. (Page 253)

159. Adi Parva of Mahabharata is the first book of the Mahapuranas (*"Adi"* means *"first"*) and contains 19 books and 225 chapters. (Page 258)

160. Garuda Purana is one of the 18 Mahapuranas, containing 15,000 verses mostly on cosmology, yoga and karma. (Page 258)

161. Max Born. 1882 – 1970, was a German physicist and mathematician who played a key role in the development of quantum mechanics. (Page 259)

162. King Himavan is the personification of the Himalayan Mountains, being the personification of the Kingdom of Ancient Nepal. (Page 261)

163. Jaiminiya Upanishad Brahmana, also known as the Talavakara Upanishad Brahmana. (Page 263)

164. Rav H. Epsten, 1860 – 1941, a Lithuanian Jewish rabbi, known for his Torah Temimah commentary on the Torah. (Page

264)

165. Hieros gamos or Hierogamy is the holy marriage between a goddess and a god. (Page 265)

166. Sage Gaudapanda was a Advaita Vedanta scholar and philosopher, the compiler of Mandukya Karika   (Page 276)

167. Sikhism is a Dharmic religion in the Punjab India (Page 292)

168. Sarvesham purnam bhavatu ("May there be peace in all") is a Shanti mantra (Page 295)

169. Sage Briahspati is a Sage who counsels the gods. (Page 296)

170. John Cramer, 1934-, known for his development of the transactional interpretation of quantum mechanics. (Page 300)

171. Rabban Shimon ben Gamliel, 10 BCE – 70 CE, was a Tanna sage and leader of the Jewish people. (Page 300)

172. Dhyanabindu Upanishad is a minor Upanishad in the Atharveda containing 106 verses. (Page 301)

173. 8 limbs of yoga are: Yamas- ethical values (Ahimsa-nonviolence; Satya- truthfulness, Asteya- nonstealing, Brahmacharya- continence and Aparigraha- noncovetousness); Niyama- self discipline (Saucha- cleanliness, Samtosa-contentment, Tapas- spiritual austerities, Svadhyaya- study of the scriptures and Isvara Pranidhana- surrender to God); Asanas-posture; Pranayama- breathing technique; Prathyahara- sensory trancendence; Dharana- concentration; Dhyana- meditation; Samadhi- ecstacy. (Page 309)

174. Sandilya Upanshad is one of the 20 Yoga Upanishads in the Atharveda. (Page 311)

ABOUT THE AUTHORS

After retiring from a career as an automotive engineer, working in the UK, Europe and Japan, Paul has finally time to do what he likes most. Paul's love is Kabbalah, which he has studied for many years. He is also involved in international communities, the "Bohm- Krisnamurti" group being one of his favourites. He is currently mentoring novices joining one of the spiritual fraternities in Auckland, New Zealand. His passion is nature. Therefore he enjoys taking long walks and connecting with trees. On Sundays, Paul occasionally joins the devotional meeting of a local the Baha'i community.

Devi runs a busy Clinical Hypnotherapy practice in New Plymouth, but after hours she enjoys playing drums, bass guitar and Indian harmonium, as well as practicing Kundalini yoga. She loves growing orchids and spending time with her dog Hendrix, who understands commands in at least three languages. She is part of several spiritual communities and the Mooji Satsang group. She is a published author of two hypnotherapy books, "You have lived many times" and "We have met in past lives". Devi's heart is in the Vedic philosophy, which she has studied for the last thirty years.

Made in the USA
Las Vegas, NV
22 August 2021